Mohini M. Chatterji

The Bhagavad Gîtâ or the Lord's Lay

Mohini M. Chatterji

The Bhagavad Gîtâ or the Lord's Lay

ISBN/EAN: 9783337167257

Printed in Europe, USA, Canada, Australia, Japan

Cover: Foto ©Lupo / pixelio.de

More available books at **www.hansebooks.com**

THE BHAGAVAD GÎTÂ

OR

THE LORD'S LAY

PREFACE.

IN the following pages an attempt is made to present to the English-speaking people the pearl of price from the ocean of Brâhmanical Scriptures.

The Bhagavad Gîtâ, as a book, is well known in the Western World. In offering a Scripture to those in search of scriptural light, who rejoice in the things of the Spirit, the first duty is to be free from the mere human spirit. This end has been striven for by following the spiritual chief of modern India, the revered Sankarâchârya, in the translation of the text and in the comments and notes. The words of the teacher have been rendered into the English tongue, and his expressions adapted to the Western modes of thought as far as was possible while preserving their meaning. For the elucidation of some topics, however, a few supplementary observations have been added, in all humility.

The interpretations of the Bhagavad Gîtâ can be divided into three classes, according to the teacher whose authority is followed. Three great teachers make the points of a triangle on which Brâhmanical orthodoxy rests.

The earliest and greatest among them is Sankarâchârya, whose influence extends over all India. The others, in order of time, were Râmânujâchârya and Madhvâchârya. Their most important difference is regarding the relation between the Spirit of God and the real nature of the spirit of man. Sankarâchârya holds that the Spirit of God is the only reality; that this Spirit is the Self in all creatures, and is yet one and attributeless, — pure Consciousness, Bliss, and Beingness. These are not properties of the Spirit, but are the Spirit of God, as a thing is itself.

The apparent existence of many egos or spirits is due to the operation of a power called Falsehood. It is called a power because it depends necessarily upon the Spirit of God, which remains unchanged in the midst of the operations of this power. It is called Falsehood because it is not the Spirit of God, which is the only Reality; yet it is not altogether unreal, because it invests with seeming reality that which is nothing, since it is not the Spirit of God. In a sense it is not a negation, and yet is devoid of community of nature with the Spirit of God. For this reason it is called Falsehood, or Lie. A lie is not an utter negation, because it concerns some reality. This creative power is called Falsehood because it produces the appearance of many egos, whereas in reality the Spirit of God is the only ego.

The supreme end of existence is the change produced in man's nature by the power called Right Knowledge. This change shows the seeming independent reality of the Self within man to be due to the power called Falsehood. In truth, it is the shadow of the one and only reality, the Spirit of God, and has no more independence of being than a shadow can have. The shadow has no being independent of the substance; nor has the self in us a being independent of the true Self, which is the Spirit of God.

The shortest way of stating the relation is this: the spirit in the individual is really identical with the Spirit of God. It is eternally identical, and the statements in the Scriptures as to individuals *becoming* the Supreme Spirit are figurative. The essence of this system is the denial of real existence to the individual spirit, and the insistence upon its true identity with the Spirit of God.

Râmânujâchârya teaches that the Spirit of God is the only reality, and shares community of nature with nothing. Conscious and unconscious nature are the two eternal powers of the Spirit. Consciousness, unconsciousness, and the Lord of both are the three eternal verities. He whose being is such that neither consciousness, nor unconsciousness, nor both, can limit Him, is the Supreme Lord, who makes no effort to escape from limitation or to prevent change of condition. To know these three verities to be what they are said to be, is to attain liberation.

Madhvâchârya maintains that the relation between God and man is the relation between master and servant. Through evil and blindness, this relation — which is an eternal verity, and not one that comes into existence after previous non-existence — is not realized. The complete and full realization of this relation, consequent upon a change of nature by God's grace, is salvation.

These three teachers have explained the Scriptures from their several standpoints, and have each founded a complete system by which to lead the faithful to salvation. Monastic orders and other institutions established by them exist to the present day. Accepting the Bhagavad Gîtâ as authoritative, each teacher has left his commentary upon it. The faithful disciple of any one of this illustrious trio, while following in exclusive devotion the path pointed out to him, will yet believe that though the roads are different, the goal to which they lead is the same.

A dutiful study of the blessed Bhagavad Gîtâ in connection with the Holy Bible will, it is believed, show that the word of God does not change with the change of time. As it was in the beginning, so it is now, and will be to the end. In order to aid this study, frequent references to the Christian Scriptures are made beside the text of the following translation; not, indeed, for verbal similarities, but to establish some points in common in the two Scriptures, in order that the reader may superpose one upon the other, and thus demonstrate their agreement. These references are believed to be sufficient for the purpose intended, although by no means exhaustive.

A few words as to some surrounding circumstances will help to show the full significance of the two sets of Scriptures, which, though differing in nomenclature, embody the same Truth. Secular scholars agree that the Vedas are the earliest known record of religious truths. It is not necessary to cite the teachings of Brâhmanical authorities on the subject of the Vedas; but it should be remembered that the revered Sankarâchârya, the greatest Vedic teacher since the time of Vyâsa, calls the Bhagavad Gîtâ the collected essence of all the Vedas.

Hence it conclusively appears that the word of God, though often well-nigh forgotten by men, remained the same from the time of the Vedas to the time of the present Scripture. The word of God as given to the people of India in the earliest time, and preserved in all the Scriptures of the Brâhmans, is to be found in the colloquy between the blessed Krishna and Arjuna. According to the sacred chronicles, Krishna lived one hundred and twenty-five years, and departed from the world in the year 3001 B. C.*

If it be found that the Scriptures of the Brâhmans and the Scriptures of the Jews and Christians, widely separated as they are by age and nationality, are but different names for one and the same Truth, who can then say that the Scriptures contradict one another? A careful and reverent collation of the two sets of Scriptures will show forth the conscious and intelligent design of revelation.

In the Bhagavad Gîtâ, consisting of 770 verses, the principal topic is the being of God; while scarcely the same amount of exposition is given to it in the whole Bible. The explanation of this remarkable fact is found in the difference between the genius of the Hebrew and Brâhmanic races, and also in the fact that the teachings of Jesus Christ were addressed to the "common people." This one consideration carries the conviction to unprejudiced minds that although Truth is eternally the same, yet, as the nature of man undergoes change, new embodiments of Truth are required in order to reconcile men to the Truth.

By a dutiful study of the subject, comparing spiritual things with spiritual, the mind is uplifted and filled with wonder at the

---

* See Bhâgavat Purâna, Book XI. Chap. vii. 20; and Vishnu Purâna, Book V. Chap. xxxviii. 8.

marvellous workings of the one Holy Spirit. If, on the contrary, in violation of the method of spiritual study, things of the Spirit are compared to things material, confusion can be the only result.

The question as to whether the Bhagavad Gîtâ and the New Testament have been in part copied one from the other, has vexed many minds; but it is apparent that the ground upon which the legitimacy of the issue is based is without scriptural support. The identity of Truth, or even of its expression, can furnish no such inference, unless it is demonstrated that all Scriptures are products of the human mind. No believer in revelation will admit this, nor, indeed, can it be maintained with reason; the supporter of this inference must adduce authority from his own Scriptures against the possible authenticity of all others. The question of priority, by itself, can have no bearing on the subject.

Fixing our attention upon the two sets of Scriptures with which we are concerned, the question is to be considered from the standpoints of the Brâhman and the Christian. From that of the first, it is not a bold statement to say that no such citation can be brought against the Christian Scriptures. On the contrary, there are abundant reasons for the opposite conclusion.

In one of the most important Brâhmanical Scriptures — Nârada Pancharâtra — a very significant epithet is bestowed upon Buddha. He is called *pâshanda çruti-gopaka*, or "the preserver of revelation for those outside of the Vedic authority." When one such revealer is admitted, there can be no reason for excluding others; indeed, the Bhagavad Gîtâ puts this beyond doubt in Chapter IV. It is also clear, upon the authority of the Vedas, that the only thing necessary for salvation is the knowledge of the true God. "The knot of the heart becomes untied, all his doubts are dispersed, all his innate tendencies are exhausted, on seeing Him, the superior and inferior." "Having known even Him, he attains to deathlessness; there is no other path."

Put side by side with these Vedic texts the words of Jesus: "And this is life eternal, that they might know Thee, the only true God, and Jesus Christ, whom Thou hast sent;"* "No man cometh unto the Father, but by me," and it is not possible to doubt that the Brâhman and the Christian are fellow-voyagers. The Brâhmanical Scriptures are of one accord in teaching that when the heart (*chitta*, in Sanskrit) is purified, God is seen. Jesus Christ declares, "Blessed are the pure in heart, for they shall see God."

The Brâhmanical sages have taught with great emphasis that the easiest road to perfect purity is love of God and love of His creatures. Does Christianity teach anything else? There is then no cause for the Christian to create antagonism between the two faiths.

The knowledge of Truth carries with itself an increased responsibility. The man who sees the wonderful workings of the Spirit of God among the nations of the earth, bringing each people to God by ways unknown to others, is thereby charged with a duty. To him, with terrible precision, applies the warning given by Gamaliel to the Pharisees: "Take heed to yourselves what ye intend to do, ... lest ye be found to fight even against God" (Acts v. 35-39). If he be a Brâhman, let him reflect, when opposing the religion of Jesus, what it is that he fights. The truths of Christianity are the same as those upon which his own salvation depends. How can he be a lover of Truth, which is God, if he knows not his beloved under such a disguise? And if he does penetrate behind the veil,— which should tend only to increase the ardor of his love, — he cannot hate those who, in obedience to the same Truth, are

---

* According to the belief of all Brâhmans the Vedas are the revelation of the Creator to Man when he first started into being. On account of coevality with the human race they cannot require faith in an especial incarnate Saviour; while the Christian dispensation, founded as it is at a definite point of time upon the pre-existing Mosaic Law, cannot be separated from the Saviour Jesus. This is the explanation of the striking and often-noted difference between Brâhmanism and Christianity. There cannot be a Saviour for the Brâhmans unless he be a re-revealer of the Truth, eternally enshrined in the Vedas, though often ignored and forgotten by the heirs to that Sacred Wisdom.

preaching the gospel of Christ to all nations. Indeed, he ought to rejoice at his brother's devotion to the selfsame God, and see that he is rendering service to God by helping others to carry out the behests given to them by the Divine Master. If, on the other hand, he be a Christian, let him remember that while he is commanded to preach repentance and remission of sins in the name of the Saviour Jesus, he is also warned against the "teaching for doctrines the commandments of men" (Matt. xv. 9).

Considerations such as these have led to the present work, which is a kind of votive offering.

It only remains earnestly to pray to the merciful Father of Humanity to remove from all races of men every unbrotherly feeling in the sacred name of Religion, which is but one! Amen.

MOHINI MOHUN CHATTERJI.

BOSTON, Mass., U. S. A.,
July 20, 1887.

CONTENTS.

		PAGE
INTRODUCTION		1

CHAPTER

I.	Survey of Army	21
II.	Right Knowledge of the Spirit	30
III.	The Knowledge of Right Action	63
IV.	Right Knowledge of Dedication of Action leading to Spiritual Wisdom	77
V.	Right Knowledge of the Renunciation of Action	93
VI.	Right Knowledge of Meditation	103
VII.	Right Knowledge of Realization	121
VIII.	Supreme Spirit named as Om	135
IX.	Right Knowledge of the Royal Mystery	146
X.	Right Knowledge of Divine Powers	158
XI.	Vision of the Deity as the Soul of the Universe	169
XII.	Right Knowledge of Devotion	180
XIII.	Right Knowledge of the Discrimination between Kshetra and Kshetrajna	189
XIV.	Right Knowledge of the Division of the Three Qualities	215
XV.	Right Knowledge of the Supreme Spirit	225
XVI.	Right Knowledge of the Discrimination between Godlike and Demoniac Attributes	234
XVII.	Right Knowledge of the Threefold Division of Faith	241
XVIII.	Right Knowledge of Liberation	249

SYNOPSIS		271
INDEX		279

INTRODUCTION.

I.

LET us pause and reflect before entering upon our work. Let us be sure of the spirit in our hearts before we enter the Temple of the Lord. For the truth as declared in the Scriptures is indeed the Temple of the Lord in which His Spirit dwells.

The Scriptures of the nations are the most glorious of all the temples that can enshrine that Spirit which is the life of our life, and the light that shineth in the darkness of our minds and hearts.

May we all feel that we come to worship, and not to read.

The reading of holy books is the fulfilling of the duty which we owe to Him whose name they whisper in our ears. Yes, they whisper His name in our ears as they proclaim Him to be beyond all names, — beyond both thought and speech.

In reading the Scriptures we touch the hem of the garments of those who have stood at the altar and have looked into the light of God and seen Him.

Yes, seen Him face to face, and — let us speak by silence, nay, let us shout it to the heavens, let it echo back from hell, let it sweep over the broad bosom of the earth — found Him as the Self.

May we all feel that there is nothing which is our Self but God.

Let us lay down all our burdens at the Gate of the Temple and enter it clothed in the dignity of our humanity. Let us enter the Temple as men, unqualified by adjectives which degrade the manhood they pretend to elevate. It is easier for the son to be the father's father, than for adjectives to ennoble the substance, man; for all adjectives originate in the mind of man.

It is only thus that we can stand alone before the Master whose voice we are to hear.

Finally, let us never forget that no one has discharged his full duty until his heart responds to each word of the Master, who lives and must always live in His Word.

II.

All Indian authorities agree in pronouncing the Bhagavad Gîtâ to be the essence of all sacred writings. They call it an Upanishad, — a term applied to the wisdom, as distinguished from the ceremonial, portion of the Vedas, and to no books less sacred.

In the book itself Krishna declares: "Whoever shall expound this most mysterious colloquy to those who have love for me shall without doubt come to me, having obtained unifying love for me. Than he there is no better performer of what is dear to me among men, nor shall there ever be on earth any one more beloved unto me. And whoever shall study this colloquy, which makes for righteousness, by him shall I be worshipped in the sacrifice through knowledge; this is my mind. The man who shall listen to it in faith and without a cavilling spirit, even he, freed from sins, shall obtain the blessed abodes of those who work righteousness, liberated from evil."

Elsewhere it is said, "The Lord's Song being well sung, what use is there in other and voluminous Scriptures?"

The revered Sankarâchârya, in the beginning of his commentary, calls the sacred Gîtâ "the collected essence of all the Vedas."

The influence of this book upon the spiritual life of India can be estimated by the fact that within the last twelve hundred years no great teacher has lived who has not commented upon it. Frequent references are also found to earlier commentaries which are no longer available.

Beyond doubt the Bhagavad Gîtâ is the best book in existence for the study of the spiritually-minded; for it is suited to all conditions of men; it is short; it is complete and not ambiguous; it is direct, speaking as friend to friend or teacher to pupil, and thus is not coldly impersonal; the teaching is preserved in the very words of Krishna, the few introductory verses being the production of the sage Vyâsa.

The great author of the Gîtâ lays down a very wise rule as to its study:—

"This must never be declared by thee to one who does not perform penance, has no devotion,[1] and is unwilling to serve this spiritual superior;[2] and also not unto one who reviles me."[3]

May we therefore realize what He says:—

"With their hearts in me, and their faculties and

---

[1] Matt. xiii. 10-16.   [2] 1 Thess. v. 12, 13.   [3] Matt. xii. 31.

senses lost in me, enlightening one another and declaring me to one another, they are ever in peace and ever in rejoicing. To them, ever attached to me and worshipping me in love, I give that wisdom by which they come to me."[1]

III.

Ye are the temples of God.[2] This is true in letter and spirit. The power of man to entertain the angel of Religion distinguishes him from the animal. His power to gaze at the sun which illumines the outstretched finger of religion enthrones him as the king of all that exist. We have heard, indeed, of the angels who dwell on glistening heights unconcerned with the ills of this mortal sphere and unconscious of the battles that rage in the human breast. But have we not also heard that the angels never have the ecstasy of hearing that shout of joy with which great Nature enthrones as her lord the liberated man in Nirvâna? Let us realize it again and again, — man is the lord of all that exist; his crown of thorns is his crown of glory.[3] That which elevates man above all other beings is his capacity for suffering, and the consequent power of asking for its extinction absolutely and forever. But Nature works in perfect symmetry; every unit in a crystal is a perfect crystal itself. The evolution of the embryo is a miniature reproduction of the progress of the ego through the various kingdoms; and the race of man presents a perfect picture of the different orders of beings. These types are eternal and not subject to evolution, although individuals evolve from one class to another.

---

[1] 1 Thess. v. 11-18.   [2] 1 Cor. vi. 19.   [3] Psalms viii. 5-8.

There is the vegetable-like man who only responds to a few of the possibilities in him; like the tree, he can only assimilate food and perpetuate his species. Next is the animal-like man who can assimilate mental food called experience, and develop the quality of prudence. To the third class belongs the godlike man who is hospitable to Universals, — to the laws of morality which are absolute. This marks the turning-point in the life history of the ego; it is beginning to disentangle itself from the bonds of mere experience, and places its happiness in a region which no mortal eye can penetrate. He is learning to worship; in his breast the infant Faith is opening her meek eyes to gaze upon a mystery. But he has not yet grasped the meaning of his personality. The relation between the finite and the Infinite is perceptible to him, but it is still an awful mystery to be contemplated with fear and trembling; to be borne in mind in order that his personality may acquire possessions that he imagines will secure him happiness. He is a suitor before the throne of God, but not an adorer. His religion is one of reward and punishment, not of love and rejoicing; but yet he is religious.

Last of all is the divine man, — the lover and knower of God. He casts not a glance at the wonderfully varied powers of God; he will none of them; they are as ashes without their possessor, the God himself. In him is born that love which casteth out fear, and to him God is void of attributes, while to others he possesses the very infinitude of attributes.

"I but know that I love Thee," is the language of his spirit.

We have asked Thee again and again what is Thy name, and have laid our faces on the earth for an answer. Our question has come back from the whole expanse of the universe, — from above, from below, from the middle regions, but no answer; in our hearts alone we have heard, — Silence is Thy name.

He who thinks that he knows Thee, by him Thou art not known. He who does not think that he knows Thee, knows Thee indeed. "I do not think that I know well, nor that I do not know." Whoever knows the meaning of this paradox knows well indeed.

But we know that He is Sweetness, and of this Sweetness the infinitude of creatures are enjoying but an atom. Who would have moved, who would have breathed, if this Sweetness had not pervaded all space?

To the true worshipper God is attributeless; it is indeed so. He is the sublime and supreme paradox. He possesses all attributes and yet is attributeless. This paradox is the language of the soul; its culmination is comprehension of Divine love.

Consider for a moment what it is to love. That baby whose infant form you have seen in the cradle, whose feeble cry you have soothed, grows to be a creeping babe, all smiles and tears. He catches the hem of your garment, and stands and falls, falls and stands. The same child becomes a man; he sways senates by his voice, armies tremble before his sword, and the world is submerged by the sky-defying billows of his fame. But where are all his attributes when, sitting by his side, you take his hand and look into the eyes of your own son?

As below, so above; God is infinite in attributes and yet devoid of attributes.[1] This is the God whom the Bhagavad Gîtâ proclaims; this the God whom the Scriptures of all nations proclaim, — the God who is the true and only Self in all creatures.[2]

---

[1] Job xi. 7; Rom. xi. 33, 34.   [2] John i. 1-9.

"I shall declare that which is to be known; knowing which a man attains deathlessness, — the Supreme Brahmă, having no beginning, and said to be neither subject to affirmation nor to negation" (because He is beyond all attributes).

"His hands and feet are everywhere; everywhere His eyes, heads, and mouths; His ears everywhere in the worlds; enveloping everything He dwells."[1]

"Manifested in the operations of all organs and faculties, yet devoid of organs and faculties. Unattached, He supports all. Though devoid of attributes, He is the experiencer of all attributes."[2]

"He is the within and without of all beings, moving and stationary.[3] Unrealizable on account of His subtlety; though afar, He is near"[4] (to the illuminated man who realizes Him as the true Self).

"Though undistributed, He appears to dwell as distributed in creatures; the same that which is to be known is the supporter of creatures, is the devourer and producer."[5]

"He is the light of lights, is said to be beyond darkness.[6] He is knowledge, that which is to be known and that which is the ultimate end of knowledge,[7] and is seated in the hearts of all." — CHAP. XIII. 12–17.

The relation between the finite and the Infinite is religion, in the true sense of the word. Its application to words and acts, in some way touching upon this relation, is a figure of speech. Every man who feels the need of God is religious. This need, however, can be felt in two ways: one may want God for the sake of the

---

[1] Psalms cxxxix. 7-17.
[2] Job. x. 4-8; Prov. xv. 3.
[3] Isaiah xlv. 12, 13.
[4] Psalms cxlv. 18.
[5] Deut. iv. 39.
[6] 1 John i. 5.
[7] Prov. viii. 22-31; Col. ii. 2, 3.

benefits He can confer; or he may want God purely for Himself, simply because God is Himself. We want Him because not to want Him is impossible. Those who feel the need of God in the first way are godlike men; those who hunger and thirst for Him in the other way, are divine.

According to the nature of these needs, religion has a twofold aspect, presenting the path of action and the path of cessation of action, or work and rest. Those who follow the first path live in the veiled light of God, ever working and ever having to work. The other path leads to the attainment of God, having obtained whom there is nothing else to attain; having become whom there is nothing else to be. The result yielded by the religion of rest is the acme of bliss, which to human imagination appears as the cessation of all suffering.

The nature of the path of action is easily understood. I want something for my personality, for the permanence of which I am also craving. A desire for anything in the future involves the desire for the continuance of personal identity. I cannot secure this end by any effort of my mind or my muscle; I therefore turn to superhuman means,—in short, I am not only worldly, but other-worldly. So far, it is clear, I am seeking happiness by changing the Infinite towards the finite, myself.

But what is the other path,—that which leads to God, Nirvâna, or Eternal Life?

In the supreme reality we are all absolutely identical with God and with one another. The difference which appears to us as real is but a seeming; in truth it is not so. For this reason the seeming reality is called illusion, error, disorder, disobedience, a mystery, in fact,—

a something which cannot be defined. If it could be, it would not have been false, but true. Being the will of God absolutely free and unconditioned, it cannot bear the limitation implied by saying "It is this."

The perception of this truth is the dawn of faith. One fact should ever be borne in mind, — that this mysterious power did not begin in time. For time itself requires variety for its existence, and variety cannot exist unless supported by this power. Hence it is plain that the mere lapse of time will not destroy this illusion. No one can attain Nirvâna by merely drifting on the stream of evolution.

Neither can action deliver us from bondage. Action can only lead to action, as animals can only reproduce their kind. The actor consisting only of the stuff called illusion, his action cannot transcend illusion. If the illusion can be supposed to be suspended for a moment, no action can take place, inasmuch as the actor, in so far as he is the actor, will disappear. It is clear that as bondage is a state of which we are conscious, some other state of consciousness alone can remove it. The state of consciousness called illusion, or false knowledge, will not exist in the state of consciousness called right knowledge.

"Those whose sins are washed away by knowledge attain to rest from conditioned existence."[1] — CHAP. V. 16.

The Buddhahood of Buddha consists in the Bodhi knowledge that arose in him under the Bo-tree. Christ says, "And this is life eternal, that they might know Thee, the only true God, and Jesus Christ whom Thou hast sent."[2]

---

[1] Prov. viii. 33-35.   [2] John xvii. 3.

This knowledge is not an expansion of the intellect, but the annulment of the intellect. Saint Paul says, "When that which is perfect is come, then that which is in part shall be done away." It is an interior state of illumination as independent of us as is our present concept that "I am this."

Such being the case, we are compelled to ask, How are we to act (since act we must, whether inwardly or outwardly) so as to be in harmony with the goal of our life, the pole toward which the magnet of our soul ever turns, "to know even as we are known"? The answer is, that if all one's acts are performed with the full conviction that they are of no value to the actor, but are to be done simply because they have to be done, — in other words, because it is in our nature to act, — then the personality or egotism in us will grow weaker and weaker until it comes to rest, permitting the knowledge revealing the true Self to shine out in all its splendor. But this path of pure, spiritual knowledge is hard to tread. Those alone are therefore fit to enter upon the path of pure philosophy whose hearts are disentangled from the bonds of worldly attachment.[1]

"Greater is the suffering of those whose hearts are attached to the attributeless. Those having self-identifying consciousness of the body find devotion to the attributeless painful indeed." — CHAP. XII. 5.

"Among thousands of men, one perhaps strives after perfection; and even among those who strive after perfection perhaps but one knows me truly."[2] — CHAP. VII. 3.

But among the sons of men there are few indeed in whom all passions are dead, and whose awakened spir-

---

[1] 1 Kings iii. 11, 12.   [2] Psalms liii. 2, 3.

itual perceptions have borne them beyond the sphere in which the majority of our race are wandering blindly, slaves to their passions, and with hearts bound to things of the earth earthy. What hope is there for such?

Will the majority of men perish in the valley of the shadow of death? Is there no hand to save us from the Slough of Despond, no light to illumine the stagnant gloom of our souls?

When the cry of the soul goes out in waves of agony to the God of mercy, Religion descends to us as the gentle companion and friend. We then perceive that God is the embodiment of infinite mercy, ever ready to dispense His grace. Have we not seen that the inspired and illuminated artist has dreamed of the Deity with the palm of His hand turned toward us as if in the act of giving? We also feel that the giver is not the same as the oppressor. The giver fills a want, but the oppressor gives without regard to the want of the receiver. We must therefore learn to ask of God. He is infinitely merciful, and will not inflict a flash of pain upon any soul in the universe. If you have a single wish other than the desire for God, He will not deny you that wish, but you will reap fruits such as will be impossible when once you become identical with God. Let every man learn to want God only for His own sake; when that is learned, there is no more to be known.

"Those, however, who worship me, having abandoned all actions in me, regarding me as the Supreme, and fixing their hearts upon me without clinging to anything beside, — whose hearts have entered into me, — for them I become before long the rescuer from the ocean of death and changeful existence."[1] — CHAP. XII. 6, 7.

This teaches us that we learn to ask only when our

---

[1] John v. 24; Isaiah xlv. 22.

souls are fixed upon God to the exclusion of all things that appear as separate from Him.

Away with all false asceticism; it is useless. All things are from God, and so must live. Our emotional longings are not to be crushed; but we must bend brain, heart, and muscle to secure their eternal gratification. We must be infinitely ambitious in desiring that beyond which there is nothing more, and in which is everything that can exist. If we crave for beauty, we must know that there can be no beautiful object which is not excelled in beauty by God. For how can that exist in a finite object which is not in the Infinite, — All, yet One? The entire beauty in the Universe is but the reflection of the absolutely beautiful God whom it obscures and hides; and so in regard to every other longing of our hearts.

If I take Infinity from Infinity, still Infinity remains. What exists in which I can so glory as I can in this, — that God is, and that He and I are one; and that all this wonderfully complex existence contains no other like me, or even unlike me, when I resign everything to God? Therefore I say that asceticism for its own sake is a delusion and a snare.

"The enjoyment that deluded men feel in objects that are transitory, — may that enjoyment never depart from my heart when my mind ceaselessly dwells on Thee." — VISHNU PURANA, PART II. CHAP. II. 17.

"He always sees himself, kingdom, wealth, as also wife and equipages, — all as of the Lord." — MAHÂBHÂRATA, BOOK X. CHAP. cccxxxvii. 12718.

If God destroys me, my enjoyment will increase, since it is He who destroys me, and not another. I do not wish to know what is to happen either in the next moment or during millions of ages from now. It is the will of God that is to be done. I do not wish Him to do anything for my sake that would not have been done did I not exist at all; I do not even wish to be saved; for from what am I to be saved? Is there anything in the universe outside of God?

It is true that this love is the supreme possession of the soul; it is also true that this love can only exist as a gift of the Holy Spirit. As mere men, we are not capable of receiving even a ray of it, however much we may long for it. We are poor in that calmness of spirit which alone is the fit habitation of God.

Faith must have grown to some extent before desire can turn inward; what then shall I do if my faith is weak, if external attractions are so strong as to prevent this turning inward for life and light? The cure of such a state cannot come to a man through his deluding himself into the belief that the inner citadel is won by a mere forcible repression of the outgoing tendencies.

"The man of deluded soul, who, having restrained the organs of action, remains dwelling upon objects of sense in his mind, is called a hypocrite."— CHAP. II. 6. "And the hypocrite's hope shall perish: whose hopes shall be cut off, and whose trust shall be a spider's web." — JOB viii. 13, 14.

The right thing to do, then, is to work on, but to work with a different motive. I must no longer work for the gain of any benefit, temporal or spiritual, but to fulfil the law of being which is the righteous will of God, — to finish the day's work in order to acquire leisure for eternal communion of identity with God, who dwells in every human breast; that the Father in whom I live, move, and have my being may be in me as I am in Him.

Whatever there is to do has to be done, but not for the sake of enjoying the fruit of action. Let me work for God like a slave; not that He wants it of me, but because He has blessed me with the wish to serve Him. If I am not able thus to dedicate to God every thought and deed, let me at least do some specific things for Him; if I cannot give Him the twenty-four hours, at least let me give Him one. But let me not forget the lesson of the widow's mite.

Beings below this are not yet fit for religious life. They must look to morality as the highest ideal of existence, and follow its dictates until the birth-throes of a new life are felt within them; until they know that sublime discontent which distinguishes man from animals. "Come unto me, all ye that labour and are heavy-laden, and I will give you rest," says the Master (Matt. xi. 28).

This, in brief, is the teaching of the Bhagavad Gîtâ, and indeed of all books that are holy. Beyond all doubt and cavilling, this is the truth declared to us by those in whose mouths there was no guile. In truth, this is the eternal revelation of God to man, the eternal oath that He has sworn. This truth requires no proof of its truthfulness; man cannot even touch it with falsehood, by observation or inference. Left to himself, man has not light enough to fabricate even a lie about God and the mystery of His relations with man.

IV.

As soon as I open the Bhagavad Gîtâ it seems to seize upon my very soul. I am face to face with antiquity. How many are the centuries that have passed since were uttered and written the words of eternal life I am about to read! The remainder of my life on this earth will not be more than a mere fraction of that time. The truth that was enshrined in this book five thousand years ago is as necessary to me as it was to him who first heard it; perhaps more so. Do I need further proof that truth abides forever? Do I require to be told that there is a something in man that neither grows nor dies?

These words were uttered by him who is one with God, and so is God. He who first listened to it was foremost among the royal warriors who assembled on the battlefield of Kurukshetra. The prowess of his mighty arms was known alike to men, gods, and demons. Among more than two millions of men present in that festival of battle there was not one whose name and fame excelled those of Arjuna. His superiority was so undoubted that he thought it a religious duty to find foemen worthy of his steel. Taking a position between the hostile ranks, he beholds the flower of Indian chivalry drawn up in battle array; and what does he see?

He there beholds uncles and grand-uncles, sons and grandsons, brothers and friends, teachers and well-wishers prepared to fight, one with another, unto the very death. The claims of blood and friendship assert their sway over him. His heart is assailed by strange and conflicting emotions. His proud warrior heart quails under them, his courage kisses the ground before grief, and for the first time he knows fear. His limbs quake, his hair stands on end, his great bow drops from his hand, and his skin begins to burn.

The strong faith of the royal warrior in his duty to fight is shaken by his love of kindred and friend, and doubts divide his mind. Of what avail is the unshaken throne on earth, without the near and dear ones for whose sake alone Prosperity has her charms? Far better feed upon the beggar's alms than enjoy blood-stained success. The sense of duty implanted in the warrior's breast by the traditions of a divine ancestry and the teaching of venerable sages still struggle for mastery, and scriptural texts are quoted to allay the qualms of a sensitive and educated conscience.

Alas! thus it always is with man. The source of evil is within us. Egotism deludes us with the feeling of possession where there is nothing to possess. This is the great enemy, — the *my-ness* in me. This is the giant weed whose roots lie deep in the human heart.

The Bhagavad Gîtâ is the epic which sings the death of this hydra-headed monster. It is a great poem, — a poem whose author must be both poet and prophet. It closes with the glorious vision of the victor standing firm in his glory: —

"O Thou unshaken one! by thy favor my delusion is destroyed. I have recognized myself; my doubts are gone. I am firm, and shall do Thy bidding."

As I close the book the Vedic hymn reverberates through my innermost being: —

"Destroyed is the knot of the heart, removed are all doubts, extinct are all hidden longings of the man, on seeing Him, Supreme and not-Supreme!"

V.

The machinery of the poem is deeply impressive. It is enshrined in the great Indian national epic, which has preserved for us the last rays of the Sun of India's ancient glory as he sank below the horizon.

Of all the royal families that flourished in India at that time, the suzerainty rested with the princes of the lunar dynasty. The king of that family bore the proud title of Râja Chakravartin, — "the Emperor from sea to sea." His capital was near the site of modern Delhi. Yes, when the stranger approaches this charmed spot in northern India, tongueless voices will call to him, —

"Stop! for thy tread is on the dust of many empires! Kurus and Pândavas, Rathors and Chohans, Pathans and Moguls have flourished on that spot and have then disappeared into the dark night of Time's insatiable maw. Stop, friend! and reflect on thyself, — thy hopes, thy disappointments, and thy hopes again renewed."

> "As we look our life fades away;
> Youth decays as day follows day;
> The days that go ne'er come again,
> And Time devours the Universe.
> Fortune flies as ripples break upon the sea;
> We flash through life as lightning on the sky."
> *Translated from the Sanskrit.*

Forgetful of this truth, one line of the royal house of Hastinâpura — as Delhi then was called — sought to rob another of its rightful sovereignty, and a battle was fought at Kurukshetra, a place sanctified by the pious deeds of their common ancestor Kuru, whose Kshetra, or field, it was called. At the time of this battle the royal family was divided into two branches, descended from two brothers.

Dhritarâshtra, the elder brother, was born blind, and was still living. He and his hundred sons, of whom Duryodhana was the chief, were called Kauravas. The other branch consisted of the five sons of Pându, the younger brother, and their descendants; these were called Pândavas, from the name of their ancestor.

Although Dhritarâshtra was the elder, by the Brahmanical law he was not competent to sit upon the throne, on account of his blindness; so Pându, and after him his eldest son Yudhisthira, ruled the country. The Kauravas, by fraud and other wicked means, forced the five Pândavas to expatriate themselves in order to keep their pledged word, and then deprived them of their royal rights.

After thirteen years of absence the Pândavas returned, having dutifully fulfilled their promise. But the Kauravas refused to restore to them their kingdom without a battle. To avoid bloodshed, the five brothers were ready to give up their rights in exchange for five villages. But the Kaurava chief would not give them as much earth as could be raised on the point of a sharp needle, without a contest. Accordingly the chivalry of India, consisting of more than two millions of men, assembled on the field of Kurukshetra to pay the debt of duty in battle.

The blind king Dhritarâshtra was led, through parental love, to approve of wrong and wickedness. The great sage Vyâsa, the poet of the Mahâbhârata, as well as other merciful men and well-wishers of the royal house, tried to awaken his conscience, but in vain. The sage then asked Dhritarâshtra if he desired sight in order to witness the carnival of slaughter about to take place on account of the wickedness of his sons. He declined the gift of sight promised by the holy man of wisdom, and begged that superhuman perception might be bestowed on his charioteer Sanjaya, who would acquaint him with all that came to pass.

INDIVIDUAL SPIRIT.

THE BHAGAVAD GÎTÂ;

OR,

THE LORD'S LAY.

CHAPTER I.

SURVEY OF ARMY.

DHRITARÂSHTRA *spoke:*

1. WHAT, O Sanjaya, do my sons and Pându's, assembled battle-bent, on the field of Kuru, the sacred plain?

SANJAYA *said:*

2. King Duryodhana, having but beheld[1] the hosts of Pându's sons drawn up in battle array, and then having approached the preceptor, said these words:—

3. Survey, O Preceptor, the vast army of the sons of Pându, guarded by thy wise pupil, Drupada's son.

Duryodhana, Dhritarâshtra's wicked son, is the very incarnation of pride, injustice, and jealousy. Evil-doers must repeatedly fortify themselves by the approval of the intellect, or they lose heart. The king praises the hostile warriors in order to rouse the martial pride of the preceptor, Drona by name, who instructed the sons of Dhritarâshtra and Pându in the science and art of war.

4. There are heroes of mighty bows, the compeers of Bhîma and Arjuna in fight; Yuyudhâna, Virâta, and Drupada, each a master of great car;[2]

---

[1] "But beheld." The Sanskrit here implies fear on the part of Duryodhana.

[2] "Master of great car" is an epithet bestowed upon a warrior who is able to fight, single-handed, 10,000 bowmen, and is thoroughly skilled in the use of weapons of offence and defence.

5. Valorous Dhristaketu, Chekitâna, and Kâçi's lord, Purujit, Kuntibhoja, and Saivya, chiefs among men;

6. Mighty Yudhâmanyu and valorous Uttamaujâ, as well as the son of Subhadrâ and the sons of Draupadî, all masters of great car.

If the enemy is so powerful, the best course is not to persist in evil and fight. It is best to abandon evil from prudence if it is not done for the sake of righteousness. Anticipating this reply from the wise preceptor, and thinking how uncertain is the triumph of good over evil, he enumerates the warriors on his own side.

7. But, O best of Brâhmanas, know those who are the flower of our side. Of the leaders of my army I shall name the select to you for your full understanding.

I am reflecting only on the principal expedients at my command; a hundred other devices will suggest themselves as occasions arise. These are but the "flower of our side." There is no reason for losing heart.

8. Thyself, Bhîshma, Karna, Kripa, — all conquerors of assembled hosts, as also Asatthama, Vikarna, the son of Somadatta, Jayadratha,

9. And many other brave warriors determined to lose their lives for my sake; all possessed of many weapons to strike and ward, and well skilled in the art of war.

"If you are so confident of success I need say nothing more, — then fight." Such a reply from the preceptor would frustrate the purpose of his speech. So Duryodhana again shows fear.

10. This our army, guarded by Bhîshma, seems insufficient, while the army of those guarded by Bhîma seems sufficient.

Bhîshma, the grandsire (grandfather's step-brother) of both the Kauravas and the Pândavas, is the most experienced of all the assembled warriors; on him Duryodhana chiefly relies. Evil must always support itself by experience, while good rests upon universal principles. Evil must rely on the power of the evil-doer, while good derives strength from faith in the absolute character of the law of righteousness. Evil is personal and good is universal; the good man feels himself to be upheld by something beyond him; he knows that the principles upon which he stands will abide, come what may. The evil-doer has no such confidence, because he seeks some definite object, and does not concern himself as to whether the laws of evil are absolute or not. For that knowledge can bring him no consolation if he loses that which he desires. Here Bhîshma, the most experienced general, is opposed to Bhîma, the most rash and reckless among the Pândava leaders. It is significant that Bhîma is named here, and not the son of Drupada, as in the third verse. The chief incitement to evil is the past experience of its success. Therefore it is that Duryodhana is so anxious for the safety of Bhîshma, whose "lion-roar" inspires him with confidence. This is expressed in the two following stanzas:

11. Let all of you, occupying properly distributed positions, guard Bhîshma at every point.

In the case of evil the inner voice can only speak from experience. Bhîshma, in whom Duryodhana declares such confidence, in return for this favor gives the king the needed encouragement, and,

12. Producing joy in him, the powerful grandsire, the most ancient among Kuru's sons, blew his conch, loudly roaring the lion-roar.

13. Then of a sudden sounded conchs and trumpets, and drums and tabors; and tumultuous grew the din thereof.

This was answered from the opposing ranks.

14. Then Mâdhava[1] and the son of Pându,[2] seated in

[1] *Mâdhava* is an epithet of Krishna implying his lordly power over Nature.
[2] The "son of Pându" is here Arjuna, who is also the son of Prithâ, whose other name was Kuntî. Bharata was the common ancestor of the Kauravas and the Pândavas.

the great car yoked to white horses, loudly blew their celestial conchs.

15. Hrishîkeça[1] blew his conch, called Pânchajanya, Dhananjaya[2] blew Devadatta, and Vrikodara,[3] of terror-inspiring deeds, blew the great conch Paundra.

16. King Yudhisthira, the son of Kuntî, blew Ananta-vijaya; Nakula and Sahadeva blew Sughosha and Manipushpaka.[4]

17. Possessed of excellent bows, the king of Kâçi, Çikhandî the master of great car, Dhristadyumna,[5] Virâta, unconquered Sâtyaki,[6]

18. Drupada and the sons of Draupadî, the son of Subhadrâ, O Lord of earth, all blew their respective conchs.

19. That terrible uproar, filling heaven and earth with sound, shivered the hearts of Dhritarâshtra's sons.

20. After that, then, as missiles were about to fall, O Lord of earth, the son of Pându, of the ape-crested car, with his bow raised, spoke this sentence to Hrishîkeça:

Arjuna *spoke:*

21. O Fall-less one, place the car between the two armies,

22. For so long that I may see these battle-desiring warriors here present, and find with whom I ought to fight in this impending battle;

23. I must survey these combatants here assembled, desiring in fight to work good to the evil-minded son of Dhritarâshtra.

---

[1] *Hrishîkeça*, the lord of senses and faculties, who dwells in us as "lord of the bosom," not only the searcher but also the designer of the workings of our hearts.

[2] *Dhananjaya* is Arjuna, "the conqueror of wealth."

[3] *Vrikodara* is Bhîma.

[4] These conchs were blown by the five sons of Pându.

[5] *Dhristadyumna* is the son of Drupada, mentioned in the third verse.

[6] *Sâtyaki*, the same as Yuyudhâna in the fourth verse.

Krishna, as the charioteer of Arjuna, shows that the Supreme God can be conquered, but by love only; at the same time the epithet "Fall-less one" shows that God is ever the same; no change of state can come to Him, although the changes in our own hearts produce apparent changes in the Deity.

Arjuna here wishes to know who among the hostile chiefs are fit antagonists for him. The strong should fight with the strong only.

SANJAYA *spoke:*

24. O son of Bharata; Hrishîkeça, thus addressed by Gûdakeça, placed the best of cars between the two armies, and

25. Said this: O son of Prithâ, see Bhîshma and Drona in front of all the kings assembled on the Kaurava side.

That is, Bhîshma and Drona are worthy antagonists for you, O Arjuna.

26. The son of Prithâ then saw there present in the two armies, sires, grandsires, preceptors, uncles, brothers, sons, grandsons, fathers, and also friends, fathers-in-law, and kindred.

27. He, the son of Kuntî, seeing all his kith and kin present, overcome with great pity, despondent, said thus:

ARJUNA *spoke:*

28. Seeing, O Krishna, these kindred, assembled battle-bent, my limbs wither and my mouth becomes parched.

These are indications of grief.

29. There is trembling in my body and my hair stands on end; the Gândiva[1] drops from my hand, and my skin burns fiercely.

These are symptoms of fear.

---

[1] *Gândiva* is the name of Arjuna's bow.

30. I am not able to remain firm seated; my mind also seems to wander; and, O Keçava, I also perceive omens of evil.

> This shows lack of endurance. Whenever a man loses faith, these three evils, grief, fear, and weakness, attack him, and he begins to delude himself into the belief that it is fruitless to persevere on the upward path. Whenever we ask ourselves, "Is the goal worth attaining?" we must know that we are falling, — losing ground. Such obstacles are presented to every one, and it is of the utmost importance not to lose confidence. The most effective weapon with which we can contend against the internal enemy is found in the study of what the sacred books have said about the successful traveller who has passed through the narrow gate. The dutiful student of the holy books may find the admonitions of some beloved teacher which may prove the very balm he needs. Meditation on the lives of spiritual heroes, the conquerors of the serpent of egotism, is also of great value.

31. Truly I do not perceive any benefit from killing kindred in battle. I long not for victory, O Krishna, nor for kingdom, nor for pleasures.

32. What, O Govinda,[1] are for us kingdoms, enjoyments, or even life? Those for whose sake kingdoms, enjoyments, and pleasures are desired

33. Are these here present in battle, abandoning desire of life and possessions, — preceptors, sires, sons, grandsires,

34. Uncles, fathers-in-law, grandsons, brothers-in-law, and also other kinsmen, O slayer of Madhu,[2] — I do not wish to slay them even though I be slain myself.

35. O Janârdana,[3] what satisfaction can there be for us in slaying the sons of Dhritarâshtra, even for the

---

[1] *Govinda*, — Krishna, who knows all that is done by our senses and organs.
[2] "Slayer of Madhu," — the demon of darkness.
[3] *Janârdana*, — the giver of all men ask of him.

sake of the sovereignty of the three worlds?[1] What then of the earth?

When the doubter begins to reason as to the nature of his gain in attaining eternal life, naturally he perceives nothing; all appears like dark and cold negation, for so it is to thought and sense. Only "the pure in heart can see God."

36. Sin indeed will cling to us for killing these, though open foes. Therefore we are not justified in slaying the sons of Dhritarâshtra together with their friends. How can we be happy in killing our own kindred, O Mâdhava?

"Open foes" is a technical term, which includes an incendiary, a poisoner, one with weapon raised ready to kill, or a robber of goods, lands, or wife. Although it is allowable to kill them, yet all violation of the supreme injunction against the taking of life is sinful. In the case of Arjuna this rule does not apply, as his duty to fight rests upon the divine command which established the system of castes.

37. If these, with hearts deluded by grief, do not perceive the sin caused by destruction of one's own family and by hostility against friends,

38. Why, O Janârdana, by us who perceive the wrong produced by the destruction of family should this not be rightly viewed as reason for desisting from this sin?

39. Upon the extinction of the family, the eternal rites of piety of the family being extinct, impiety overcomes the whole family.

By the theocratic law of the Brâhmans it is enjoined upon every householder to labor for the perpetuation of the good qualities of his ancestors. If he allows the family to die out, he has to answer for the impoverishment of the race consequent thereupon. The

[1] "The three worlds," — the habitations of men, gods, and semi-divine beings.

home is sacred, and to fulfil the duties of home is an act of worship. There is no one in the world superior to the righteous householder; for all others — the spiritual mendicant and all — are dependent upon him. Therefore whoever looks upon the state of a householder as a sacred duty, and not a privilege, is blessed indeed.

40. From the domination of impiety, O Krishna, the women of the family become corrupt. By the corruption of women confusion of castes is produced.

41. Confusion of castes [thus] causes the abiding in hell of the family of those who destroy the family. Their ancestors fall into hell owing to the cessation of the offering of ..ral cake and water.

When the principal members of a family are destroyed, the survivors follow the path of lawlessness; and owing to the absence of fit persons to perform the funeral ceremonies required for the peace of the manes of the ancestors, these last lose their celestial estate.

42. By these wrongs, productive of the confusion of castes, the eternal, pious rites of the family and of the caste of those who destroy their families are extinguished.

The institution of castes secures to a man the knowledge of what he must do to inherit eternal life. The family and caste duties being well known and rigorously fixed, an ego is born in a particular family and caste in accordance with its needs. Thus a man has not to search blindly and waveringly for a full knowledge of his duty, but starts with it in life's great journey. Hence to create a confusion of castes is a greater moral wrong than to remove the sea-marks which guide the mariners in their course.

43. For those men, O Janârdana, whose family piety becomes extinguished there is continued abiding in hell; this we have heard.

44. Alas! we are bent upon committing a deadly sin,

since we are ready through greed of empire and enjoyment to slay our own kindred.

45. If me, unresisting and weaponless, the weapon-handed sons of Dhritarâshtra slay in fight, — that for me will be better.

> SANJAYA *spoke:*

46. Having said this, Arjuna, shaken in heart by grief, in the midst of battle's ranks sat down on the car, abandoning his bow[1] together with the arrows.

> This ends chapter the first, called the "SURVEY OF ARMY," in the blessed BHAGAVAD GÎTÂ, the sacred lore, the divine wisdom, the book of divine union, the colloquy between the blessed KRISHNA and ARJUNA, and contained in the Bhîshma Parvan of the blessed MAHÂBHÂRATA, which is a collection of a hundred thousand verses by VYÂSA.

[1] "Abandoning his bow," etc., as a sign of his resolve to adopt the life of a religious mendicant.

CHAPTER II.

RIGHT KNOWLEDGE OF THE SPIRIT.

IN this chapter, as well as in those succeeding, it is taught that the only reality is Consciousness, or the Supreme Spirit, which, being absolute, has no relation to any object or action. But there is a mysterious power, which though really non-existent, except in identity with the Supreme Spirit, yet appears as if possessed of a co-ordinate being. This seemingly real power presents two poles, namely, the perfect and ruling, and the reverse; each of these appears as though conscious, owing to a mysterious connection between the power and consciousness. The one pole is the personal God, called the "Son of God" in the Christian Scriptures; the other, man. As consciousness — that is to say, in reality — they are identical. Conditioned existence ceases for him who realizes this identity, but not for others. The only right course for those bound by conditions, and therefore under the necessity for action, is to follow scriptural commands in perfect faith that the power to act, as well as the results that ensue, belongs to the Supreme God, — even the Father, — who is eternally free from all conditions as well as from all attributes that are given to the personal God, — the first among all the sons of God.

SANJAYA *said:*

1. Then the Slayer of Madhu said these words to him, thus overcome with pity, despondent, and with eyes full of perplexity and tears: —

THE BLESSED LORD *spoke:*

2. Whence, in this place of danger, is come to thee[1] this sinful darkness, shunned of the worthy,[2] heaven-marring, and unmaker of name and fame?[3]

---

[1] "Thee," who art the best of warriors.
[2] "Worthy," that is, versed in holy lore.
[3] "Name and fame." It was a religious duty for the warriors to keep these unsullied.

3. Fall not into eunuch-hood,[1] O son of Kuntî;[2] this is not worthy of thee. Arise, O harasser of thy foes,[3] casting aside this degrading faintness of heart.

Arjuna *said:*

4. How shall I, O Slayer of Madhu, in battle with arrows contend[4] against Bhîshma and Drona, worthy to be adored, O Slayer of thy foes?

> This last epithet, "Slayer of thy foes," is used here to show that all that can possibly be done is eternally accomplished by the Blessed Lord. Arjuna is only the harasser, Krishna is the Slayer. The one is trying to do what the other has already and forever done, — eternally accomplished. The Deity, as absolute and perfect, can have nothing to attain. The moment that we conceive that He has anything to gain, we also perceive that He is possessed of the same from all time and forever. The Blessed Lord, being one with the Deity, reveals to mankind the Supreme Spiritual nature.

5. Better in this world[5] to eat even the beggar's bread, without slaying the great-souled, adorable ones, than by slaughtering those worthy to be worshipped, to enjoy on this earth alone[6] blood-stained pleasures, lusted after by those desiring possessions.[7]

6. We know not this, — which for us is preferable, that we should conquer, or that they should conquer us. Those, whom slaying, we wish not for life, are present before us, — Dhritarâshtra's sons.

---

[1] "Eunuch-hood," that is, want of firmness.
[2] "Son of Kuntî." This epithet is intended to make Arjuna feel that he is a man, and
[3] "Harasser of thy foes" is meant to remind him that he is a hero.
[4] "With arrows contend," when I ought not to contend even with words.
[5] "Better in this world," as opposed to spiritual welfare in the world to come.
[6] "On this earth alone." The enjoyments are blood-stained, and only obtained by forfeiting heaven.
[7] "Those desiring possessions." The natural man striving to perpetuate the enjoyment of worldly objects.

7. Thee I ask, with nature defiled by blindness to Spirit[1] and heart, in delusion about the Supporter,[2] tell me that which is truly best. I am thy pupil;[3] instruct me, who in thee have refuge sought.

I seek for Nirvâna because

8. I do not perceive that which can remove the grief that withers my senses and organs and mind, even on obtaining footless empire on earth and also the sovereignty over gods.

SANJAYA *spoke:*

9. Gûdakeça, the harasser of foes, after thus speaking to Hrishîkeça, became silent, saying, "I shall not fight, O Govinda."[4]

10. O son of Bharata, to him, despondent in the midst of the two armies, Hrishîkeça, as if in mockery,[5] said these words: —

The despondency of Arjuna offers the most suitable opportunity for the Blessed Lord to proclaim the truth to the world and point out the way of the Spirit. It is clearly shown that without perception of the Spirit, which is the true Ego, power, virtue, and learning are useless. The feeling of *my-ness* is the real enemy which shrouds knowledge with ignorance and severs man from the path of duty. The only effective remedy against this spiritual evil is the recognition of the truth that as the personal ego is beginningless in time, its work throughout past eternity has not

---

[1] "Blindness to Spirit." The state of one who departs this life not knowing "this indestructible God," the truest Self.

[2] "Supporter." The Supreme Spirit, comprehending all, — both what is caused and what causes.

[3] "I am thy pupil." The mysteries of the Spirit should only be revealed to a son or pupil, — such is the injunction of the ages. Cf. Matt. iv. 11.

[4] *Govinda*, he who knows the workings of our senses and faculties. Arjuna, unable to express all that is in his mind, relies upon Divine Omniscience; hence this epithet.

[5] "As if in mockery." To impress him with the folly that prompted his thought, word, and deed.

ended its suffering, and no work is therefore capable of securing "surcease of sorrow" during the future eternity. Without a just motive, a man must not abandon his duty although its performance is of no use in reaching the desired goal, — the peace that is eternal life or Nirvâna. The delusion that induces an abandonment of duty because it offers no positive benefit is the great stumbling-block. True spiritual knowledge dawns upon no man who does not selflessly perform his duty, although the mere performance of duty does not necessarily result in illumination which depends on Divine grace. This is the gist of the teaching of Krishna.

The Blessed Lord proceeds to show that egotism is the cause of grief, suffering, and violation of duty.

The Blessed Lord *spoke:*

11. Thou mournest those who ought not to be mourned, though thou speakest words of learning.[1] Those wise in things spiritual mourn not the living or dead.

The reason why he says "ought not to be mourned" is, that as the true Ego of all is the Deity, death is not a reality; it is also evident that in so far as they *are in reality* they cannot become *naught* by operation of cause or lapse of time.

The "wise in things spiritual" are those who have realized the identity of the Deity and the Ego. "Although thou speakest words of learning, yet thy behavior discloses thy ignorance of spiritual truth."

12. Verily it is not so that ever I *was not*, nor thou, nor these lords of men: nor is it that we, every one, shall hereafter[2] *be not.*

The idea of plurality of egos, as suggested by "I," "thou," and "lords of men," refers only to the body. The true identity of all egos with one another and with the Deity is the supreme truth here declared as the basis of the immortality of all individuals.

---

[1] "Words of learning." See Chapter I. verse 38 *et seq.*
[2] "Hereafter;" that is, after the dissolution of the body.

13. As for the lord of the body, there are in this body childhood, youth, and decay; so is there the attaining of another body; by this the man of wisdom is not deluded.

Arjuna reasons within himself that though there is no reason to grieve for the true self, or the spirit, which is immortal, yet the present feeling of the "pair of opposites," heat and cold, pleasure and pain, is a sufficient cause of grief. To remove this it is said:—

14. O son of Kuntî, the senses and their objects are producers of heat and cold, pleasure and pain. They are transitory, appearing and ending; abandon them, O son of Bharata.

"The senses and their objects." The original Sanskrit phrase can also be rendered as "the contact of the senses with their appropriate objects." It is here shown that the pair of opposites are the only things known to human beings; pleasure and pain in reality include heat and cold.

In the beginning of the verse, where the nature of heat and cold is declared, Arjuna is addressed as the son of his mother,— Kuntî; but when he is exhorted to abandon pleasure and pain, he is reminded of his heroic ancestor Bharata, from whom India is called by her people "the land of Bharata."

The command to "abandon them" means to be above the senses by realizing the truth that the Ego is independent of them. What follows superiority over the pair of opposites is next declared.

15. O best of men, the man who is equal in pleasure and pain, is undisturbed by them, and is possessed of wisdom, is fit for immortality.

This mode of addressing Arjuna is intended to imply that he ought to aspire for immortality, the eternal life of Nirvâna, which is attainable by any man who is free from the influence of the pair of opposites and possessed of wisdom.

Further reasons to show the necessity or dispassion:—

16. For the Naught no aughtness can there be, nor naughtness can there be for Aught. By the truth-seeing [1] the ultimate characteristic of these both [2] has indeed been seen.

"Naught" signifies those things that have a cause: for example, *heat* and *cold*, which are really non-existent because they are not conceivable without their cause. With the eye an earthen pot is seen, but if the earth be absent the eye cannot at all perceive the pot; nor was the pot seen before it was made nor will it be seen after it is destroyed. The perception of the pot therefore shows nothing but itself; in other words, does not demonstrate its own reality but manifests the reality of its cause. It may at first appear that to proceed in this manner is to accept a *regressus in infinitum* and maintain universal negation. But it is not so. For whatever happens, the perception of reality — that something *is* — never can be absent.

Every fact of consciousness involves in itself two elements; namely, substance and quality, noun and adjective, subject and predicate. When we speak of different substances we really mean qualities; among which without any logical reason one is assumed to be the substance.

In the term "black horse" it is usually assumed that "horse" is the substance and "black" the attribute. In reality it is not so. For no one can represent to his mind a horse without a color. Hence in dealing with "horse" divested of attributes, as the substance, we are really dealing with an abstraction or attribute, — with *horseness*, in fact. This is strengthened by the consideration that if the word "horse" is spoken before a number of people, each one figures to himself a different horse. Which of them is the horse corresponding to the word "horse"? In the absence of any reason for specialization it is clear that the word "horse" is the power to indicate all the individual horses in existence. The word "black"

---

[1] "The truth-seeing." The word translated "truth" is "that"ness. Being the name applicable to all and everything, "that" is taken to mean the substance of the universe. Hence "thatness" implies the essential reality of "that," or Supreme Brahmā.

[2] "The ultimate characteristic of these both;" that is, Naught is Naught and Aught is Aught. Relying upon this, feel convinced that so far as these creatures are real they will forever remain real, there being no power to alter that. In so far as they are unreal they do not exist even now. So there is no occasion for grief.

restricts the operation of that power by the operation of another power, namely, *blackness*. The mutual relation between these two powers, as shown by the position of the words, is that their area of operation is identical. It is clear from this that neither of them is the substance, or both are. The necessity for excluding one of them from the category of substance shows that there *is* a substance independent of them in which they both inhere as attributes or powers. Therefore the existence of an attributeless substance, and the insubstantiality, and in that sense non-existence, of attributes, cannot be denied.

It is also clear that everything observable or inferable is included in the class of attributes. By themselves, separated from the substance, the attributes are non-existent; but in relation to the substance they are identical with it. For otherwise they would be *absolute* negation, which is evidently not the case from their power of simulating the substance. Now, what is the substance?

To determine this we must consider what is the peculiar characteristic of the substance. If all that is observable and inferable is attribute, the only thing that *is* and yet cannot be the object of a probative operation must be the substance. It is clear that the ego alone fulfils these requirements; for there can be no probative operation that is not preceded by a doubt, and no doubt can exist without the existence of the doubter, or ego.

The substance is the Self, and the not-Self, embracing the whole universe, is its power. In this power is contained the power of perceiving the power separated from the Powerful; but this separating power is power, and not the Powerful, — in other words, is an adjective and not a noun, and hence by the above reasoning has no substantiality except in identity with the substance. This is the reason why the power of viewing the power as separate from the Powerful is called illusion, — neither real nor unreal; in fact, indescribable.

The argument set forth above may lead to this inference: Granted the omnipresence of substance and quality, it does not necessarily follow that the Ego is immortal or real. For obviously substance and quality are mutually convertible expressions. Hence it is clear that the Ego is only a quality of the non-ego, and as such is unreal, except in identity with it. In so far as Nature is the Ego, the Ego has existence; otherwise it is a figment of the imagination. This reasoning is false.

The question is whether the Ego is the power or quality of the non-ego, or the reverse. It is evident that nothing *is* except Ego and non-ego. Now, let us suppose that the Ego is the property of the non-ego. This would mean that the Ego knows itself to be non-existent except as a property of the non-ego, and therefore in identity with it. But the Ego cannot know itself, except through some objective medium, and consequently cannot under any circumstances be really identical with the non-ego.

Therefore the other alternative must be true. Ego is the substance, and non-ego the power or quality. The Ego is immortal, for how can power destroy the Powerful, who alone can exercise it? One power can destroy another power, but not the powerful, without whom the power cannot exist. Evidently the power cannot do what it could only do if it did not exist. A thing cannot do what its negation can do. This is declared in the following verse:—

17. And[1] know him as indestructible by whom all this is pervaded.[2] Of him who remains unchanged nothing can produce destruction.

Next is declared what is Naught from the standpoint of *supreme truth*, in other words, what is and is yet not real in its being.

18. These bodies, subject to dissolution, are said[3] to belong to him, the eternal,[4] indestructible,[5] unprovable,[6] who is in the body; therefore fight, O son of Bharata.

The word "fight" in this verse is not used as an injunction, but a statement of Arjuna's mental state, which has been temporarily clouded by doubts. Wisdom does not require the co-operation of any act whatever to compass the supreme end of existence, and the Bhagavad Gîtâ is not meant for enjoining any course of action, but for the extinction of conditioned existence, which consists of

---

[1] "And." This conjunction is to show that the "Aught" in the preceding verse is the immortal Self.
[2] "By whom all this is pervaded." Without the Ego nothing can exist; therefore space is nothing but the pervasive power of the Ego.
[3] "Said," that is, by the unwise.
[4] "Eternal," that is, is not liable to be annihilated.
[5] "Indestructible," that is, not subject to change of character.
[6] "Unprovable," that is, self-evident.

grief and delusion. To strengthen this impression the Blessed Lord cites the two following Vedic texts. The first is intended to disabuse Arjuna of the idea that he is acting or is to act in the ensuing battle; the whole thing is but the baseless fabric of a dream.

19. He who knows it as the slayer, and also he who knows it as the slain, they both know not rightly: it kills not, nor is killed.

Next it is declared that the Ego is not subject to change. In regard to the true Self the six classes of change are denied in detail.

20. Never is this[1] born, nor does it die, nor having been does it ever cease to be; unborn,[2] eternal,[3] undecaying,[4] ancient;[5] this is not disintegrated by the disintegration[6] of the body.

"Nor having been does it ever cease to be," requires some thought for its right understanding. No object can be conceived of by the mind as continuing to exist, except in relation to its beginning and end. That which having been does not cease to be, does not also persist in existence. All objects which come into existence at any definite point of time cannot cease to be at that very moment, nor can it be conceived of as remaining absolutely the same as at the moment of its appearance. The idea of a beginning, an end, and an interval separating them invariably accompanies the conception of all objects that are non-eternal. This is here denied of the Ego.

The proposition laid down in verse 19 is proved by the Vedic text forming verse 20, and is now being repeated as proved.

21. Whoever knows this[7] unborn and changeless, as

---

[1] "This." The real identity of the Self with the divine Self is implied.
[2] "Unborn," that is, not subject to the change called birth.
[3] "Eternal," denies death.
[4] "Undecaying," denies decay.
[5] "Ancient," denies growth; the same that was, is now.
[6] "Disintegration" denies change of substance.
[7] "This," that is, the Ego, mentioned in the foregoing verse.

undying[1] and eternal,[2] O son of Prithâ, whom does he, the Spirit,[3] kill or cause to be killed?

In the preceding verse all kinds of action are generally negatived in regard to the Spirit, or true Ego; here the identity of the illuminated sage with the Spirit is declared, and the class of action called killing is set forth to strengthen the general truth by application to the case of Arjuna. But how is this identity to be understood? The actionlessness of the âtmâ or true Ego being granted, how does that apply to him who knows the âtmâ?

The illuminated sage, in so far as he is the illuminated sage, is *not* âtmâ, and therefore is not actionless. To this the reply is that the illuminated sage, in so far as he is the illuminated sage, is *really* non-existent, and what is said here does not apply to him, as it is addressed to one who is not illuminated. The aspirant will understand what is meant by the identity of the sage and the Spirit only when he becomes himself what others would call a sage. In the mean time he can but try to understand it.

Another question also arises. If the âtmâ is actionless it cannot be known, for that would connect it with action as its object. Not only the actor is in delusion, but also the one who is acted upon; they both know me not rightly, says the text (v. 19). This is perfectly true. The Vedas teach, "That by which everything is known by what is that to be known." "Not he is the Supreme Spirit who is worshipped here."

How can there be a spiritual philosophy if this is the case? If the Spirit is utterly unknown, how can any one teach or learn anything about it? In supreme reality there is no one to teach or to be taught. And yet there is a false knowledge about the âtmâ, — a groundless belief that it is known; this false knowledge is what every man calls "himself," the centre of all that is done and experienced. Spiritual philosophy teaches the nature of this self, and shows it to be the misconception of the âtmâ, and no reality

---

[1] "Undying," that is, supremely unmodifying.

[2] "Eternal," that is, never appearing as of a different substance. These two attributes declare the supreme independence of the Ego. They show that the Ego undergoes no change either in form or substance.

[3] "He, the Spirit." The possessor of this knowledge is the same as the Supreme Spirit. The truth is here stated in the form of a question, to show that although limbs may appear to move and mind to think, there is no egotism claiming their ownership.

except in so far as the misconception is identical with the thing about which it is a misconception; as is seen in the case of the rope which is mistaken for a serpent. The misconception called the serpent is nothing but the rope. When this is seen, the process of inquiry about the serpent and its nature comes to an end. In order that this illustration may be fully understood, it must be borne in mind that if the serpent is the personal self, then on the removal of the misconception there can be no one to say, "I am the self that was," for I never was the self spoken of; nor that "I am the âtmâ," for he who can be supposed to say this is really a misconception, and therefore on being realized as such can say nothing. The wisdom implied by realization ceases to exist on realization, for it has nothing to realize; and further, it has realized nothing, for that which it is said to have realized is a misconception and not a thing. Spiritual philosophy cannot manifest the Spirit that is self-manifest, but what it is not; and when that is realized, the Spirit, which is the true Self, is, by a figure of speech, said to be known owing to its self-manifestness. In reality the Spirit and the knower cannot exist together as co-ordinate realities.

What is meant here by the illuminated sage is the âtmâ, — both by him who asks and him who is asked. In so far as any other answer is expected, the expectation is no reality. Being no reality itself, it can have no real answer. The questioner and replier are both *really* an illusion. The answer is also an illusion, yet it is capable of removing the other illusion, namely, the existence of the questioner and replier, and the necessity for their act; and when the truth declared by it is understood, the sufferings of conditioned life cease.

If anywhere reality is assumed, — for instance, if it is imagined that either the questioner or he who replies is real, — the identity of the sage with the Spirit is real, and ought to be accepted as such; that is to say, will be accepted as such if this is the only illusion requiring consideration; in other words, if the only desire is that of knowing the truth. Hence it is that all spiritual teachers lay so much stress upon the moral purity of the pupil. "To know the doctrine one must live the life;" "the man without faith comes to destruction."

In order to show that the Ego is unchangeable, and thus to remove the grief lingering in the thought that the change of body is itself a great calamity, it is said : —

22. As, abandoning clothes that are decayed, a man takes other clothes that are new, so the dweller in the body, abandoning bodies that are decayed, goes into other bodies that are new.

23. Not this [1] the weapons pierce; not this does fire burn, nor this does water wet, nor the wind dry up.

The âtmâ is beyond the four elements, earth (weapons), fire, water, and wind. This is the negative aspect.

24. This is called unpierceable, unburnable, also unwetable and undriable; eternal,[2] all-pervading, constant this,— changeless, ever the same; [3] unmanifest [4] this, uncognizable [5] this, and unvarying.[6]

The "this" is all-pervading, because if there was any place from which it was absent, it could only be so through the presence of something else. The cognition of this something else would exclude the presence of "this" for a time, and prevent its being eternal. This epithet is also meant to deny that the Ego is an atom; therefore it is constant, and therefore unchanging, which is not the same thing as constant, for a thing may be constant in changing. Nor is it to be understood that the unchangeableness of the Ego is here inferred from its being constant ; it rests upon all the attributes taken together. Yet again it is not to be forgotten that these epithets are meant to facilitate the realization of the objective universe as not-Self, and intended to describe what the Ego really is, — "unmanifest," unthinkable.

25. Therefore, knowing this to be such, thou oughtest not to be able to mourn.[7]

This completes the topic commenced in verse 11, and forms one unit in the harmonious whole.

---

1 "This," that is, the Ego, the dweller in the body through the power of illusion.
2 "Eternal," that is, not subject to the conditions of time.
3 "Ever the same," that is, is uncaused.
4 "Unmanifest," that is, irresponsive to sense and mind.
5 "Uncognizable," that is, not answering any faculty in us.
6 "Unvarying," that is, not subject to change, even such as milk turning into cream or curds.
7 "Not to be able to mourn," not merely to abstain from so doing.

26. Again, if thou considerest this to be constantly born and constantly dying, still thou, O mighty armed one, oughtest not to be able thus to mourn.

Even if thou shouldst adopt the opinions of the worldly-minded, and conclude that with the birth of every body a new and separate ego is born, and dies with its death, even then, being a mighty armed hero, thou oughtest to be above grief. For in that case it follows : —

27. Of that which is born death is certain, and certain also is the re-birth of the dead. Therefore, owing to its unavoidableness, thou oughtest not to be able to mourn.

28. Unperceived[1] is the origin[2] of creatures and unperceived is their end;[3] only their middle, O son of Bharata, is perceived; what is there in it to lament?

This being the case, how can you lament and feel attachment to those about whom you know so little ? Like logs of wood floating on the ocean current we meet on earth for a moment, and then we part, each following his own path. Therefore such thoughts as " I am theirs " and " They are mine " are merely a delusion.

The next verse seeks to encourage Arjuna by showing him that his want of right perception of the Ego is due to the inherent difficulties of the process, and not to any extraordinary defect on his part.

29. Some consider[4] the âtmâ as a marvel; others again speak[5] of it as a marvel; and still others hear[6] of it in wonder; and even having heard, not one realizes it.

Isa. vi. 9.

---

[1] "Unperceived," that is, by physical senses.
[2] "Origin," that is, ante-natal condition.
[3] "End," that is, state succeeding death.
[4] "Consider," etc., that is, do not realize that it is the innermost Self.
[5] "Speak," etc. Many who repeat what the sages say of it still wonder if those sayings are true.
[6] "Hear," etc., shows the increasing difficulty of the various stages of spiritual perception.

30. The indwelling spirit that is in every body is indestructible, being eternal. Therefore thou oughtest not to be able to mourn any creature.

The indwelling spirit, or the dweller in the body, is the One Spirit viewed in relation to a variety of bodies. The Spirit, though one, appears as separated, owing to the separateness of bodies; like light from one and the same source appearing as varied, owing to differences in the reflecting surfaces. This is the " I " which every creature takes as his own.

This gathers together all the units of crystals in the teachings of the Blessed Lord and combines them in one great crystal. The idea introduced in verse 11, having been clearly shown forth more than once, is here fully completed.

This section of the present chapter makes the folly of grief manifest from a purely philosophical point of view. With the following verse begin other considerations leading to the same result. The teaching slowly descends from the height of spiritual philosophy, and by degrees comes home to the hearts of all kinds and classes of men.

Having spoken of the final goal and the ultimate reality, the Blessed Lord puts forth other considerations, — not to strengthen the truth, for that requires no support, but to increase the receptive powers of the hearer, to help his unbelief. The method of all divine teachers is, first of all to declare unto us the ultimate truth, the final goal, and then to remove all obstacles which stand in the way of our receiving the truth. "Believe me that I am in the Father, and the Father in me : or else believe me for the very works' sake " (John xiv. 11). These auxiliary means of strengthening faith when received as final in themselves and out of connection with the whole produce blindness and bigotry. The reference to Arjuna's caste morality in the ensuing verse is to be taken as auxiliary teaching.

31. Because for a Kshatriya nothing exists which is superior to lawful fighting, therefore viewing this as natural duty thou oughtest not to waver.

Kshatriya is the second or military caste of India. The caste duties are the natural proclivities of the man as shown by his birth in a particular caste. Arjuna's duty is to fight, and not to hesitate to kill when lawful occasion for it arises.

The meaning of this verse is that nothing on earth is absolutely perfect; the wisest thing, therefore, is to follow one's nature. But this is impracticable for those who do not understand their natures nor their own final good. Ethical codes are intended to guide us in acquiring this knowledge. If a man has nothing in him to respond to ethical laws, all teachings would be of no value to him. Whenever we accept an ethical principle, it is only because we recognize its meaning as a part of our nature. The relation of ethics to spiritual life is most beautifully explained by Saint Paul (Romans vii.).

The true duty of a man is the true need of his nature. There can be no duty which is not a natural need viewed in the light of the complete destiny of man. The majority of mankind, not knowing the destiny of man, are blind to duty. The code of ethics which is associated with religion is an invaluable aid to us in the recognition of our duties; but owing to its high spiritual standpoint it requires to be supplemented. For the understanding of our real, as opposed to our conventional, duty the following are necessary: —

1. A dutiful study of religious ethics.
2. Diligent observation of the practice of the faithful followers of spiritual ethics.
3. Right understanding of the practical morality of one's own people as shown in the ethical foundation of the social and political institutions.
4. Study of the tendencies of one's own nature; that is to say, listening to the still, small voice of conscience. No one of these singly can be the infallible guide in all possible situations in life, but all of them must be harmoniously combined for the purpose.

32. Only fortunate Kshatriyas, O son of Prithâ, obtain such a fight as this, which has come unsolicited, like the gates of heaven unclosed.

The general injunction against taking life is here pushed aside by the special injunction which makes it the indispensable duty of the warrior caste to fight. One of this caste who fights as a matter of religious duty, and looks upon slaying and being slain as of no importance, goes to Indra's heaven if slain on the field of battle. If he wins, he acquires possessions wherewith he can fulfil such religious obligations as are imposed upon his caste. Fighting is "like the gates of heaven unclosed," especially to him who is slain, for he goes forthwith to heaven; whereas the slayer gains that benefit only by the performance of duty during the rest of his life.

In order to strengthen Arjuna's faith in the performance of duty, the Blessed Lord declared in the last verse what would result from it; he next says what will follow its non-performance:—

33. Contrariwise, if thou dost not engage in this lawful battle, then thou shalt incur sin by abandoning thy natural duty as well as fame.

Not only shalt thou incur the sin of omission shutting thee out of heaven, but even on this earth

34. Men will speak of thy ill-fame forever. For those much esteemed ill-fame exceeds death.

35. Masters of great car will consider thee as turning away from fight through fear, and before them thou shalt grow low, having once been so high.

36. Enemies, reviling thy prowess, will utter many unbefitting[1] sayings directed against thee. What can be more painful than this?

The next two verses sum up the section of the discourse commencing with verse 31.

37. If slain, thou shalt attain heaven; if victorious, thou shalt enjoy this earth; therefore arise, O Kunti's son, with resolve fixed on battle.[2]

Fight thou must; then listen as to what state of mind thou oughtest to fight in, so that thou mayest escape sin.

---

[1] "Unbefitting,"—not justly applicable.
[2] "Resolve fixed on battle." Because this is thy natural duty, and not because action extinguishes suffering.

38. Having made pleasure and pain equal,[1] as also gain and loss, victory and defeat, then engage in fight; thus thou shalt not incur sin.

Here commences a new section. What has been said hitherto is from the standpoint of pure spiritual philosophy, which would be quite sufficient for the wise man whom the world can ensnare no more. But so long as we have passions and the world has charms, the spirit may aspire to those serene heights, but the flesh will still be weak. For such men the Blessed Lord declares the path, which, though in reality the same, appears to be different, owing to the difference in the development of the aspirants. It must never be forgotten that the right performance of action is declared throughout to be of value only as the means of leading to the knowledge set forth in the seven verses, 12-18. Otherwise, no act of any kind leads to eternal life, or Nirvâna.

39. To thee has been declared[2] the knowledge regarding the pure spiritual philosophy; now listen to this [knowledge] regarding the philosophy of action:[3] O son of Prithâ, being united to this knowledge thou shalt escape the bondage of action.

The "knowledge regarding the purely spiritual philosophy" is the right knowledge of the supreme reality, — the absoluteness of the Ego, — which extinguishes conditioned existence in all phases and forms. It is called "purely spiritual," because those alone can comprehend it without any preliminary training who are entirely purified from all passions and thirst for life. This shows that the preceding verses are not intended to enjoin any course of action.

The "philosophy of action" is that of the means for attaining spiritual knowledge. It consists in performing the religious and moral duties pertaining to a man's station in life, free from liking or aversion by dedicating them to the Deity, and in removing the

---

[1] "Equal," that is, having purified thyself from attraction and repulsion. This is the secret by which the world is conquered.

[2] "Declared" — in verses 12-18.

[3] "Action" comprehends all that can be related to the actor, — good and evil action as well as complete inaction.

germs of desire embedded in the super-conscious self by the practice of all-absorbing meditation on the mystery of the Spirit. That spiritual knowledge is the crown of righteousness, and hence of all existence, is the truth also taught by Jesus (John xvii. 3). Saint Paul explains it further in 1 Corinthians xiii. 9–12.

"Being united to this knowledge, thou shalt escape the bondage of action;" for although the knowledge of the philosophy of action does not by itself remove the "bondage of action," yet it renders the man pure enough to receive the knowledge of the Spirit which does cut asunder the knot of action. The knowledge of spiritual philosophy is one with the knowledge of the philosophy of action; for the means and the end can but form together one harmonious whole. The subject will be quite clear on reference to Chapter IV. verses 33–38.

40. In this[1] no initiation is lost,[2] nor are there any evil consequences,[3] and even a little[4] of this practice saves from the great danger.[5]

41. In this path the certainty-souled faith is one; but many-branched, infinite-fold are the faiths[6] of those devoid of this faith of which the soul is certainty.

The "certainty-souled faith;" that is, the deep faith which excludes the infinity of possibilities. "I am certain that by devotion to God I shall attain Nirvâna through the illumination granted by His grace." The interior change in us represented by these words is the "one faith" which arises as the consummation of the anxious

---

[1] "In this," that is, path to liberation through the right performance of action.

[2] "No initiation is lost." Labor spent upon a field one season becomes exhausted after producing the crop; but not so in regard to the practice of the philosophy of action. Whatever is begun takes its character from the state of mind in which it is begun, and is independent of the end. The beginning is the end; the rest but an echo.

[3] "Evil consequences," that is, failure to attain the end.

[4] "Even a little," as seen by men. The character and amount of our work for the Deity are perfectly immaterial. If our natures change, then all is done, — all is gained.

[5] "The great danger," that is, conditioned existence.

[6] "Faith" is used in this and the following verses in the sense of "conviction as to the reality of anything sensuous or spiritual."

questionings and deep yearnings of our nature, and the unswerving search for the light veiled by the words of the Scriptures. When this faith produces spiritual illumination, the universe — which is but the infinite-fold modification of faith, in other words, infinite states of consciousness — merges in the glorified Ego that is absolutely identical with God, as energy merges in substance.

The term "many-branched" refers to the unstable character of desire and the transitoriness of that which is not spiritual. Faith in one absolutely perfect God — One without a second, either similar to or different from Him — extinguishes forever the impulse for creating hypotheses, while unending and infinite is the brood of Desire and Error; hence "infinite-fold" is false faith.

The three following verses explain why this "certainty-souled knowledge" is not found in every human heart.

42. The unwise [1] are lovers of the praise in the Vedas of the fruit of ceremonies prescribed therein, and are sayers of "there is nothing else," [2] and repeaters of flowery shadows of speech

Rom. ix. 32.

43. (Full of special ceremonies, — yielding birth as the fruit of action, and leading to power and objects of enjoyment), desire-souled and aspiring to celestial abodes as the supreme goal, —

44. Of these, devotedly attached to power and objects of enjoyment, and with hearts snatched away [3] by such speech, the certainty-souled knowledge does not become fixed [4] in casting away [5] all things for the enjoyment of the Spirit.

The "lovers of praise in the Vedas" are those who through the darkness of desire cannot find in the Vedas the real truth, but rest satisfied with such sayings as "inexhaustible is the merit of him who performs the Châturmâsya sacrifice."

---

[1] "Unwise," that is, devoid of right discrimination.

[2] "Nothing else" besides the objects of their cravings set forth in the Vedas.

[3] "Hearts snatched away." This is the reason why they are unwise and devoid of faith.

[4] "Certainty-souled knowledge... fixed;" that is, their faith is not established.

[5] "Casting away," etc., that is, self-oblivion in the Deity.

"Shadows of speech" means mere semblances of speech, and nothing more. Thus the praise of ceremonials is to be taken merely as the inducement for their acceptance, and having no other value. For instance, the text in praise of the Châturmâsya sacrifice, cited above, does but mean that that sacrifice is to be performed.

The expression "yielding birth" signifies that all the ceremonies can do is to secure to the performer birth in heaven or in a royal family, and kindred benefits. The performance of ceremonies lusting after their fruits does not have the purifying effect which comes from their dedication to God. Therefore it is said, "leading to power," etc. The chief question is not what is done, but how it is done. If ceremonies are performed for love of God, the performer proceeds on the road to Nirvâna. Otherwise, as in the case of the "desire-souled unwise," the result is only as here set forth.

45. The Vedas have for their object only the assemblage of the three qualities; be free from the three qualities, O Arjuna; free from the pairs of opposites, constant in the quality of *satva*, free from acquisitiveness and desire for the preservation of what is possessed already, and not dominated by any object of sense or mind.

Rom. iii. 20; iv. 15; vii 1, 6.

"The assemblage of the three qualities" is the manifested universe, or conditioned existence. These qualities and their functions will be described in Chapter XIV. The entire universe may be considered as the modifications of the three qualities roughly to be spoken of as goodness, passion, and darkness or stupefaction. To be "free from these qualities" is to be purified from desires, and the method for accomplishing this is shown by the attributes that follow.

Satva is goodness, or that power in Nature which allows a man to transcend the limitations of his personal nature by embracing some absolute principle. In its perfection it is that power which preserves the eternal perfection of God, although He is the doer of all that is done.

The next verse shows how the performance of works for the sake of God alone is better than working for heavenly enjoyments and the other gains before mentioned.

46. As much benefit as there is in a limited expanse of water, so much is there in water stretching free on all sides:[1] similarly, as much benefit as there is in all the Vedic rites, so much is there for the truth-realizing Brâhman.[2]

<small>Rom. viii. 4.</small>

"The truth-realizing Brâhman" is one who has consummated the knowledge of spiritual philosophy. That which is attained through inner illumination transcends every possible object of desire. For as the whole universe is nothing but illusions that simulate the One Reality which is the true Ego or God, so when this Reality is attained there cannot possibly remain any want for any object in the universe.

But then, O Lord, thinks Arjuna, why art thou inclining my mind to the philosophy of action, consisting in the dedication of all actions to God? Is it not better to enter upon the path of spiritual knowledge at once, since the immediate antecedent of liberation is knowledge? The next verse clears this doubt. No one can put his foot upon that path unless he goes through the path of right action first.

47. Thy right is only to action;[3] let thy right be never to the result; nor may thou be the cause of the result of action,[4] nor may there be in thee attachment to inaction![5]

<small>Matt. vi 1-4;
1 Cor. x. 31;
Rom. xii.11;
2 Tim. iv. 2.</small>

"Let thy right be never to the result" means, though thou must tread the path of action, do not enter into action with thirst for it. Do not thou deceive thyself into the thought that "I am obliged to be on the path of action, therefore it is right that

---

1 "As much benefit . . . all sides." The usefulness of a limitless expanse of water includes the usefulness of a limited sheet.

2 *Brâhman* has no reference to caste here, but simply means an illuminated sage.

3 "Only to action," and not to actionless devotion to spiritual philosophy, owing to thy spiritual immaturity.

4 "Cause of the result of action." If thou shouldst engage in action, thirsting therefor, thou shalt surely be tied to the future experience of its results.

5 "Attachment to inaction." Do thou not think, Why should I do anything at all, when it is, so difficult to pass through the fire unhurt?

I should engage in all action." Whoever thinks thus is sure to be entangled in useless actions through his passion for action. The right course is either to do only such works as are declared on scriptural authority to be acceptable to God; or if it be not possible to restrict one's acts to these alone, then perform whatever action is absolutely called for by the sense of duty until the change of heart comes. In either case dedicate the fruit of action to God, and do not impute to yourself the power to perform action rightly, as it is not comprised within the self-conscious being, — the man as known to himself. To this end is Romans viii. 26.

48. Firmly seated in yoga,[1] perform action, abandoning attachment,[2] O Dhananjaya,[3] and being equal-minded towards success or ill success. Equal-mindedness is called yoga.

<small>Luke xvii. 7-10; Job xxxv. 6-8.</small>

Success here means the spiritual illumination in the gift of God. For the complete purification of the inner nature it is necessary to resign even the desire for illumination and salvation.

49. O Dhananjaya, by far inferior is action to union with knowledge;[4] seek refuge in knowledge; those who become causes of fruit of action[6] are spiritually blind.[7]

<small>Isa. i. 11-17; Matt. xxiii.23; Rom. iii. 28.</small>

Now listen to what arises from the performance of acts of natural and scriptural duty in the state of union with knowledge or faith.

---

[1] *Yoga* is one-pointed devotion to God. The word generally has a larger acceptation, as, for instance, at the end of this verse. When the thinking principle is at rest and images the Ego in serenity, it is yoga.

[2] "Abandoning attachment." This is not a repetition of what is said in the preceding verse. It means the surrender of the desire that God may be pleased with the actor in consequence of his acts.

[3] *Dhananjaya* literally means "conqueror of wealth." The epithet implies exhortation to rise superior to all desires.

[4] "Union with knowledge," that is, yoga, the union with the realization of the equal-mindedness or peace before described. "Knowledge" is to be understood in its two aspects as related to action and philosophy.

[6] "Causes of fruit of action," by acting under the impulse of desire.

[7] "Spiritually blind," those who die without the knowledge of the Supreme Spirit, — who die in their sins (John viii. 21).

50. On this earth he who is united to yoga[1] abandons both virtue and sin;[2] therefore aspire for yoga; yoga is the skill in action.[3]

How does it happen that the man who dedicates his acts to God escapes from the wheel of conditioned existence? Listen:—

51. Because, being united to knowledge, and abandoning action-born fruits, the sage of mature wisdom, freed from the bondage called birth, goes to the troubleless seat.[4]

In this and the two preceding verses "knowledge" may mean not the yoga, which is equal-mindedness or peace, but the spiritual knowledge that arises from the practice of the philosophy of action, or yoga through action. This interpretation is supported by the statement about its extinguishing virtue and sin (v. 50), which spiritual knowledge is alone competent to do.

When does the light of the Spirit dawn upon the heart purified through action performed in the above manner?

52. When the forest of delusion[5] thy heart shall cross over,[6] then shalt thou attain dispassion[7] both as to what is heard[8] and what is yet to hear.

Col. ii. 8; Tit. iii. 9.

---

[1] *Yoga*,—the interior state of peace produced by devotion or spiritual knowledge.

[2] "Both virtue and sin." One rises above the bondage of sin, and therefore of virtue also, by the spiritual light that illumines the perfectly pure heart.

[3] "Skill in action." The secret of being in action and yet not bound to the wheel of conditioned existence which action would surely necessitate if not surrendered to God.

[4] "Troubleless seat," that is, Nirvâna.

[5] "Forest of delusion," in the midst of whose dark shadows thou hast lost the discrimination between thy real Self and that which is illusive, and in consequence thy heart is inclined towards objects of sense and mind.

[6] "Cross over," that is, when thy nature shall be exceedingly purified.

[7] "Dispassion," that is, want of interest in them by perceiving their ineffectuality in thy search for Supreme light.

[8] "What is heard ... to hear." All books and discourses not connected with the way of the Spirit.

53. When thy heart, thoroughly confused[1] by all that <small>Col. ii. 9.</small> is heard, shall attain unwavering rest in the Supreme Spirit,[2] then shalt thou attain to the realization of the Spirit.[3]

"Then" here means this state of unwavering rest in the Supreme Spirit. No man can ever come to God by mere lapse of time, but through various stages of illumination. All adverbs of time describing spiritual mysteries indicate the orderly comprehension of these states, and not the movement of heavenly bodies. Time refers to spiritual order, ascending and descending.

The chapter closes with a vision of the glorification of the spirit in man. Wishing to know of the blessed condition of those who attain to the supreme knowledge spoken of in the previous verse,

Arjuna *said:*

54. How, O Keçava,[4] does he whose power of cognition[5] is at rest in the Supreme Spirit speak when spoken to? How does he, whose heart is at rest, speak himself? How does he remain, and how does he go?

In the preceding verses (39-53) the Blessed Lord has declared the steps that the self-conscious man can and does take in his progress Godward. The internal steps which the real man, the super-conscious self, takes, are super-ethical, and therefore inexpressible as injunctions, but can be apprehended in spirit through love of those who have gone beyond the cloudy peak. For that which is natural to them is the means or the steps which the inner man must take. From this point there is no help from any

---

[1] "Thoroughly confused;" that is, when all that men say about the way to God is no longer of any interest, and the need of external knowledge — that is, knowledge that comes from words — has disappeared.

[2] "Supreme Spirit," the only and true Self.

[3] "Realization of the Spirit;" that is, the truth that sets us free; the knowledge of identity between the universal and individual spirit.

[4] *Keçava*, that is, "he whose rays manifest themselves as omniscience." This epithet gives the reason for asking him such a question of divine and mysterious import.

[5] "Power of cognition . . . Supreme Spirit," refers to the words of the preceding verse. The "power of cognition" is the "thoughts" which "shall be established" if thou "commit thy works unto the Lord" (Prov. xvi. 3).

other source than the divine love, or knowledge, as it is variously regarded by us who know not, but hear and believe.

The purpose of the rest of the chapter may be perceived from this, — that the illuminated sage, being one with God, really has no attributes. Fatal errors would arise if we take this part of the discourse as having any ethical value. Let no man apply this teaching about the obliteration of good and evil to himself. For the applying of it, or even the conscious tendency towards it, is an unmistakable proof that the necessity for action still exists; "thy right is only to action;" consequently find out the best way of performing action, and strive not for the characteristics of the spiritually illuminated sage, which are not attainable by mere striving. They are in the gift of God, and none else; they do not pertain to the personality of man that thinks, acts, and wills. When the personality is so thoroughly renounced, or, in other words, when resignation to the mysterious and inscrutable will of God is so complete, as to extinguish all sense of effort, then these attributes become natural. If perfection is attained, there can be no need for further effort: effort is of value only because perfection is attainable. Efforts made by a man without regard to the final cessation of effort in perfection, which is rest, are without doubt misdirected and useless.

THE BLESSED LORD *spoke:*

55. When he completely casts out all desires[1] which are seated in the heart, and is content in the Self, through the Self,[2] then is he called one whose knowledge[3] is at rest.

The meaning of "content" is, that identity with absolute bliss which is independence of everything. The outward signs of activity seen in a sage are like those in a madman or a child; no action on his part is preceded by the determination "I shall do it." To the question as to how he speaks when spoken to, the reply is,

---

[1] "All desires . . . the heart;" that is, the state where there is not even the desire to cast away desires. This at once shows that this state of illumination is beyond the reach of the personal will, and therefore of all injunction and restriction.
[2] "Self through the Self," — the realization of the Supreme Spirit as the Self.
[3] "Knowledge," that is, heart, cognitive power, "thoughts."

Like a madman or a child. "We are fools, for Christ's sake," says Saint Paul (1 Cor. iv. 10).

Whatever we perceive in one "whose heart is at rest in God" is just what we seek from him. He is merged in the Infinite, and has therefore all desires, and none; consequently what he gives us is exactly what we ask. "All things are lawful unto me, but all things are not expedient" (1 Cor. vi. 12). Hence it is certain that no external sign can ever prove the divinity within the divinely illuminated sage. When Peter declares the Christhood of Jesus, the Master says, "Blessed art thou, Simon Bar-jona, for flesh and blood hath not revealed it unto thee, but my Father which is in heaven" (Matt. xvi. 17). He spoke to the same effect on other occasions; for example, 'Blessed are they who have not seen and yet have believed" (John xx. 29).

56. Having mind unperturbed in pain [1] and devoid of craving in pleasure,[2] the man of renunciation, without attachment,[3] fear, or anger, is said to be one whose knowledge is at rest.

57. Who in every condition [4] is devoid of attachment, and in every condition receiving that which is favorable as well as that which is unfavorable, neither likes nor dislikes, — his knowledge is established in rest.

The question as to how he speaks is now answered; he speaks without any personal motive.

58. When he completely withdraws [5] in every condition all his senses from their objects, after the manner

---

[1] "Pain" includes everything opposed to the Self, whether coming from things outside the body or from the body, as well as from acts of God, accidents, etc.

[2] "Craving in pleasure;" that is, absence of desire for the perpetuation of any of the three kinds of pleasure, corresponding to the three kinds of pain, when it comes, and also absence of increase of appetite by what it feeds on.

[3] "Attachment," the tendency to repeat a past experience on account of the enjoyment once derived from it. After an enjoyment is over it is never missed, nor is there the fear of losing it while it lasts, nor a desire to hurt another who possesses the enjoyment which the man of renunciation has not.

[4] "Every condition," that is, in regard to the body, life, etc.

[5] "Withdraws." This shows that the character of the senses is so changed that they can range over objects without being entangled in them.

of the limbs of the tortoise,[1] then is his knowledge established in rest.

This verse does not refer to the *real* condition of the sage, but only to his gaining a firm foothold on the path of knowledge, because the senses are said to be withdrawn, or rather indrawn, like the limbs of the tortoise, and not perfectly established in harmony of action ; this is really the case with the illuminated sage who is so thoroughly independent of the flesh as to have no concern of any kind about the senses.

A misconception may here arise. In illness, distress, fatigue, anxiety, and other similar conditions, the senses become withdrawn, like tortoise-limbs; also in the case of the deluded ascetic, who by penance and austerities suppresses the outward activity of the senses, and is yet devoid of spiritual illumination. Wherein, then, lies the difference?

59. From a man who gathers not objects of sense, the objects fall back; but on seeing the Supreme, even the taste for objects falls back from him.

The necessary condition for inner illumination is the effacement of taste for things; in other words, the latent desires which enable us to attach pleasure or pain to experiences when they come. Things in themselves are neutral, neither pleasurable nor painful, as can easily be seen from the fact that they do not affect all men in the same manner, nor do they produce the same effect on the same man under different conditions. "Taste" here means the element which colors objects with pleasure or pain. This taste cannot be obliterated by any external effort, but only by *Samâdhi*, or self-effacing rest in God, described in Chapter VI. All aspirations being gratified, no further impulse towards any object can remain. In the presence of fulness, how can hunger and thirst exist?

God is the plenitude of all enjoyment, and all the enjoyment of the universe can be but an atom of that. For as the Deity transcends the infinite universe and is also infinite, the derived infinity will have infinity beyond it. The same thing can be seen from a different standpoint. Nothing is pleasant nor unpleasant except in relation to the Ego; that which the Ego approves is pleasant. The

---

[1] "Limbs of the tortoise," withdrawn into its shell when it is frightened.

Deity is the true Ego, and therefore the essential reality, by a mysterious connection with which things can be either pleasant or unpleasant ; the true Ego is the absolute bliss.

Although the germs of desire latent in the mind are the most important enemy of the seeker of liberation, yet active desires are not to be given way to. For eternal life or liberation is liberation from all desire, without limitation. The necessity for self-restraint is inculcated in the two following verses. Those who aspire for spiritual illumination must bring the senses under control at the outset, because, —

60. The turbulent senses and organs violently snatch away [1] the heart, even of the wise man striving after perfection.

"The wise man" is one who perceives the evil of conditioned existence and also the truth beyond. He has the feeling that one should not desire worldly objects because they are vain and the reality is beyond them. These two together form the dawn of spiritual perception. So long as they are not co-existent the religious life cannot be said to begin, although there may be a semblance of it. Therefore, —

61. He,[2] having controlled the senses [3] and organs, remains at rest [4] on me [5] his true Self.[6]

Col. ii. 2-10.

Whoever has the senses and organs under control,[7] his knowledge is at rest.

[1] "Snatch away," that is, unsettle and drag towards worldly objects.

[2] "He," that is, "the man of renunciation," spoken of in verse 56.

[3] Controlled the senses," that is, the senses are his, but he is not theirs ; this is real control, and not merely the determination to stop the manifested activity of the senses. (Cf. Col. iii. 4, 5 ; Rom. viii. 13.)

[4] "Remains at rest." This is in reply to the question, How does he remain ? (v. 54.) "At rest" means without tendency to change in any direction whatever.

[5] "On me," the one Ego of all, as his highest and truest Self. "This Ego of all, I am." Without this recognition there is no liberation.

[6] "His true Self." That is, without any thought that "this is my own Ego, and this is the Ego of all."

[7] "Under control," owing to absence of any inducement to work, the whole universe being undesirable ; or, by reason of having broken their tendency to work by the rest attained through long communion with the Deity.

62. For the man contemplating objects is born appreciation[1] thereof; from appreciation arises desire; from desire[2] springs forth anger.

63. From anger comes delusion;[3] from delusion, loss of memory; from loss of memory, loss of discrimination; and from loss of discrimination the man is destroyed.

When delusion exists loss of memory follows; for the truth may be recognized at one time, yet through anger there will be failure to recall it at the right moment. If this continues long enough, there comes the loss of discrimination, or the faculty of judgment. Not merely are erroneous conclusions formed, but the faculty itself is lost. This is the utmost annihilation that can come to the man.

The Ego is immortal, but the power of making judgments as to what is the nature of the Ego, and uniting such judgments into various centres, makes so many persons, or personal egos. If through a long course of bad judgments there comes at last the extinction of the faculty to judge, and an unquestioning submission to blind propensities of nature, the final result is that the personal Ego, or centre of judgment, becomes merged in the great Nature without recognizing the fact that the true Ego is independent of Nature. This recognition is the highest function of the faculty of judgment.

On the other hand, when through divine illumination judgment ceases as the culmination of a long course of wise judgments, there is the judgment that the Ego, being identical with the perfect God, does not want anything, and never did. The difference between the two is quite obvious; not to want because all that can be desired is obtained, and not to want because nothing can be obtained, are not the same.

The source of evil having been described, the next verse proceeds to show the way to liberation. If, as has been said, the thought of objects is so dangerous, and yet the forcible suppres-

---

[1] "Appreciation" includes an intellectual preference. By dwelling on things we notice peculiarities which distinguish them from similar things seen before. Obviously this is the beginning of desire.

[2] "From desire ... anger;" that is, from opposition to desire comes anger.

[3] "Delusion," that is, incapacity to use the power of judgment rightly. Wrong appears as right.

sion is condemned, what, then, is the path? Especially as some thought is necessary for the maintenance of the body, without which we are destitute of means for obtaining knowledge of the Supreme Spirit. The reply follows: —

64. He however who experiences objects[1] through the senses and organs, freed from attachment and repulsion,[2] and controlled by his heart, and his heart[3] obedient to the will,[4] attains to peace.[5]

65. Upon the attainment of peace arises the end of all his sufferings, and the knowledge of him whose heart is tranquil quickly comes to all-embracing rest.

"All sufferings" includes physical pain. When the aspirant's heart is at rest, he is free from bodily ailments, at all events is not conscious of pain, because the body requires pulsatory attention in order to be conscious of its workings. So, when the man is no longer subject to the present conditions of consciousness, he does not know of the existence of bodily pain.

This is one result of tranquillity of heart. The other is firmness or rest of the cognitive power, which in this case perfectly reflects the true Ego.

The "all-embracing rest" is the final consummation, — being as the perfect image of the Ego, which is formless. In every act of cognition the cognitive power assumes the form of the object cognized. When the true Ego is known, — in other words, when the objective universe is known as the non-ego, of which the Ego is independent, — the cognitive power is in absolute rest, because there is no object for it to cognize; the true Ego or consciousness it is satisfied is uncognizable; that which leads to this supreme satisfaction is the perfect image of the Ego, the "form of God" (Phil. ii. 6). The cognitive power is not the same as consciousness, which does not cognize, but renders cognition possible; just

---

[1] "Objects," that is, such as are necessary to the maintenance of the body.

[2] "Attachment and repulsion." The senses of the unregenerate act under the impulsion of these two powers. But not so of the man whose heart is purified by scriptural studies and other methods of spiritual training.

[3] "Heart," that is, desires, feelings, judgment, etc.

[4] "Will," that is, the spiritual will, or aspiration for the highest blessing; namely, realization of identity with the Deity.

[5] "Peace." This answers the question, How does he go? (v. 54).

as sovereignty does not govern, but renders it possible for the sovereign to rule.

The next verse shows the value of the control of the senses in the attainment of this rest.

66. For one whose heart is not at rest there is no spiritual knowledge; for him whose heart is not at rest there is no joyous aspiration towards spiritual illumination; and not for the unaspiring is peace, and for one without peace where is happiness?

The faith that the Ego is absolute, the spiritual gift of hope, is the sense in which "aspiration" is here used. And the reason why there is no spiritual knowledge for one whose heart is not at rest is declared in the next verse.

67. The senses and organs being in activity, whichever the heart follows, the same snatches away his knowledge, as wind the boat on the water.

If there is a single sense out of control, the aspirant must fall. Let us, therefore, be warned against being lulled into a fancied security when the senses do not seem to be as turbulent as before. For this is very often entirely due to the fact that other senses are gaining strength, and not to any increase of purity in us. Frequently vices reassert themselves after long intervals of apparent death; so long as there is one unruly sense, we must not forget the teaching given here, as well as in Matthew v. 29, 30. It should also be borne in mind that the best remedy for evil is not the suppression but the elimination of desire; and this can best be accomplished by keeping the mind constantly steeped in things divine, as said in Chapter IX.; patient resistance is the only safeguard against the active onslaughts of desire.

In the "heart," spoken of as following the senses, is included the faculties of imagination and reflection. The knowledge of what is the true Ego and what is not, is snatched away by engaging the mind in brooding over or contemplating with pleasure the objects which correspond to the unruly sense. And as the wind drives the boat out of its proper direction, so the uncontrolled heart wrenches the cognitive faculty away from spiritual things and links it to matter. The topic commenced in verse 60 is summed up in the following verse.

68. Therefore, O thou mighty-armed, his knowledge is firmly established whose senses and organs are in every respect regulated in regard to their objects.

The manner in which the characteristics of the illuminated or beatified sage are here stated is noteworthy. The description opens with the statement that he is free from all desires and *knows* that the true Ego or the Supreme Spirit alone is happiness; all else is pain. Then it follows that he is free from attachment or repulsion towards whatever may befall him, and that he acts without determination. Lastly comes the subjugation of the senses, which is useless, and frequently injurious, as breeding hypocrisy and spiritual pride without the second; and that again is not of much value without the first. It is very important to keep this in mind. The teaching here is an expansion of the Vedic text: "He who does not abstain from unrighteous conduct, is not of peaceful mind, whose heart is not one-pointed and free from desire, never finds the true Ego."

69. What is night to all creatures[1] there is awake the man of restraint;[2] that in which[3] all creatures are awake is viewed as night by the seeing sage.

Col. iii. 3;
1 Cor. ii. 13-17;
iii. 19.

"Viewed as night by the seeing sage" emphasizes the truth that the sage who has realized the identity of the Ego with the Supreme Spirit cannot have egoistic consciousness in regard to any object, whether the body appears to be awake or asleep. Therefore all scriptural injunctions as to specific works as well as ethical rules, so necessary for ordinary men, are to him perfectly meaningless. He has no wish either to violate or follow them; they relate to the false self-conscious life of the personality, which he knows to be illusive. Even the aspirant for the realization of the Truth must give up the ambition to be good; in other words, must feel spiritual poverty and devote himself entirely to the

---

[1] "Night to all creatures," that is, divine illumination.

[2] "Man of restraint." This does not mean the mere prevention of the senses and organs from wandering; but the elimination of the dispersive and enveloping powers — passion and ignorance — which constitute bondage.

[3] "That in which . . . awake," that is, the delusion in which they appear to be awake, though really buried in the sleep of false knowledge; their state is comparable to dreaming.

increase of Faith, the consummation of which is Truth. In fact, every desire must vanish before Truth can be truly seen. For the innermost thing in us is Truth, and the only expedient necessary for its realization is the removal of falsehood, which is the warp and woof of the self-conscious life.

70. As waters enter the sea, fixed and changeless though ever filled, whom thus all desires enter,[1] he alone attains to peace, not he that cravings crave.

71. The man who, abandoning all longings, wanders[2] void of desire,[3] and feels not himself to be the actor or possessor,[4] attains to peace.

72. This is rest in the Supreme Spirit, O son of Prithâ, having obtained it the sage is deluded no more; established herein at the time of death, he attains Nirvâna in the Supreme Spirit.

> Thus ends chapter the second, called the "RIGHT KNOWLEDGE OF THE SPIRIT," in the blessed BHAGAVAD GÎTÂ, the sacred lore, the divine wisdom, the book of divine union, the colloquy between the blessed KRISHNA and ARJUNA, and contained in the Bhîshma Parvan of the blessed MAHÂBHARATA, which is a collection of a hundred thousand verses by VYÂSA.

Salutation to Krishna, who by the declaration of this spiritual philosophy rescued his devotee Arjuna from the mire of grief and despair.

---

[1] "Whom thus all desires enter." As they enter, so they die; as fresh water entering the sea loses its own character without affecting the sea.

[2] "Wanders," for food necessary for the support of life.

[3] "Desire," all but for maintenance of life.

[4] "The actor," etc. But even then does not feel the effort made as made for *himself* or for the preservation of *his* life.

CHAPTER III.

THE KNOWLEDGE OF RIGHT ACTION.

IN the preceding chapter it has been declared that the devotion of men is twofold; namely, that to pure spiritual knowledge, and that to right action. Then, from verse 55 to the end of the chapter it is shown that the sage, devoted to pure spiritual knowledge, and not bound to action of any kind, attains to Nirvâna (v. 72). Yet the Blessed Lord teaches Arjuna (v. 47), "Thy right is only to the act; . . . let not for thee be attachment to inaction." In other words, Arjuna is enjoined to perform action with the right knowledge of action; in consequence, perplexities arise in his breast. "When I pray to the Lord to be taught the best means for attaining supreme welfare, he replies that it is devotion to spiritual philosophy, and yet commands me to engage in action which can but mediately lead to the goal; how is this?" Thus confused,

ARJUNA *said:*

1. If, according to thy intention, O Giver of all men ask,[1] knowledge is superior to action,[2] then why, O Keçava,[3] engagest thou me in acts of cruelty?

If it had been the intention of the Blessed Lord to teach the need of works for salvation, Arjuna would not have asked this question, unless he very grossly misunderstood the teaching. It will presently appear that there is no such misconception in his mind; and, indeed, this is quite clear from (II. 49), "By far action

---

[1] "O Giver of all men ask." In Sanskrit, Janârdana. "Thou givest all that men ask of thee, thou wilt also grant this prayer," so hopes Arjuna.

[2] "Action," as explained in note on Chapter II. verse 39.

[3] *Keçava*, being lord of all, thou canst save me from the necessity for cruel deeds, if thou shouldst choose.

is inferior to knowledge," which throughout this book means real consciousness, and not acquirements of the intellect.

2. With words, as though confused, thou seemest to delude my reason. With certainty declare one method by which I may attain well-being.

The Blessed Lord *spoke:*

3. Two paths of devotion for the world were declared by me in the beginning,[1] O sinless one,[2] — devotion as wisdom of the spiritually wise,[3] and devotion as action[4] of the men of action.

The same man cannot be devoted to pure spiritual knowledge and also to action. This is the solution of all possible doubts. There is one stage in a man's life when work and forms are necessary for him, but subsequently they become unnecessary.

It is here taught that those only should renounce the world who are detached from it by absence of natural affinities for it, and not those who must wrench themselves away. The twofold character of devotion depends upon the purity or impurity of the nature of the devotee.

Then why not let Arjuna adopt the path of wisdom? Because,

4. A man does not attain to freedom from action by not engaging in action merely, nor is the goal gained by simple abandonment of action.

Action is not merely that which is technically called works by Bráhman theologians, but it also includes outward acts of divine worship. The spiritually wise man worships in spirit and truth by the realization of identity with the Supreme Spirit.

---

[1] "In the beginning," that is, at the foundation of the world.

[2] "O sinless one." This means that only those who are pure in heart can receive truth. Arjuna's fear on account of his confusion of mind is baseless, because he is pure, and therefore fit for the reception of truth.

[3] "The spiritually wise," that is, those who from early life renounce the world by perceiving its vanity.

[4] "Action," that is, duties enjoined by Scriptures.

On the other hand, freedom from action is the interior illumination which puts an end to all interest in objects and renders action impossible by revealing the identity of the Ego and the Supreme Spirit. The abandoning of action from spiritual pride is not spiritual wisdom.

Why one does not gain wisdom by simply abandoning action is next declared.

5. Verily no one [1] ever rests an instant without being a performer of action; all creatures are made to act without independence [2] by nature-born qualities.

In regard to nature-born qualities it should be explained that the Indian sages teach that Nature is the totality of all qualities, and that which is not quality is the Ego. Conditioned existence is due to the acceptance of some group of qualities or conditions as the Ego. So long as this erroneous view of the Ego is entertained, the man feels himself drawn into endless series of changes. He cannot stop them by simple wishes, and certainly cannot even wish to stop them unless he hears and believes that some other state is possible and ought to be aspired to. Thus the mind of man is in perpetual rotation through the influence of the qualities that compose it.

These qualities, though infinitely divisible, fall under three classes:—

1. Goodness, enlightenment, and pleasure (in Sanskrit called *Satva*).
2. Badness, passion, and pain (*Rajas*).
3. Indifference, dulness, and darkness (*Tamas*).

These are perpetually active, and the bondage of man consists in the mistaken notion that he is a bundle of qualities.

The reason why every one not spiritually illuminated should engage in action is because,—

6. He who, restraining the organs of action and sensation remains dwelling upon objects of sense,

---

[1] "No one," that is, except the spiritually wise as described in the final verse of the preceding chapter.

[2] "Without independence." No man who is subject to desires is master of himself.

is deluded in heart, and is called a hypo-crite.

<small>Matt. xxiii. 25-27.</small>

7. But he who, having restrained the organs by the mind engages in devotion through action, is superior.

"Superior" to the hypocrite, because by degrees he will attain to wisdom.

8. Perform thou proper action; action is superior to inaction. By inaction even thy bodily voyage cannot be accomplished.

Proper action is made up of religious and moral duties, and our bodily voyage is the fulfilment of the purpose of existence. Whoever attains to Nirvâna before death is in Nirvâna after death; but whoever departs this life without attaining that blessed goal does not attain it on account of death.

If one should think that action leads to action, and therefore it is best absolutely to desist from it, that would be an error; for,—

9. All actions performed, other than those for God's sake, make the actor bound by action. Perform action for His sake, O son of Kuntî, devoid of attachment.

Renunciation is not abstinence from action, but the doing of action for the sake of God; in other words, knowing that it is not done by thee or for thee, although with thy body and mind. It is not necessary to give up anything except desire. Further on, certain kinds of action, it is declared, are not necessarily to be given up even by the illuminated sage (Chap. XVIII. 3).

10. In the beginning, the lord of creatures, having produced creatures together with sacrifice,[1] said: With it multiply; may this be your milch-cow of desire![2]

11. Nourish the gods with this; may those gods[3]

---

[1] "Sacrifice," that is, works prescribed by the Theocratic Code, by which the Brahmanical people are governed.

[2] "Milch-cow of desire." The cow of plenty, whose milk takes the form of the object desired by the milker.

[3] "Those gods," that is, thus nourished. The gods correspond to angels of the Lord.

nourish you; mutually nourishing, may ye both attain well-being!¹

12. The gods nourished by sacrifice will give you wished-for enjoyment. He who enjoys their gifts without giving them is even as a thief.

<small>Prov. iii. 9, 10.</small>

All good things that come to us are from the gods, and it is the ordinance of the Creator that a portion of it should be used for nourishing the gods through sacrifices.

13. Being the eaters of the leavings after sacrifice, they become free from all sins. Those incarnate sins who cook for themselves eat sin.

Giving a wider significance to sacrifice than its mere technical import, we may interpret the first part of this verse thus: whoever performs duty and has no other enjoyment than what is gathered from its mere performance is beyond the reach of sin.

"Those incarnate sins" are men who receive this world's goods, which are the gifts of the gods, and offer no portion of them in sacrifice, — they are sins in the forms of human beings. They "eat sin," because the objects they enjoy are sins, being used in an unrighteous way.

Action is needed to keep in motion the wheel of cause and effect which forms the universe. The co-eternity of these two, as of tree and seed, is shown in the next verse.

14. From food come creatures; food comes from rain; rain comes from sacrifice; sacrifice is born of action.

15. Know action to be Veda-born, and Veda as born of the Exhaustless Spirit; therefore the all-pervading Spirit is ever established in action.

Religious duties derive their final authority from the Vedas. Although everything that takes place is owing to the power of the

---

¹ "Well-being," that is, prosperity on earth and at death liberation, or abode in any heavenly sphere that is desired.

Supreme, yet that power is especially revealed by religious rites, as all-pervasive light appears to be especially present in a transparent object.

16. The wheel thus set in motion, whoever does not turn according to ancient practice, he, O son of Prithâ, of sinful life and sense-delighted, lives in vain.

This concludes the topic begun in verse 4. So long as a man must live in the world, let him live in accordance with the principles inculcated by his religion. But when he receives spiritual illumination and stands alone with his God, he becomes a law unto himself. This is the highest spiritual state, which but very few attain, though all ought to aspire for.

17. But he whose delight is in the Spirit, the man who is filled by the Spirit, who is contented with the Spirit, there is nothing necessary for him to do.

Those whose delight is in the Spirit find as much delight in spiritual things as is found in objects of sense by the carnally minded. Being filled by the Spirit and one with that Spirit, no desire for anything can exist. As a lighted lamp does not require another lamp in order to be seen, so the spiritually wise want nothing for their enjoyment beyond the Spirit, or the true Self, which is the very essence of delight.

18. In the world, verily, there is not for him any interest in what is done, nor even in what is not done. Nor for any object is his dependence on any creature.

But thou art not thus.

19. Therefore, unattached, always perform those acts that have to be performed. A man performing action without attachment attains to the Supreme.

He attains to the Supreme because he becomes fit for divine illumination through the purification of his nature.

20. Verily through action[1] Janaka and others attained the goal.[2] And even[3] seeing the need of keeping men fixed to duty, thou oughtest to perform thy duties.

How men are kept faithful to religious and temporal duties is now explained.

21. Whatever is performed by the superior, the same is done by the inferior. Whatever he accepts as authority, even so does the world.

He cites his own case in illustration : —

22. O son of Prithâ, there is nothing for me to do in these three worlds, — nothing unattained that is possible to attain; still I am present in action.

23. If for once I do not ceaselessly remain in action, all men will follow my way, O son of Prithâ.

The Holy One, thus speaking, can only be said to remain in action through the mysterious power of the Deity, who cannot be compelled to work by any extraneous power. Man's conception of himself changes with every new act; but not so with the Deity, even though He be said to act or remain in action.

24. If I do not perform action these creatures will be lost[4] and I shall become the author of confusion, and shall have slain all these creatures.

This being the case, the general rule is as follows : —

25. O son of Bharata, as the unwise one acts, being attached to the fruit of action, let the wise man, without

---

[1] "Through action," that is, obtained purity of nature through righteousness of life, and through that the real knowledge of the Supreme Spirit.

[2] "Goal," that is, spiritual wisdom. The phrase may also mean that Janaka, Açvapati, and other royal saints carried on their original work for the benefit of the world even after their spiritual illumination.

[3] "Even," that is, even if thou considerest thyself free to enter the path of wisdom.

[4] "Creatures will be lost," by the complete extinction of the sense of duty.

attachment, act in the same manner, striving for the world's fidelity to duty.

Further,

26. Let not the wise man create confusion in the minds of the unwise[1] who are attached to action, but being himself engaged,[2] engage them in all action.

The reason why the unwise become attached to action is explained.

27. All actions are performed by the qualities of Nature, but the heart deluded by egotism[3] fancies that "I am the actor."

The reason why the wise are not attached is next given.

28. But, O mighty armed one, the truth-knower about the distinctness of the Ego from quality and action is not attached, being convinced that qualities[4] only act upon qualities.[5]

29. Those deluded by the qualities of Nature become attached to the actions of qualities; them, of dim discrimination and devoid of complete knowledge, he of perfect knowledge must not unsettle.

The foregoing teachings can be summed up thus:—
1. Action is indispensable for all but the spiritually wise.
2. Even they may at their choice act for the benefit of the world.
3. The unwise are bound by the desire for the fruit of action.
4. The wise are freed by knowing that the Ego is distinct from quality and action.

[1] "Confusion in . . . unwise;" not to disturb those who cannot act except for the sake of the fruit of action.

[2] "Himself engaged," that is, through his example.

[3] "Egotism" is the conviction that the body, its organs and the mental faculties taken together, form the real Ego.

[4] "Qualities," that is, organs and faculties.

[5] "Upon qualities," that is, objects appertaining thereto.

30. Giving up all actions to me, and with heart fixed on the mysterious link[1] between man and the Deity, do battle without expectation, free from the feeling of my-ness and free from anguish.

31. Those men who always follow these my words with faith and without reviling, they also become liberated from action.

Faith is the conviction that things that are imperceptible and not inferable, are true upon the authority of the Scriptures and that of illuminated teachers. This is the path of gradual emancipation, and will be further described in Chapter VIII. verse 24.

32. But those who revile them and do not follow them, know them to be deluded in regard to all knowledge,[2] lost[3] and void of discrimination.[4]

Why men still follow the wrong course is next declared.

33. Even the wise man acts in accordance with his character; all creatures follow nature; what can restraint do?

"Character" is the aggregate of the tendencies embodied in a creature, resulting from causes generated in the beginningless past.

"Nature" is the totality of the forces which form a conscious personal being by a mysterious relation to consciousness, which is the divine essence.

---

[1] "Mysterious link," etc. Knowing that existence simply as man is incomplete; there is another pole of being, the Spirit. Reality or Being as itself is one, but it manifests in two poles, Spirit and Flesh. What man has to do, the Spirit causes to be done. If all acts are done with this knowledge, then the one-ness of Being is manifested as divine illumination, and man's suffering comes to an absolute end. (Cf. Luke xvii. 10.)

[2] "All knowledge," that is, whether derived from sacred authority or from real illumination.

[3] "Lost," that is, unfit by nature to be proper vessels for the reception of truth, and therefore liable to the danger alluded to in Chapter II. verse 63.

[4] "Discrimination," spiritual perception.

This relation is called false knowledge, illusion, or simulation; because, although each creature seems to be a distinct centre of consciousness, yet in reality consciousness, not being an object, is not liable to partition.

The restraint referred to is that which teachers and Scriptures seek to impose. The idea is that a forcible alteration of the nature of any one — that is to say, to make a man into what is totally different from himself — is the same thing as to efface him from existence; for such a process involves a dissolution of continuity.

For this reason the Deity stands in the relation of a giver to man, granting what is asked; and not as a tyrant, imposing what is not solicited.

The final sentence, rendered "What can restraint do?" can also be thus translated, "What can mere attempt to restrain the senses do?" That is, a mere desire for things of the Spirit and an external conformity to laws of righteousness, unaccompanied by the purification of nature (usually called heart), does not make a fit vessel for the spirit of Truth. Faith without good works is dead, but good works without faith are a mockery.

If all creatures work according to their nature, — and there are none who are entirely independent of nature, — what is the object of the ordinances of the Scriptures and the commandments?

The answer, in brief, is that nature's work is twofold; it causes creatures to recede from truth and it draws them to it. The relation between spiritual teaching and the latter mode of nature's operations is the same as that between the allurements of the world and the former mode. Those who are of the flock will hear the shepherd's voice.

34. In the objects of every sense are established relish and distaste. Do not be subject to them; they are the enemies of man.

The perception of objects as pleasant or unpleasant is imprisonment in flesh. It is true that nature is irresistible, yet this nature can only be set in motion by the feeling of relish or distaste in objects of sense. If worldly desires are resisted through faith in spiritual truth, nature, through want of incentive, is finally vanquished.

35. Better is one's own proper duty, even though not fully performed, than the duty of another perfectly accomplished. It is better to perish in one's own duty; the duty of another is full of danger.

Even if one cannot fully perform one's own proper duty, it is better to attempt it than to do what is the lawful duty of another — that is to say, duties not pertaining to one's own station in life — in a flawless manner. Because the question is to do one's duty, and not any particular act or acts. Righteousness consists in obedience to divine commands or spiritual truth, and not in what results from such obedience.

ARJUNA *said:*

36. Now then, by whom led, does a man, O descendant of Vrishni,[1] practise sinfulness, as though unwilling and impressed by force?

THE BLESSED LORD *spoke:*

37. This is lust, this is anger,[2] born of the quality of rajas.[3] Know this to be a great devourer,[4] great sin,[5] and the enemy[6] on earth.

38. As by smoke fire is enveloped, and the looking-glass by rust,[7] as the womb envelops the fœtus, so by this[8] it[9] is enveloped.

39. By this — the eternal enemy of the wise man,[10]

---

[1] "Descendant of Vrishni" is Krishna.
[2] "Lust and anger" are really one, for every desire opposed becomes anger.
[3] *Rajas*, the driving power of Nature.
[4] "Great devourer," that is, knows no satiety.
[5] "Great sin" is the root of all sin.
[6] "Enemy," because this is the cause of this life of suffering.
[7] "Rust," because the native Indian mirror is made of burnished metal.
[8] "This," that is, lust and anger.
[9] "It" is discriminating knowledge.
[10] "Eternal . . . wise man." Because he knows the root of all evil to be desire, and therefore regards it as the enemy; while the unwise man, thirsting for enjoyment, can never recognize the true character of desire, and so regards it as a friend.

desire-formed,[1] hard to be filled, insatiate — discrimination is enveloped.

40. The senses and organs, the thinking faculty, as well as the faculty of judgment, are said to be its seat. It — enveloping the discriminative faculty with these — deludes the lord of the body.

> The "lord of the body" is the Ego in apparent connection with the body. It should always be borne in mind that in reality the lord of the body *is* and *not becomes* one with the Lord of all; it is God, and not *crude* God. A man while thinking of what he ought to do, or of the results of his acts, has in reality nothing whatsoever to do with the true Ego, which is the same as the Deity, for whom there is no thinking or "may-be." The Deity and Ego are one to that man alone in whom self-consciousness is extinct. The man for whom necessity for action has any meaning is in ignorance, and will always remain so if he does not completely obey the law of righteousness and aspire to true spiritual knowledge.

41. Therefore thou, O best of the descendants of Bharata, at the very outset, restraining the senses, conquer this sin, which is really destructive of communicated knowledge, as well as its realization.

42. Great are the senses and organs said to be; greater[2] than senses and organs is the thinking self; greater than the thinking self is the principle of judgment; and that which[3] is greater than the principle of judgment is He.[4]

> It is spiritual death to invest with divinity anything that is connected with self-consciousness. It is not possible to obtain any specific knowledge of things spiritual except when self-consciousness

---

[1] "Desire-formed," that is, able to assume any form at will. This refers to the chameleon-like character of desire.

[2] "Greater," on account of greater subtlety than belongs to gross objects. The classification ascends in the order of subtlety.

[3] "That which . . . than . . . judgment," that is, the ego in the body.

[4] "Is He" that is, the Supreme Spirit; that which is the true Ego in relation to the body is identical with the Supreme.

— which includes the sense of egoistic existence of every kind — is obliterated, and the sense of within and without is entirely effaced.

The beginning of all spiritual life must lie in the recognition of truths which at the time of recognition leave no doubt of their origin outside of the recognizer. This is to say that spiritual truths are only representable by words that can never be connected with any object of normal experience. Therefore spiritual life begins with submission to some authority in the belief that it is absolute. At the same time it must be seen that such a submission becomes the most degrading superstition, unless the authority itself rejects everything that is of practical benefit to the being conditioned by experience, and embodies the annulment of self-consciousness. (Cf. John v. 18.)

No authority can be spiritual if it does not uphold, as ultimate truth, the falsehood of that being with whom the idea of will, action, or knowledge can in any way be associated. He who does not teach the perfect renunciation of will, action, and knowledge can never be a true prophet. Every other thing must be subordinate to this ideal. In other words, no promise of eternal life can be valid which does not stand upon the ashes of the present life.

The doctrine of the identity of God and the Ego is liable to be misunderstood with the most frightfully evil consequences, and this is why the injunction against "throwing pearls before swine" is so strict and universal. God is, and the Ego is, and they are one, being Consciousness; this is not the same as the denial of God and the investiture of self-conscious being with the glory of God; on the contrary, it is a denial of the reality of self-consciousness. This doctrine does not enthrone experience as the supreme authority; it denies the validity of experience altogether. Materialism and worldliness are the lawful offspring of the authority of experience, and spiritual truth represented by the doctrine presented is its implacable foe. Nothing that is not God can ever be the Ego in reality; to imagine that the Ego is anything else is spiritual death.

43. Thus realizing[1] that which is greater than the faculty of judgment, and bringing the self to rest by

---

[1] "Thus realizing," that is, being convinced of the identity of the Ego with the Supreme Spirit.

the self,[1] O thou of mighty arms, conquer the enemy, desire-formed and difficult to seize.

It is to be noted that throughout this chapter the internal faculties are taken to be three, namely: —

1. MANAS, or the thinking self, which manifests itself as the power of making hypotheses, — "is it this," or "is it that?"

2. BUDDHI, or the principle of judgment which selects one out of the endless possibilities conjured up by the manas by investing it with the conviction of certainty, — "it is this."

3. AHANKÂRA, or egotism; that within us which says, "I am the actor; for my benefit all this is being done."

This analysis of the inner faculties is the same as that of the Sânkhya philosophers. The orthodox Brahmanical system, the Vedânta, adds to these three a fourth, CHITTA, the principle of desire, or the power of searching for things agreeable to the ahankâra.

Thus ends chapter the third, called the "RIGHT KNOWLEDGE OF ACTION," in the blessed BHAGAVAD GÎTÂ, the sacred lore, the divine wisdom, the book of divine union, the colloquy between the blessed KRISHNA and ARJUNA, and contained in the Bhîshma Parvan of the blessed MAHÂBHÂRATA, which is a collection of a hundred thousand verses by VYÂSA.

Salutation to Krishna, who has taught mankind to attain salvation through worship of the Supreme Spirit by the selfless performance of duties pertaining to the station of life in which a man is born.

---

[1] "Self to rest by the self," that is, the restless mind by the purified mind, which is the conviction mentioned above.

CHAPTER IV.

RIGHT KNOWLEDGE OF DEDICATION OF ACTION LEADING TO SPIRITUAL WISDOM.

THE two previous chapters show that there are apparently different paths through which the striver for salvation reaches Nirvâna. For those completely purified from worldly attachments there is nothing left but devotion to pure spiritual knowledge; while for those who, though struggling to be free, are yet tied to the world by desires there is no other way than by all-absorbing meditations on the mystery of the Supreme Spirit, preceded by the fulfilment of the duties pertaining to the station of life in which they are born, and the pure-hearted performance of good works for the sake of the Deity alone. In this chapter is declared the eternal permanence of this law, which is preserved for men by spiritual succession and the mystery of divine incarnations.

THE BLESSED LORD *spoke:*

1. This exhaustless,[1] eternal, spiritual truth[2] I declared unto Vivasvat;[3] Vivasvat declared it unto Manu,[4] and Manu declared it unto Ikshvâku.[5]

---

[1] "Exhaustless," because leading to Nirvâna.
[2] "This ... spiritual truth;" the right performance of action which by purification of the nature of man renders him fit for the reception of spiritual illumination.
[3] *Vivasvat* literally means "the Sun;" it here signifies the first manifestation of divine wisdom at the season of creation.
[4] *Manu* is the spirit of the sensuous universe.
[5] *Ikshvâku*, the son of Manu, was the first king and the founder of the solar dynasty of Indian history.

2. Thus successively transmitted, this the royal sages knew. By this great lapse of time that spiritual truth was lost,[1] O harasser of thy foes.[2]

3. That same secret,[3] eternal, excellent truth is this declared unto thee to-day by me, because thou art my devotee [4] and friend.[5]

Prov. viii. 25.

This doctrine, herein unfolded, is the truth declared at the foundation of the world, and all who have entered the eternal life have travelled by this path and no other.

Arjuna *said:*

4. Later thy birth, earlier the birth of Vivasvat — how is this to be realized that thou wert the declarer in the beginning?[6]

John viii. 58.

The mystery of the divine incarnation is next declared. The Spirit never is born but by the inscrutable power of the Deity; a human being is made, not for his own benefit but for the spiritual well-being of the world, to manifest Divine grace, wisdom, and power unto men. None of the Christs of God are to be known after the manner of the flesh; it is only through the power of the Spirit that there can be recognition. There can be no change in the Divine Substance.

Whether the mystery as declared here is or is not properly apprehended in its positive aspect, its negative aspect is perfectly clear. God is one and indivisible. Millions upon millions of men may realize their identity with the Deity; innumerable may be the number of "divine incarnations," yet their identity is with the One God.

---

[1] "Lost." Owing to want of fit recipients of truth the succession was broken. The unfitness consisted in submission to passions which are the implacable enemies of man.

[2] "O harasser of thy foes," thou art a fit recipient because thou hast these foes under control.

[3] "Secret." that is, it must not be communicated to unfit persons, and the Blessed Lord therefore declares it only unto His

[4] "Devotee," or one whose heart rests in peace by depending on another.

[5] "Friend," that is, one of about the same age who is an affectionate fellow-worker.

[6] "In the beginning," that is, at the foundation of the world.

If the numerous children of a man separately call him "Father," his personality is not multiplied into the number of his children. Of all spiritual sins the belief in a plurality of gods is the most deadly.

It is not difficult to perceive the position of beings whose perfection is not in any sense the product of evolution, in the harmony of the universe. Individuals evolve from one form into another, but the archetypes of these forms are not produced by evolution. Otherwise the determination of evolution into the forms it actually does take, out of the infinite number of possibilities, remains unexplained. If it is believed that perfect knowledge of the Deity is possible for man, — to know even as he is known, — the archetype of such perfection must be a reality, and an eternal reality.

In order to remove from the minds of carnal men the doubt of the divine incarnation and the omniscience of Krishna,

The Blessed Lord *spoke:*

5. Many births have passed of mine, and also of thine, O Arjuna. I know them all; thou knowest not, O harasser of thy foes.

"I know," because my power of wisdom is unconditioned and I am of nature eternally pure, illuminated, liberated, and true, while thou art conditioned by the consciousness of some things being peculiarly thine.

How can there then be birth for the Divine Spirit, since it is not limited by any cause?

6. Being even birthless, exhaustless in essence, and being even the lord of all creatures, I am born through my inscrutable power and controlling nature.

John i. 13, 14.

All that men can know of the Deity by observing the history of any divine incarnation is not the Deity himself, but his unsearchable, mysterious power. Be it always remembered that God is one, and forever the same. He is Krishna, and yet Himself, and Krishna knew that the consciousness within him was the Deity; therefore it is true that the human being was not Krishna the Supreme Spirit. To be a man is to know one's self to be a man, and not to know the Self to be the Deity. The Deity being one, eternal and secondless, to know the Self as the Deity is the same thing as not to know one's self as being one among the many and transitory.

The truth therefore is that a man who thinks himself to be the assemblage of the body and the inner faculties may believe the body with which the name Krishna was associated to be God; but Krishna never thought so himself. Within himself there was no personality accepted as the Deity, who was the only Self that Krishna knew himself to be. The Deity is the true Self of all creatures, but they do not know it. Krishna knew it, and consequently all the incidents of his life emanated from a full knowledge of divine identity unstained by the human personality which in the case of an "incarnation" is perfectly pure and in absolute accord with the Divine will. Owing to this reason the glory, power, and truth of the Supreme God manifest themselves in their fulness through the "Word made flesh," as sunlight is transmitted, in its perfect form, through an absolutely transparent medium.

The words here translated "inscrutable power" are usually rendered "illusive power;" but the present form is preferable because it clearly conveys the idea that it can only be known as the unknowable. No one is to think that this unknowableness is due to defective perception on the part of the knower; for he knows it perfectly when he knows it as the unknowable. It is no defect in him that the thing is unknowable. In other words, it is only that which we should call unknowableness, and to know it as such is to comprehend it fully.

"Nature" is that which we know a thing to be. Coldness is the nature of ice. The nature of God is that by which He is known to us; and He is known to us only through His power, which appears to us in three aspects, namely:—

1. Power of producing change.
2. Power of exercising all power; in other words, absolute free-will.
3. Power of knowing the power of will and action.

The only way in which these three powers can be spoken of as a whole is as the absoluteness of the Deity. But if we regard the power as power, it is not the Deity, because it is imperfect and requires the idea of the powerful, the lord of the power, to give the mind that rest we call completeness. But when that completeness is obtained we do not find any power as separate from the Deity.

The term, however, is here to be understood in a restricted sense, for reasons that are obvious. As the nature of the Deity includes knowledge of truth, and this knowledge is the agent which sets a man free from bondage, then it is clear that this element must be wanting in what produces birth, which from the point of view of the Deity is illusory. "My nature" is the nature of which the Deity is the Master, and therefore not His *real* nature which is Himself. Here is meant the power which is the substance of the objective universe and the cause of that blindness by the working of which a man does not know that he is identical with God.

To sum up: This verse denies the possibility of the Deity's ever being born; and declares that such an apparent (real from man's point of view) incarnation is produced by the inscrutable power of the Deity.

The times of divine incarnations are next declared.

7. O son of Bharata,[1] whenever there is decline of righteousness[2] and uprising of unrighteousness, then I project myself into creation.

Rom. i. 16–32.

The purpose of divine incarnations is next declared.

8. For the protection of the righteous and the destruction of the evil-doer, and for the proper establishment of the law of righteousness, I appear from age to age.

The purpose of divine incarnation is to judge mankind and bring peace to the world. To know the divine mystery of such incarnations is to inherit the everlasting life.

9. Whoever knows in truth[3] my divine birth and works, he, abandoning the body, does not incur re-birth, O Arjuna; he comes to me.

John v. 24.

The true knowledge of "my divine birth and works" is the spiritual perception of this, that I am never really born, although

---

[1] "Son of Bharata," being a descendant of so just a king, thou shouldst not permit the decline of the law of righteousness.

[2] "Righteousness." If the law of righteousness is preserved inviolate, all creatures will have prosperity on earth, and at death final rest in the Deity. If it be completely extinct, the race of man will also become extinct.

[3] "Knows in truth," that is, realizes it as it is, and is not blindly attached to mere outward appearance, thinking that the Father of the universe is a conditioned being.

appearing to be so; that I have nothing to achieve for personal gain, but yet I work for the establishment of truth and righteousness in the hearts of men, and thus I protect them. The Blessed Lord also means that whoever works for the same purpose really works for Him. The supreme duty for us all, then, is to recognize through faith that we are nothing but incarnations of the Deity, unborn and eternal, for the same purpose as is shown forth here. Thus we shall attain the life that is hidden in God.

The path of liberation as herein pointed out is not new, but eternally founded upon truth.

10. Many, devoid of attachment, fear, and anger, filled with me,[1] depending on me alone,[2] through penance of wisdom[3] purified, have attained my estate. *Isa. lvii. 15.*

The question may arise as to why the Deity, devoid, as he is, of personal preferences, gives His own estate — the life that the Father has in Himself (John v. 26) — to those alone who are free from attachment and are possessed of the other qualities. If He is a merciful God, why does He not grant Nirvâna to all?

11. Whoever approaches me in any form,[4] in the same form do I approach him. In every case and condition[5] men follow but my path, O son of Prithâ. *Ps. lxxviii. 29; cxi. 15.*

Righteousness and unrighteousness are both ordained by the Supreme Power. Those who follow the path of righteousness find eternal life; the others remain immersed in darkness, — this is also His ordinance.

The reason why all men do not wish for liberation is next declared.

---

[1] "Filled with me," that is, recognizing identity with the Deity in the way hereafter explained.

[2] "Depending on me alone," that is, following the path by devotion as knowledge (Chap. II. 55 *et seq.*).

[3] "Penance of wisdom" refers to the purifying effect of wisdom.

[4] "In any form," that is, with whatever object one approaches me, the same object is granted to him by me.

[5] "In every case and condition." This is universal. There is no single case in which I do not grant the prayer of all creatures as expressed in their wishes. The Divine Author bestows free-will on all His creatures to approach Him or not.

12. Those desirous of success through action[1] worship gods[2] on this earth. Action-born success comes quickly in the world of men.[3]

Rom. vii. 1.

Thus is shown how all men follow his path, and it is also specifically stated that only in the world of men are religious injunctions concerning forms and ceremonies operative.

13. According to the classification of action and qualities the four castes are created by me. Know me, non-actor and changeless,[4] as even the author of this.

1 Cor. xii. 4-27.

"Classification" here refers to caste. The Brâhman caste has a preponderance of the quality of *Satva* (goodness, joy, and enlightenment), and its effect is mental and bodily tranquillity, penance, etc. The warrior caste has a greater proportion of the quality of passion mixed with goodness, and its effect is heroism, etc. The commercial and agricultural caste has a preponderance of the quality of passion over the quality of darkness, ignorance, and the like, and its effect is trade and agriculture. The Çudra, or lowest caste, has the quality of darkness dominant over the other qualities, and its effect is subordination to the other castes.

The paradox of the eternal Deity engaging in action is further amplified.

14. Acts do not touch me,[5] nor in me is relish [6] for

---

[1] "Success through action," that is, promise of heavenly enjoyments attached to the performance of religious ceremonials.

[2] "Gods," that is, other than the true God. The Vedic injunction against idolatry is very strict and explicit. "Whoever worships another god, thinking 'This god is one, and I am another,' he knows not; like a domestic beast is he to the gods."

[3] "The world of men." In other worlds the divine ordinances as to religions and moral duties do not exist. All creatures other than man never aspire to higher conditions, and live in stagnant satisfaction with that which they have.

[4] "Non-actor and changeless." The action is done by divine power, and not by the Deity Himself.

[5] "Do not touch me," because I have no egotism or personality.

[6] "Relish," etc. When action is performed by me I do not feel as if I have gained something I did not possess before.

<small>Isa. xlv. 5-24; Amos iii. 6, 7.</small> the fruit of acts. Whoever knows me thus is not bound by acts.¹

From reference to Krishna apparently as to a person this might be mistaken for a new doctrine and produce confusion. Therefore it is said:—

15. By previous aspirants for liberation action has been performed; knowing this, therefore, perform thou action performed by the ancients ² in ancient times.

This closes the section.

The authority of the ancients extended only to the bare performance of action, and does not apply to the nature of the action. Therefore it is said:—

16. Even the wise are in delusion in regard to what is action and what is not action.³ Therefore I shall declare to thee what is action, knowing which thou shalt be liberated from evil.

17. Enjoined acts are to be known, as also acts forbidden, and also inaction. The path of action is difficult to discern.

<small>Heb. v. 14.</small>

The highest benefit derivable from ethics is the comprehension of these three classes of action.

18. Whoever sees inaction in action, whoever in inaction action, he, among men, is possessed of spiritual illumination; is the man of right action and the doer of all action.

These paradoxes mean that the Supreme Spirit being in reality absolute is actionless; the Ego, being in reality identical with the

---

<small>1 "Bound by acts." For such a man the acts observed as done by his body do not touch the Spirit, which is unconditioned.

2 "Ancients." Work for the purification of thy nature if thou art unwise; otherwise, for the good of the world. The instance of Janaka is here especially meant. He was a king remarkable for wisdom and sanctity.

3 "Action . . . not action." It is not to be understood that "action" means all movements of body or mind, and "not action" its opposite. It means what is, and what is not to be done,—right action.</small>

Supreme Spirit, is therefore also actionless. Yet the existence of suffering shows that embodied egos are not independent of action. To be entirely disconnected from action is to realize identity with the Supreme Spirit, and thus to completely lose the consciousness of being one among many egos. To act and to suppress the impulse towards action are both forms of action, which is connected with the true Ego or Supreme Spirit only through error or false attribution.

Whoever realizes that action belongs to the assemblage of body and mind and is only attributed to the Ego through error, and also realizes that abstinence from action through indolence is in truth action, and therefore charged with all its properties, is one with the Supreme Spirit. This realization is the same as spiritual illumination and perfect independence of the law of cause and effect; it is the accomplishment of all that can be done, because there remains nothing to be done when the eternal life is attained.

Sometimes this verse is erroneously interpreted to mean that a man ought to abandon the sense of right and wrong and act according to his impulses, thinking all the time that he, being one with the Supreme Spirit, cannot act; and in this manner it is imagined that inaction is perceived in action. It is easy to see that if the principle of this verse is rightly applied, thinking is to be regarded as action. No thinking can in consequence make wrong right. Furthermore, how can a man who is conscious of egoistic impulses, and for whom there is therefore action still to be done, be called "the doer of all action"? With the cessation of these impulses such thinking becomes meaningless.

In fact, what is here stated has no ethical bearing, and is merely the declaration of the want of relation between action and the true Ego, which is absolute. This is quite clear from the succeeding verse which commends the knowledge, by which is meant a new consciousness.

19. The spiritually discriminating call him wise whose initiatives are devoid of desire and determination, and whose action is burned up by the fire of knowledge.[1]

The man described above — "whose initiatives . . . determination" — is one who not only feels no interest in the fruit of action,

---

[1] "Fire of *knowledge*," described in the previous verse.

but is also unconcerned as to the nature of that fruit, owing to his want of determination or motive in relation to action. Some difficulty arises as to how such a man can act at all. But it must not be forgotten that such wise men, from want of a motive to put an end to life, will perform the action necessary for the maintenance of life, and their existence on earth leads to the establishment of the law of righteousness among men.

20. Abandoning attachment to the fruit of action, ever satisfied, on nothing dependent,[1] he does nothing, even though engaged in action.[2]

21. Devoid of expectation, with mind and body tranquil,[3] having abandoned submission[4] to enjoyment of objects in any form, doing only acts of the body,[5] he does not incur re-birth.

22. Contented with what is obtained without effort,[6] beyond the pairs of opposites,[7] free from hostility[8] against any creature, equal in success and ill-success, even though performing action he becomes not bound.[9]

Having thus lauded spiritual illumination, which sets a man free from the bondage of action, he proceeds to show how the bondage

[1] "On nothing dependent." Free of the consciousness of the existence of any such objects as means.

[2] "Even though engaged in action," which was commenced before the time of his illumination. Since the body is non-existent for the sage who knows himself to be really pure consciousness, and as such is identical with the Supreme, there is no motive for stopping the wheel already in motion.

[3] "Tranquil," that is, perfectly harmonious in all their relations.

[4] "Abandoned submission," that is, having no consciousness of enjoyment in any action.

[5] "Acts of the body," that is, such acts as the body does for its own maintenance.

[6] "Obtained without effort," that is, even for the barest necessity for maintaining the body he is contented with what comes without effort, and even if this is denied it is the same to him as if obtained, because his egotism is quite dead.

[7] "Pairs of opposites," that is, heat and cold, pleasure and pain.

[8] "Free from hostility," that is, in speech, act, or thought, disconnected from the suffering of any creature.

[9] "Becomes not bound," that is, is not liable to experience pleasure or pain in the future in consequence of action so performed.

does not continue, even though, owing to previous causes, outward action may go on.

The thread dropped with verse 20 is now resumed.

23. Of him, devoid of attachment, freed from bondage,[1] and with heart resting in knowledge, all actions, being performed for the sake of the Supreme,[2] become destroyed.

The reason for the destruction of such action is set forth because no one can attain Nirvâna so long as there is any earthly tendency which has to exhaust its effect.

24. The Supreme Spirit is the act of offering, the Supreme Spirit is sacrificial butter offered by the sacrificer, who is the Supreme Spirit, into the fire which is the Supreme Spirit; even the Supreme Spirit is the goal for him who is merged in action which is the Supreme Spirit.

Because for the illuminated sage nothing exists which is not really the Supreme Spirit, consequently the result of his acts is also the same.

Having thus imaged the supreme knowledge as a sacrifice, he proceeds to show the merits of the various forms of sacrifice, and then concludes by crowning knowledge as the highest of all.

25. Some men of right action perform sacrifice to gods; others offer as sacrifice the individual ego in the fire that is the Supreme Spirit.

"Sacrifice" here means all things that prepare us for the final emancipation. Therefore two most important forms of sacrifice are mentioned. First, sacrifice through pure philosophical studies and through symbolical worship, herein referred to as "sacrifice to gods;" secondly, the "individual ego" is consciousness in mysterious connection with the body and mind; the Supreme Spirit is the

---

[1] "Bondage," of the personality.
[2] "Sake of the Supreme;" it is not possible for him to act otherwise.

attributeless, absolute consciousness; and the sacrifice is the perception of their identity by rejecting as utterly non-existent the sense of within and without.

26. Others sacrifice the senses, beginning with hearing, in the fire of restraint. Others sacrifice sound, and other objects of sense, in the fire of sense.

The senses, considered as including the organs of action, are the ear, eye, tongue, nose, and skin; speech, hands, feet, and the organs of generation and excretion. The senses are not the various limbs of the body, but super-sensuous powers, which, pervading the whole body, are localized in special parts.

"Restraint" is the unification of these various powers in the mind. He who perceives that all senses are really one, and as one are related to the mind, is the man of restraint. It is not an act, but a certain interior perception or power.

The "sacrifice of sound ... in the fire of sense" consists in applying the senses to their appropriate objects only, as sanctioned by the law of righteousness.

27. Others again, illuminated by knowledge, sacrifice in the fire of firm rest in Self[1] all functions of sense and vitality.

28. Others again perform sacrifice through objects,[2] also sacrifices through austerities,[3] and also sacrifices through mystical practices. Aspirants quite firm in their vows also perform sacrifices of knowledge through study.

29. Others again sacrifice the upward life-breath in the downward life-breath,[4] or the downward life-breath in the upward life-breath;[5] others become fixed in the

---

[1] "Fire of ... Self," that is, all thought and action are extinguished by all-absorbing meditation from the Supreme, which gives rise to spiritual wisdom.

[2] "Sacrifice through objects," that is, by giving alms, etc.

[3] "Through austerities," that is, practising austerities as given in Chapter XVII. verses 14-17, regarding it as a sacrifice for the sake of attaining supreme liberation.

[4] "The upward ... life-breath," that is, breathing in without holding the air within the body, or breathing it out.

[5] "Downward ... life-breath," that is, the reverse process.

regulation of breathing by stopping[1] the movements of both the upward and downward life-breath; others, regulated in food, sacrifice life-breaths in life-breaths.[2]

These practices pertain to a branch of mysticism which requires special study for its proper comprehension.

30. All these, knowers of sacrifice, with sins exhausted through sacrifice, eating according to rule after performance of sacrifice,[3] go to the Eternal Spirit.[4]

31. O best of Kuru's sons,[5] not even this world is for him who is without sacrifice; what then about the other?

Who does not perform any of these sacrifices is not fit even for this life, much less for the life to come.

32. Thus many kinds of sacrifice are spread out in the mouth of the Vedas;[6] know them all to be action-born.[7]

33. O harasser of thy foes, superior to sacrifice through objects is sacrifice through knowledge: the whole universe of action, O son of Prithâ, is comprehended in spiritual knowledge.

Spiritual knowledge is the greatest of all things that be,— the most precious possession; therefore strive for it. The "sacrifice through knowledge" (v. 24) is "superior" because it is the im-

---

[1] "Stopping, etc.," retention of the breath within the body.

[2] "Life-breaths in life-breaths," that is, obtaining mastery over the vital functions.

[3] "Eating . . . sacrifice," that is, partaking of food only after performing sacrifice.

[4] "Go to the eternal Spirit," by spiritual knowledge acquired after purification in this manner.

[5] "O best of Kuru's sons." Being the best of the descendants of so righteous a king as Kuru, it is easy for thee to perform the necessary sacrifice.

[6] "Mouth of the Vedas," that is, declared authoritatively by the Vedas.

[7] "Action-born," that is, not done by the true Ego which is perfect and, therefore, not under the necessity for action; this being known, salvation is attained.

mediate antecedent of liberation, whereas action can only lead to liberation through knowledge.

So long as a thing is not fully comprehended there remains some interest in it; but to comprehend it is the same as to realize all that can possibly be done with it. In this sense spiritual knowledge comprehends the whole universe of action; in the purified mind of the illuminated sage all possible relations of objects are realized. When final emancipation is reached no want remains.

How then is this knowledge to be acquired?

34. Seek to know it by prostration,[1] by question,[2] and by service;[3] the truth-seeing wise will communicate this knowledge to thee.

It is next declared what this knowledge is.

35. Knowing which, O son of Pându, thou shalt never fall into delusion like this, by which the infinity of creatures thou shalt see in thyself and then in me.[4]

The glory of the knowledge is such that

36. Even if thou wert the greatest evil-doer[5] among all the unrighteous, thou shalt cross over all sins even by the bark knowledge.

How knowledge does this the following verse explains.

37. O Arjuna, as blazing fire reduces fuel to ashes, so the fire of knowledge turns all action into ashes.

---

[1] "Prostration." By humility before the teacher; without this sentiment one can never learn.

[2] "Question," for example, as to the nature of knowledge, liberation, individual and universal spirit.

[3] "Service." By constant service to the teacher the pupil comes into the necessary harmony with him.

[4] "In thyself and then in me," that is, the result of such knowledge is the perception of the identity between the individual and the universal spirit.

[5] "Evil-doer;" religious works and ceremonies performed otherwise than for the love of God are here included in evil.

The "fire of knowledge" destroys ignorance, which produces the idea that "I am the actor." Consequently in the absence of the consciousness of being the actor no action can take place, nor can effects of past actions persist after their basis is thus removed. This is how knowledge removes sins, which cannot exist disconnected with the agent, the personality.

That this knowledge is the highest of all things is repeated.

38. There is nothing on earth which is as sacred as knowledge; this the man befitted by right performance of action himself realizes within himself in course of time.[1]

Having said (v. 34) what the aspirant for knowledge must do in order to gain his end, the Blessed Lord here declares what inherent qualities, such as are not dependent upon mere personal exertion, are essential for the reception of the spiritual knowledge which leads to Nirvâna.

39. The man possessed of faith,[2] and devotion to his Master, with senses and organs restrained, gains knowledge; having gained knowledge he quickly attains to the supreme peace.[3]

Why doubt is dangerous.

40. The ignorant man, the man devoid of faith, the doubt-souled,[4] are destroyed. For the doubt-souled man there is happiness neither in this world, nor the next, nor in any other.

How doubts are removed.

41. O conqueror of wealth, actions do not bind[5] him

---

[1] "Course of time;" the long time that is required to render one fit for perfect knowledge.

[2] "Possessed of faith," that is, believing firmly in the truth of the teaching of the Scriptures, as well as of teachers. This faith is not subject to conscious determination in the individual; it has a compelling power.

[3] "Supreme peace," that is, Nirvâna.

[4] "Doubt-souled," that is, the man who has no faith of any kind; he suffers, not only in the next world, but here also, through unending anxieties concerning his own worldly affairs.

[5] "Actions do not bind," being either for the benefit of the world, or merely natural.

whose actions are renounced in consequence of having obtained spiritual discrimination, and whose doubts are cut asunder by the knowledge of identity with the Supreme, and who is not heedless.[1]

<small>John iii. 8.</small>

"Spiritual discrimination," as the result of the right performance of action, has been explained. In brief, it is said a man must always try to gain certainty, faith, etc., through the right performance of action and the study of spiritual philosophy.

42. Therefore having cut asunder with the sword of knowledge ignorance-born doubt, seated in thine own heart,[2] engage in right performance of action;[3] arise,[4] O son of Bharata.

Having removed all doubts as to the divine authority of the blessed exponent, it is declared that all who do not enter upon either the path of right performance of action or of knowledge are in danger of great suffering.

Thus ends chapter the fourth, called "RIGHT KNOWLEDGE OF DEDICATION OF ACTION LEADING TO SPIRITUAL WISDOM," in the blessed BHAGAVAD GÎTÂ, the sacred lore, the divine wisdom, the book of divine union, the colloquy between the blessed KRISHNA and ARJUNA, and contained in the Bhîshma Parvan of the blessed MAHÂBHÂRATA, which is a collection of a hundred thousand verses by VYÂSA.

Salutation to the remover of all doubts, the blessed Krishna, by whom has been declared the twofold path of faith, action and knowledge, applicable to men according to their condition.

---

[1] "Heedless," forgetful of the identity of Self with the Supreme.
[2] "Own heart," therefore none but thyself can remove it.
[3] "Right performance of action," dedicating all fruit of action to the Deity.
[4] "Arise," since that is the right action for thee.

CHAPTER V.

RIGHT KNOWLEDGE OF THE RENUNCIATION OF ACTION.

The praise bestowed in the previous chapter (vv. 18-41) upon renunciation of action, that is to say, works of merit prescribed by the Brâhmanical law, gives the idea of its superiority over action. But the chapter closes with exhortation to action (v. 42). This makes it difficult to understand the real intention of the Teacher. The declaration in the third chapter (v. 3) shows that the paths are different for different men, — "the right knowledge of things spiritual, of the illuminated sages, and the right knowledge of action of the men of action;" but not so in this instance. Nor is there anything to suggest two different stages in the great journey, — first to perform works, and then to renounce them; no limit of time being mentioned as to when works are to be abandoned.

Furthermore, the illuminated sage who has realized identity with the Supreme Spirit cannot possibly perform action, therefore it would be useless to enjoin upon him any rules of conduct. Hence it is clear that the intention here is that the two injunctions — about works and abandonment of works — are capable of being applied to the same person at the same time. In other words, two alternatives are here put before the devotee for election.

He who sincerely aspires for the life eternal may renounce all action if he chooses, or may engage in right performance of action if he thinks best. That Arjuna understood Krishna to mean this appears from his question.

Arjuna *said:*

1. Renunciation of actions,[1] and again their right performance, thou praisest, O Krishna. Of these two which is better,[2] declare unto me with certainty.

1 "Actions," that is, both religious and other works of merit.
2 "Better;" this implies comparison and selection.

The Blessed Lord's reply shows that Arjuna rightly apprehended His meaning.

THE BLESSED LORD *spoke:*

2. Renunciation and right performance of action are both producers[1] of the supreme good,[2] but of these two, better[3] is the right performance of action than renunciation.

It is "better" for the mere aspirant that he should rightly perform religious and human duties in the world than that he should, abandoning them, retire into solitude; for the hardship of the ascetic life is greater, its observances stricter. As a means for the proper assimilation of truth a life of right action is invaluable. Only a few are so constituted as to be fitted for the life of renunciation.

3. He is to be known as always a man of renunciation who neither dislikes nor likes, being truly beyond the pair of opposites, O thou of mighty arms; with ease he escapes from bondage.

Although action forges fresh links in the chain of conditioned existence, yet when performed in the right manner it frees from bondage. Thus action rightly performed produces the same result as renunciation, but without the same hardship.

It is further explained that renunciation and right action, though not practicable by the same individual, are identical in their results.

4. Fools say, and not the wise, that renunciation and right performance of action are different. He who practises one perfectly, receives the fruit of both.[4]

5. The seat[5] that is obtained by practisers of renun-

---

[1] "Producers," not indeed directly, but in being instruments fitting one for the reception of spiritual knowledge, which leads to the

[2] "Supreme good," or Nirvâna.

[3] "Better;" this implies comparison and selection.

[4] "Fruit of both," because either one of these paths leads to spiritual knowledge, culminating in Nirvâna.

[5] "The seat," that is, Nirvâna.

ciation, the same is obtained by men of right action.[1] He who sees renunciation and the right performance of action as one,[2] sees rightly.

If the same result is produced by renunciation as by right performance of action, how is the preference of the latter to the former to be understood? The answer is that renunciation is of two kinds,— one accompanying true spiritual knowledge, and the other without such knowledge. It is the last named that is inferior to right performance of action.

6. O thou of mighty arms, it is difficult to attain true renunciation[3] without right performance of action; the devotee, rightly performing action, attains to true renunciation before long.

John xvii. 15.

The heart of man is never purified except through right performance of action and that one-pointed devotion to the unsearchable Supreme Spirit. He that retires from the world with the purpose of seeking the Deity undergoes needless suffering.

Although the right performance of action, as before explained, is superior to solitary meditation, yet it is not to be imagined that he who follows the other path incurs any sin on account of his abandonment of action. For the specific nature of the act is not the purifying agent, but the inner feeling that accompanies the act.

The interior state from which action springs being the same, the question of right and wrong does not arise in this matter; that which is here involved is the minor consideration of expediency.

7. Steadfastly devoted to the means for the attainment[4] of spiritual knowledge, pure in heart,

Prov. ii. 1-5;

---

[1] "Right action," that is, action of which the fruit is given up to the Supreme Spirit.

[2] "As one," that is, as leading to the same goal, which is Nirvâna.

[3] "True renunciation" is the same as the Supreme Spirit. A Vedic text says, "Renunciation is the Supreme Spirit."

[4] "Means for the attainment," etc. Through faith the heart is purified from passion and folly; from that comes mastery over the body, and, last of all, subjugation of the senses.

<small>Matt. v. 8; 1 Cor. ix. 25-27; John i. 4</small> with the body conquered[1] and the senses subdued, for whom the only Self is the Self of all creatures, is untouched, though performing action.

8. Absorbed in right knowledge, the knower of truth feels, "I am doing nothing," while seeing, hearing, touching, smelling, eating, moving, sleeping, breathing. <small>1 Cor. xv. 10.</small>

9. Even while speaking, giving up, taking, opening the eyes and shutting them, he feels only that "the senses and organs are in relation to their objects."

The reason why he is not touched, even though performing action, is, that owing to absence of egotism he is not conscious of action. The devotee who retires from the world through the study of spiritual philosophy, meditation, and the instruction of sages, becomes emancipated from egotism, and that cuts asunder all ties to action and its consequences. The man who is not free from egotism must devote himself to the right performance of action in the way now to be described.

10. Whoever performs actions, dedicating them to the Supreme Spirit and abandoning all attachment,[2] is not touched by sin,[3] as the lotus-leaf is not wetted by water. <small>Prov. xvi. 3.</small>

11. Those possessed of right knowledge of action, abandoning all attachment, perform action with mind, judgment, and the bare senses[4] for the purification of the heart. <small>2 Cor. v. 6, 8.</small>

---

[1] "Body conquered." Body means the desires seated in the body; namely, hunger, thirst, movements, sleep, generative and excretory functions. Conquered, not suppressed.

[2] "All attachment," including the desire for salvation or Nirvâna,—not having even that as the object. For Nirvâna not being an object that can be possessed, to desire its possession can be due only to blindness.

[3] "Sin" here comprehends both virtue and vice, in so far as they are considered as attributes of the Spirit within us, which is essentially identical with the Deity. In fact, the difference between the innermost Spirit and the Supreme Spirit is merely one of nomenclature.

[4] "Bare senses," that is, unaccompanied with longings.

Because thou hast the right to action, therefore thou shouldst follow the principle declared in the ensuing verse.

12. The right performer[1] of action, abandoning fruit of action, attains to rest[2] through devotion;[3] the wrong performer of action, attached to fruit thereof on account of desire, remains bound.

<small>Luke vi. 35; Matt. vii. 21-23.</small>

13. The conqueror,[4] having by right knowledge renounced all action, dwells in peace in the city of nine gates,[5] neither performing action nor causing it to be performed.

<small>Romans viii. 9, 35-37.</small>

14. The Spirit creates not for the world actorship[6] nor acts,[7] nor even the bond[8] between action and its results; but Nature[9] works on.

15. The Lord receives not any man's sins nor deeds of merit. By untruth truth is shrouded; by this creatures are deluded.

<small>Job xxxv. 6-13.</small>

There are two aspects of the mysterious, inscrutable power of the Supreme Spirit; namely, Truth and Untruth, — real and false knowledge. The meaning of the universe is the being of this

---

1 "Right performer," that is, performer for the sake of the Deity.
2 "Rest," that is, liberation, Nirvâna.
3 "Through devotion," that is, by degrees; through purification of heart comes spiritual knowledge, from knowledge renunciation, and then rest in Nirvâna.
4 "Conqueror," that is, he who has no consciousness of effort, peaceful at heart, wanting nothing outside of the Self. The sage does not die on attaining illumination, for then the world would be soulless and mankind teacherless.
5 "City of nine gates," that is, the body; as an ordinary man sits on a seat, knowing it to be an external thing, so a liberated man remains in the body for the benefit of the world.
6 "Actorship," the universal principle of action.
7 "Acts," such as are the results of the action of special actors.
8 "Bond," that is, the sequence of events.
9 "Nature," that is, the Divine creative energy, further elucidated in Chapter VII. verse 14. In the teaching of the Blessed Lord the independent existence of Nature is never asserted. It is taught here that the Supreme Spirit, being changeless, is not liable to create; but the divine creative energy is the cause of all things, though it is itself nothing independently of the Supreme Spirit.

power in its twofold aspect and the real identity of the power and the Powerful. This mystery is more fully declared in Chapters VII.–XII.

16. Those creatures in regard to whom this Untruth becomes deprived of being by Truth, to them knowledge, sun-like, reveals that Supreme.[1]

John xvi. 13.

17. Those whose self-conscious principles[2] have entered into the Supreme,[3] whose Self the Supreme is,[4] whose devotion the Supreme is,[5] and whose goal that is,[6] attain non-evolution,[7] having their taints[8] washed away by Truth.

John xvii. 21–26.

In what manner do such sages view the Supreme Truth?

18. The sages are equal-sighted[9] in regard to a Brâhman[10] versed in Vedic lore, in letter and spirit, and devoid of egotism, a cow,[11] an elephant,[12] a dog, and an outcast.

19. By those whose minds are fixed in equality heaven has been attained even here, because the stainless equality is the Supreme; therefore they are at rest in the Supreme Spirit.

---

[1] "Supreme," that is, Absolute Reality.

[2] "Self-conscious principles," usually called souls.

[3] "Entered into the Supreme," by receiving that spiritual power called divine illumination, the Holy Ghost.

[4] "Self the Supreme is," by realization of identity.

[5] "Devotion the Supreme is," that is, those who have gone through the various degrees of devotion — right performance of action and renunciation — as before described.

[6] "Whose goal," that is, men of renunciation.

[7] "Non-evolution," that is, freedom from bondage, Nirvâna.

[8] "Taints," that is, separation from the Deity, desires and their mode of manifestation, — the causes of bondage.

[9] "Equal-sighted," that is, in all such creatures the sage perceives nothing but the Supreme Spirit. The sage's independence of all the qualities of Nature is thus shown.

[10] "Brâhman" represents satva quality.

[11] "Cow" represents rajas.

[12] "Elephant" represents tamas. These qualities are explained in Chapter XIV.

The question arises as to whether the ignoring of such palpable differences as those mentioned does not involve a penalty. The answer is in the negative, because the ignoring them is not the result of an effort of will, but comes through the realization of the Supreme Spirit, in whom all things are comprehended and are thus equal.

The absence of the idea of difference in the perception of those who have become merged in the One Consciousness leads to the same absence of difference in their action. The remainder of this chapter declares this truth.

20. The knower of the Supreme Spirit, with heart[1] perfectly at rest, not deluded,[2] and fixed in the Supreme Spirit,[3] does not rejoice at obtaining what is pleasant, nor is he troubled by obtaining what is unpleasant.

21. He whose heart is not attached to objects of sense which are external finds that within himself which is bliss; he, resting in identity with the Supreme Spirit, enjoys bliss eternal.

1 John iv. 12, 13.

The sage does not feel external pleasure and pain, because he enjoys the bliss within himself which is the peace that passeth understanding. He enjoys Nirvâna, which is eternal bliss; but no one who is conscious of any pleasure outside of himself can rest in the Deity even for an instant. Therefore it is right constantly to recognize the unsatisfactory character of existence.

22. Pain-wombed are the enjoyments, born of the contact of senses and organs with objects, and have beginning and end; the sage, O son of Kuntî, does not find relish in them.

Eccl. ii. 3-17.

Worldly pleasures are but pain in their origin, because they begin by putting an end to a previous state of things and then end themselves. If pleasure were not pain-wombed it would not

---

[1] "Heart," that is, the thinking Self.
[2] "Not deluded," that is, not accepting any object as the Supreme Spirit.
[3] "Fixed in the Supreme Spirit," that is, having attained to perfect renunciation of action in the Deity.

end. If any pleasure ceases to be pleasant after brief enjoyment, then it is quite clear that from its inception it carried pain within itself. Those upon whose authority our faith in a future life depends, have declared that there is no rest in the other world except for those who live in the Deity while on earth. The absolute, infinite, unconditioned Consciousness of Nirvâna, the everlasting life, is the only bliss ; all else is misery and delusion.

Now the Blessed Lord points out the root of evil and exhorts us to be assiduous in its destruction.

23. The man who is able on earth, until the departure of life, to bear the pressure springing from desire [1] and anger, is possessed of right knowledge, — is blessed.

Gal. v. 24.

The words here rendered "until the departure," may also without inaccuracy be translated "before the departure," meaning that as the body after death is neither pleased by the possession of pleasant objects nor angry at being deprived of them, so ought a man to be prior to the departure of the breath from the body. The sage Vasishtha says: "Life being gone, the body knows not pleasure or pain ; if it be so for the man possessed of life, he is in the condition that leads to Nirvâna."

The Blessed Lord declares the positive qualities of the illuminated sage.

24. He whose joy is within,[2] whose diversion is within, and whose light also is within,[3] is the man of right knowledge ; becoming the Supreme Spirit,[4] he attains to effacement in the Supreme Spirit.

Gal. v. 22 ; John xvii. 21–23.

25. Effacement in the Supreme Spirit[5] is gained by

---

[1] "Desire" is the attachment to or thirst for objects of pleasure directly perceived, heard of, or recollected as having been enjoyed.

[2] "Joy is within," that is, in the true Self and not in objects.

[3] "Light is within," that is, the true Self is his light, and not senses, mind, etc.

[4] "Becoming the Supreme Spirit," even before death. The sage is dead to all outside himself; his life and joy are within.

[5] "Effacement in the Supreme Spirit," that is, Nirvâna.

the right-seeing [1] sage, with his sins exhausted,[2] doubts cut asunder,[3] senses and organs under control,[4] and devoted to the well-being of all creatures.[5]

Phil. i. 21;
Gal. ii. 20.

26. For men of renunciation,[6] whose hearts are at rest from desire and anger, and knowing the Self,[7] there is, on both sides of death, effacement in the Supreme Spirit.

Matt. xi. 28, 29;
John vi. 56, 63.

The patient endurance of the onslaught of desire and anger was spoken of in verse 23; it has now been shown by what means these enemies may be extirpated. Having described the immediate Nirvâna of the sage, the Blessed Lord now declares the interior process of development suited to those whose hearts are purified by right performance of action.

27. Having driven out [8] external objects, fixed the eyes between the eyebrows,[9] and unified [10] the upward and downward life-breaths, which remain within the nostrils,

28. He whose senses [11] and organs are under control, as also the thinking and ascertaining principles, — who is devoted to inner knowledge [12] and ever free from desire, fear, and anger, is liberated.[13]

1 Cor. ii. 14.

Now is declared what will be realized when action has dropped off from him who has performed it rightly.

---

1 " Right-seeing," or illuminated by knowledge of truth.
2 " Sins exhausted," by right performance of action.
3 " Doubts cut asunder," by the reception of the spirit of truth.
4 " Senses and organs under control," that is, each engaged in its appropriate work under the law of universal harmony.
5 " Devoted to the well-being of all creatures," that is, an embodiment of divine grace and mercy.
6 " Men of renunciation," illuminated sages.
7 " Knowing the Self." It is the absence of this spiritual knowledge which keeps us in bondage even though our passions are somewhat controlled.
8 " Driven out," by abstaining from thoughts about them.
9 " Fixed the eyes . . . eyebrows," that is, not opening them completely for fear of the attraction of external objects, nor shutting them lest sleep should creep on.
10 " Unified," etc., letting breath neither go in nor come out of the body.
11 " Senses," etc., as explained in verse 25.
12 " Devoted to inner knowledge," desiring the assimilation of spiritual truths.
13 " Liberated," that is, is in need of no other means for the attainment of liberation from the bondage of changeful existence.

29. Knowing me, the Enjoyer [1] of all sacrifice and penance, the Supreme Lord of all worlds [2] and the friend [3] of all creatures, he attains rest.

John xvii. 3.

Thus ends chapter the fifth, called the "RIGHT KNOWLEDGE OF RENUNCIATION OF ACTION," in the blessed BHAGAVAD GÎTÂ, the sacred lore, the divine wisdom, the book of divine union, the colloquy between the blessed KRISHNA and ARJUNA, and contained in the Bhîshma Parvan of the blessed MAHÂBHÂRATA, which is a collection of a hundred thousand verses by VYÂSA.

The external process, as given in verse 27, is easy to be imitated even by those, not purified by dedication of the fruit of action to the Supreme Spirit. But this is not the chief element in the process of spiritual illumination. The last verse completes the description.

Whoever knows the Supreme as the Great Spirit of the Infinite Universe, as well as the Spirit that dwells in every human heart, attains Nirvâna.

This chapter shows that for one not divinely illuminated the right performance of action is a more effective instrument in rendering the heart a fit temple for the Spirit of God than renunciation of action. But the right renunciation, in other words the natural dropping off of action, is superior to its performance, inasmuch as it is immediately followed by everlasting life.

Salutation to the all-wise Teacher who has so clearly solved the doubt about right performance of action and the solitary meditations of the recluse, and has shown what renunciation is superior and what inferior.

---

[1] "The Enjoyer," that is, I am the doer as well as the Deity for whose sake this is done.

[2] "Lord of all worlds," that is, because I am the Enjoyer, it is not to be understood that there is anything higher than I. Although I am all things, yet no thing is I.

[3] "Friend," that is, one who does good with no expectation of reward.

CHAPTER VI.

RIGHT KNOWLEDGE OF MEDITATION.

In concluding the preceding chapter the Blessed Lord declared interior illumination to be the spiritual part of meditation. The three verses containing this declaration are like aphorisms, to which the present chapter serves as the commentary. Herein it is said that before interior illumination can take place religious and moral duties are to be performed, dedicating the result to the Supreme Spirit; but as soon as receptivity to this illumination has been developed, renunciation becomes natural. Thus, for the man of action there are three stages,—performance of action, meditation, and true illumination.

THE BLESSED LORD *spoke:*

1. Whoever performs action that has to be done, without depending upon the fruit of action, is the man of renunciation [1] as well as the performer of right action, and not the mere giver up of consecrated fire [2] and works of the law.

Phil. iii. 7, 8.

The renunciation here spoken of is that renunciation which is but a means for the attainment of true renunciation; so also is the right performance of action here mentioned the means for attaining the absolute right performance. The next verse declares the absolute right performance of action to be identical with absolute renunciation.

[1] "Is the man of renunciation," etc. The only renunciation that is of value as a means for the attainment of the supreme good is the renunciation of the desire of possession.
[2] "Consecrated fire" has to be kept up under the Brâhmanical Law by householders for the performance of daily and periodical sacrifices.

2. That which they call[1] renunciation, know that to be the right performance of action, O son of Pându. Without having renounced intentions[2] no one becomes a right performer of action.

The difficulty is to see how renunciation, which conveys the idea of cessation from action, should be the same as action, howsoever performed. But on reflection it will appear that ceasing to do any particular thing is in itself an act; the acme of renunciation is that state in which the intention to renounce is also renounced. While on the other hand, in the case of the right performance of action it is soon discovered by those aspiring to it that there is no intellectual representation possible for that which is right. Everything that we can think of is imperfect. Still, the hope which supports us in the search for the right shows that the right exists and that we do not know it. The natural effect of this is the absence of desire for action, including the form of it called cessation of action. The supreme truth thus represented to our intelligence is realized when Nirvâna is reached.

Having shown the importance of right performance of action by its praise, the Teacher next points out that it is the means for the attainment of right meditation.

3. For the wise man,[3] desirous of mounting to meditation,[4] action is said to be the means for the same. When thus mounted,[5] cessation of action is said to be the means.

The time of attaining meditation is next described.

4. When the man has abandoned all intentions and

---

[1] "They call," that is, those versed in the Vedas and the Sacred Law.

[2] "Intentions," that is, the feeling that "I shall do it," preceding action.

[3] "The wise man" is the performer of right action in the sense explained in the preceding chapter.

[4] "Meditation" as described in the last three verses of Chapter V.

[5] "When thus mounted," etc. Each time that in right action an interior peace and a feeling of having no responsibility is experienced, a step is taken towards right meditation. When one has begun to obtain these glimpses of the great peace, right meditation is not far from him. The power to remain fixed in meditation is the purification of the heart from desire of action here called cessation of action.

has no attachment leading to action in regard to objects of sense, then is he said to be mounted on meditation.

Psalm cxix. 97.

"Intentions" here includes unconscious tendencies. When intentions in this sense are removed there can be no prompting to action. All desires are but manifestations of these unconscious tendencies; these form the stuff, and the manner of its behavior is Karma in its strict sense. Sometimes, especially in English, the law as well as the substance is called Karma.

All tendencies, conscious or unconscious, are to be removed. When tendencies become dynamic they can be suppressed by patience and moral fortitude, but not so with latent tendencies. Since the tendencies in man are infinite in variety, it is not difficult to see that it is useless to wait for them to become dynamic in order to suppress them. The complete exhaustion of all tendencies by such a process would require infinite time. A supplementary method, more effective than the obvious one, is therefore necessary. This method is the dedication of all acts, as well as the power of action, to the Deity, or the study of spiritual philosophy. There is no other means by which the ever-burning fire of desire can be quenched, the insatiable thirst for life can be satisfied. It may be added that the dedication to the Deity of the fruit of action is not complete if the desire for the attainment of salvation, or Nirvâna, is kept back. Resign yourself to the Deity, and know through faith that the final end of existence is to attain perfect obedience to God, who is all in all. You can have no power, not even to work for the attainment of Nirvâna; all is of God.

5. Upraise the self by the self — do not sink the self; the self is the friend of self, and even the self is the enemy of self.

To "upraise the self" one must strive to "mount to meditation;" and in order not to "sink the self" one must not forget that there is no other way to escape from the ceaseless wheel of evolution than that herein described. In this way the soul is saved from all danger of falling into conditions even more miserable than its present lot.

The "self is the friend of self" because in seeking the eternal life the friends and relations who can aid us in all other matters may hinder rather than help us; the very love of them may itself become an obstacle. In the struggle for life everlasting a man is alone with his God.

The "self is the enemy of self" because the real enemy of man is his own heart, and even external enemies are such in consequence of our own nature. The pure heart is the self that rescues us from death, while the impure heart leads to destruction.

> 6. That self is the friend of the self by which the self is conquered; the unsubdued self prevails in enmity against the self even as an enemy.

1 Cor. ix. 27.

The combination of the body and mind ordinarily considered as "the self" is "conquered" when its perpetual restlessness is ended. When this is accomplished the Ego abides in its own form, — in other words, as it really is, identical with the Supreme Spirit, — and the soul receiving the perfect image of the Ego suffers no more.

How the "self is the friend of the self" is amplified.

> 7. The self of the man who is self-subdued[1] and free from desire and anger, is as the Supreme Self; and remains equal[2] in heat and cold, and also in honor and disgrace.

Romans viii. 13, 14.

"As the Supreme Self." When the self or heart of a man is perfectly at rest in God, it is said to be in the image or form of God.

The excellence of meditation is declared by praising the man who succeeds in it.

> 8. He whose heart is content with formal[3] and real knowledge,[4] and who is unshaken[5] and the conqueror of the senses, is said to be at rest in the Divine; he

---

[1] "Self-subdued," that is, mind and body at rest.
[2] "Remains equal," etc.; in consequence of divine illumination.
[3] "Formal," that is, knowledge contained in scriptural instruction.
[4] "Real knowledge" is finding confirmation within one's self of what is taught in the Scriptures.
[5] "Unshaken," by blasts of desire and anger.

is the illuminated sage to whom stone and gold are one.

The equal-mindedness of the sage is not confined to stone and gold, but embraces all things.

9. Excellent among them all is he whose heart is even in regard to friends, comrades, those who are indifferent, well-wishers to himself, and also to those opposed, to enemies and to kinsmen, and also in regard to the righteous and evil-doers.

Matt. v. 43-48.

There is another rendering for the first part of this verse, which is, "he attains liberation whose heart," etc. "Among them all" refers to those who have attained to meditation. Such an one being the most excellent, perpetual effort is to be made for final success through meditation. From the next verse to the thirty-second, instruction in the practice of meditation is given.

10. Let him who has attained to meditation always[1] strive to reduce his heart to rest in the Supreme,[2] dwelling in a secret place,[3] alone, with body and mind under control, devoid of expectation as well as of acceptance.[4]

Next is declared how the sage is to sit for meditation.

11. Having placed in a clean spot one's seat, firm,[5] not very high[6] nor very low,[7] and formed of skins of animals[8] placed upon cloth, and Kuça grass upon that,

---

[1] "Always," without intermission; continued and loving assiduity is implied by this word.

[2] "Reduce his heart ... Supreme," that is, realize identity with the Supreme.

[3] "Secret place," — mountain, cave, or any place free from all chance of interruption or interference of any kind. This and the following four conditions give all the requisites for meditation.

[4] "Acceptance," that is, sense of possession, even in relation to the rags of clothing and bits of food given to him by others.

[5] "Firm," not liable to be disturbed by instability.

[6] "Not high," for fear of falling.

[7] "Nor low," for fear of illness from damp, etc.

[8] "Skins of animals," etc.; the order of placing these three articles is reversed by some authorities.

12. Sitting on that seat, strive for meditation, for the purification of the heart, making the mind one-pointed, and reducing to rest the action of the thinking principle as well as that of the senses and organs.

The mind is "one-pointed" when it is abstracted from all other things than that to which it is applied. There are three mental states:—

1. Distracted, that in which the mind cannot apply itself to the desired object.
2. Discursive, a condition in which attention cannot be fixed on any one object without reference to its being the object desired.
3. One-pointed, which alone is conducive to meditation.

The result of meditation is the purification of the heart.

13. Holding the body, neck, and head straight and unmoved, perfectly determined,[1] and as if beholding[2] the end of his own nose, and not looking in any direction,

14. With heart in supreme peace, devoid of fear,[3] fixed in the Brahmachâri's vow,[4] with thought controlled[5] and heart in Me as the supreme goal, he remains.

Psalm cxii. 7.

It is not enough to have the heart fixed on the Deity, but he must be recognized as "the supreme goal," the finality of everything. It is possible that the heart should be absorbed in something which at the same time is not considered as the highest object in the universe.

These directions will be entirely barren of results unless the nature is first purified by faith. The most minute description

---

[1] "Perfectly determined," that is, with the whole nature bent upon this one end.

[2] "As if beholding;" the meditating mystic does not really look at his nose, but in consequence of his not looking at anything and not shutting his eyes, the lines of sight from the eyes naturally converge near the tip of his nose.

[3] "Devoid of fear," as to the violation of law, moral and religious. The perfect love that casteth out fear (1 John iv. 18).

[4] "Brahmachâri's vow;" such as celibacy, mendicancy, service to the Master.

[5] "Thought controlled," that is, having absorbed into the mind all its functions except that his "heart is in Me," the perfect Deity.

of the physiology of pleasure is not necessarily productive of pleasure in us.

Having described the process, he proceeds to describe the result in case of success.

15. Thus always tranquillizing the heart in the Supreme, the sage, with thought controlled, attains the supreme rest in Nirvâna that is my essence.

The highest conscious being in the universe is the Lord, or Içvara; but his essence is consciousness, which is the same wherever manifested, — in the ant as well as in the greatest of celestial beings. The realization of this truth is Nirvâna. The idea of subject and object does not exist in Nirvâna, and consequently the notion of difference, including the difference between the individual and universal spirit, has no place in the Absolute, which is the Spirit.

Further instructions about the food, etc., of the meditating sage now follow.

16. There is no meditation for the man who eats too much or too little, nor for him whose habit is to sleep too much or too little.

According to the sacred authority the proper amount of food is half of what can be conveniently eaten; and the same rule applies to the quantity of drink which is taken.

17. For him who is regulated in food,[1] in walking,[2] in exertion of work,[3] — regulated as well in sleep and waking,[4] — meditation becomes the destroyer of all suffering.[5]

He who perseveres in this discipline at last attains to meditation, at the time described in the following verse.

---

[1] "Regulated in food," as above.
[2] "In walking;" never to walk more than about eight miles.
[3] "Exertion of work," such as talking, etc.
[4] "Sleep and waking;" keep awake during the first four and the last four hours of the night, and sleep during the rest.
[5] "Destroyer of all suffering," that is, preventing continuance of conditioned existence by the rise to spiritual knowledge.

18. When the completely regulated heart remains at rest in the true Ego, then is the sage, free from attachment to any object of desire, said to be in yoga.

The "heart" is the combination of the principles of will, thought, and egotism. "Remains at rest," being applied to the true Ego, which is the same as the Supreme Spirit in exclusion of all objects. This stage is not final emancipation, for individual consciousness is not yet merged; it has yet an object, namely, the Supreme Spirit.

This condition, described above, is the conscious beatific vision. But in Nirvâna (to be described vv. 20–22) there is nothing which can specialize consciousness as individual or universal.

Yoga is the state described; it is defined by its greatest master as the cessation of the activity of the "heart."

19. The simile for the sage in yoga, with the heart at rest, and continuing in meditation is thought[1] to be as a lamp[2] in a windless place.

20. When the heart, restrained by the practice of yoga, rests from the final struggle, when it, viewing the Self[3] by the Self,[4] receives content in the Self,

21. When the objectless, self-perceived[5] acme of bliss he knows, and being where he never falls from the Reality,[6]

22. Having gained which no other gain is considered

Phil. i. 21.   superior thereto; in which one fixed is not moved, even by great grief.

The self is that which every one considers the greatest object of interest, so that when the self is gained there is no other gain desired. Death may be considered an example of "great grief." The idea is not that death is borne with patience, but that even

---

[1] "Thought," by those who have realized it.
[2] "Lamp," etc.; that is, the heart of the sage in yoga is steady in its illumination, with no flickering shadows of doubt on its limitless expanse.
[3] "Self," that is, the Universal Spirit, the Lord of all.
[4] "By the self," that is, as identical with "thou," the individual spirit.
[5] "Self-perceived;" that is, perceived by the principle called perception.
[6] "Reality" is Nirvâna.

death will not produce any feeling of a character requiring the exercise of patience.

The practical application of the theory of yoga, described before, is next shown in relation to the hearer.

23. Know this [1] disconnection from union with pain as yoga which ought to be striven for with faith [2] and without indifference.[3]

How this meditation is to be striven for is next described.

24. Abandoning all desires born of intentions, together with the intentions themselves, and controlling by the mind [4] the senses and organs which tend to action in every direction,

1 Pet. ii. 1, 2.

25. By degrees find rest in the inner self, possessed of patience; having brought the mind to rest in the true Self, think of nothing at all.

The expression "by degrees" shows that without attempting to fix the mind at once on the Supreme Spirit the aspirant ought to proceed step by step from the more gross to the less gross, thus: let the principle of perception (the inner self) dwell at first exclusively on the element earth and then absorb it into the next subtler element of water, and that into air, and then by degrees air into âkâsa, or free space; âkâsa into the reflective principle (manas), that into egotism, egotism into the principle of perception (buddhi), and buddhi into the unmanifested cause of all things, Prakriti, and finally that separated from the self or ego, Purusha; the Ego thus rendered independent of nature is one with the Supreme Spirit without any difference at all.

When this is done there comes rest free from all tendencies of every kind. The great Master of yoga, Patanjali, says that it is injurious to attempt to fix the mind at once on the Supreme Spirit.

---

1 "This," that is, what has been described in verses 20–22.

2 "With faith," that is, with full conviction as to the truth of the teaching of the Scriptures and Masters concerning it.

3 "Without indifference;" persevering in the effort, even though no success is readily achieved.

4 "Mind," which can perceive the harm with which the objects of sense are impregnated.

26. To whatever object goes out the mind, ever active and inconstant, restraining it from that, reduce it into subjection in the Spirit.

Whenever the mind, which, owing to natural discursiveness, is repugnant to concentration, is snatched away by any object, the best thing to be done is to perceive how worthless that object is in comparison with the prize that awaits the aspirant on the successful termination of his labors.

The result of this subjection of the mind is next stated.

27. Supreme bliss comes truly to the sage in meditation, whose mind is in peace,[1] whose passion[2] is exhausted, who is one with the Supreme Spirit, and free from both good and evil.

28. Thus devoting the heart, the sage in meditation,[3] free from imperfections, obtains without difficulty[4] the acme of bliss by union[5] with the Supreme Spirit.

Now comes the declaration of the nature of the ultimate goal, Nirvâna. It is first the extinction of all suffering, and then, for him who attains to it, it is the pure, unmixed, perfect, eternal bliss. Nirvâna is reached by the spiritual knowledge arising from yoga.

29. He whose heart is at rest through meditation, and who everywhere perceives the unity, perceives the Ego which is in every creature, and every creature in the Ego.

Restfulness of the heart is the only medium through which comes the perception of unity. He who "perceives the Ego in every creature," etc., realizes that the Ego is but one, although the forms of which it is the ego are many, and that the multitude of

---

[1] "Mind is in peace," on account of its fixed application to the true Self.
[2] "Passion" is the quality of *rajas*, producing delusion, restlessness, etc.
[3] "Sage in meditation," he who perseveres in yoga, unhindered by indolence, sickness, absence of mind, retrogression, restlessness, want of faith, erroneous perception, pain, dulness of mind, and attachment to objects of enjoyment.
[4] "Without difficulty," that is, without effort, through divine grace.
[5] "Union," that is, perception of identity.

forms can exist only as the power of the Ego. The individual spirit is here spoken of, — the spirit that is "own." The spirit that is not "own" is the Lord, Krishna. The individual ego is the spirit within, while the Lord is the spirit without. The next verse declares their identity, — that which is "own" is the Lord, and the Lord is the "own."

30. Who sees me everywhere, and sees everything in me, for him I am not lost, nor is he lost for me.
<small>John xvii. 20-23.</small>

That is, the individual spirit knows the universal spirit as the self, and the relation is reciprocal. This is the acme of identity.

31. Whoever, relying on spiritual one-ness,[1] worships me, who am in all creatures, he, the sage in yoga, in whatever condition existing, is present in me.[2]

32. Whoever among the sages, O Arjuna, perceives everywhere the same sorrow and joy[3] by measuring with his own self, is considered to be the most excellent.
<small>Matthew xxv. 34-40.</small>

Arjuna said:

33. O Slayer of Madhu,[4] this Yoga by thee declared as being tranquillity,[5] — of this I do not perceive uninterrupted continuance owing to restlessness of mind.

34. Restless, indeed, is the mind, O Krishna[6] turbu-

---

[1] "Relying on spiritual one-ness," realizing as the Ego the absolute consciousness without which no object can exist, and yet which is no object.

[2] "Is present in me," that is, attains liberation.

[3] "Same sorrow and joy," etc., that is, thinks that whatever is painful to himself is painful to others, owing to the non-duality of the Self. Do unto others as you would that they should do unto you.

[4] "Slayer of Madhu." Krishna slew the giant Madhu, who represents the quality of passion in nature.

[5] "Tranquillity," that is, the rest of the mind in the Self, freed from discursiveness as also from inaction.

[6] "Krishna," that is, he who is beyond all change, the supreme object of all meditation.

lent,[1] wild,[2] and firm;[3] the restraint of it I think is as greatly difficult as that of the wind.

THE BLESSED LORD *spoke:*

35. Without doubt, O thou of mighty arms, the mind is restless and hard to restrain; but, O son of Kuntî, it is reducible by long-continued practice and absence of desire.

"Long-continued practice" is that of holding the mind fixed in any particular function, without interruption, for a long time. "Absence of desire" is loss of relish in enjoyments, present and future, by realizing their evil consequences. According to the great Master of yoga in India, these two are the chief means of attaining to meditation, — all others are secondary to these.

36. Yoga is difficult to be attained by him whose heart is not controlled, but is attainable through proper means[4] by him whose heart is controlled.[5]

ARJUNA *said:*

37. O Krishna, who comes in faith, but whose mind is shaken,[6] — not finding the success through yoga, what end[7] does he obtain?

38. Does he, fallen from both,[8] become destroyed like a broken cloud, without any support,[9] O thou

---

[1] "Turbulent," because it destroys peace.
[2] "Wild," because its activity is subject to no rule.
[3] "Firm," because it is difficult to be bent from its object.
[4] "Proper means," that is, cessation of the functions of the thinking principle after its purification by being kept under control.
[5] "Heart is controlled," by long practice and absence of desire.
[6] "Mind is shaken," at the time of death, owing to the restlessness of the senses.
[7] "End," that is, state of being.
[8] "Both," that is, the good resulting from deeds of merit as well as from spiritual knowledge through yoga.
[9] "Without any support," from any promise contained in the theocratic Brahmanical law. The law-abiding man may hope for the fulfilment of the divine promise supporting the law.

of mighty arms, being deluded on the way of the Spirit?¹

39. This my doubt, O Krishna, thou art able to remove without leaving any remnant; there can indeed be no remover of the doubt other than thee.

The Blessed Lord *spoke:*

40. O son of Prithâ, neither here nor hereafter is there destruction² for him; never, my son, does a worker of righteousness come to an evil end.

Ps. lv. 22.

41. Attaining to the sphere of the workers of righteousness³ and dwelling there endless years,⁴ he that is fallen from yoga is born in the family of the pure and prosperous,⁵

42. Or even in the family of the wise, firm in meditation.⁶ On earth a birth like this is even more difficult⁷ to obtain.

43. There he gains union with that knowledge⁸ which belonged to the former body, and with that he again strives for perfection, O son of Kuru.

44. Because, by reason of that past practice, even against his will, he works; and though he be a mere inquirer about meditation, he reaches beyond the promise given by Vedic rites.

---

1 "Way of the Spirit," that is, in the acquirement of spiritual knowledge.
2 "Destruction;" exclusion from the society of the righteous on this earth and suffering after death, followed by re-birth in a position worse than before.
3 "Workers of righteousness," that is, those who perform acts of religious and moral merit.
4 "Endless years," that is, so long as to appear endless to mortals.
5 "Prosperous," because of his desire which led to his fall from meditation.
6 "Wise, firm in meditation," that is, men spiritually illuminated.
7 "More difficult," than the former, because it is free from all the temptations to which prosperity is subject.
8 "Knowledge" here means spiritual character; aspirations Godward.

"Even against his will" means that if he has committed any acts sufficiently unrighteous to produce evil tendencies stronger than the upward aspirations, then he has to exhaust those tendencies by experiencing their results ; and as soon as these tendencies have become for a moment powerless, as all tendencies do become while changing their form, the upward aspirations assert their sway. If, again, the downward tendencies are not so great, he walks the right path, but with trembling and trepidation, and in the darkness of doubt.

"Though he be a mere inquirer" does not mean that any one having a mere sentimental desire to know what meditation is attains to the result mentioned ; but that if one neglects all duties of life to know the nature of meditation he is superior to the performer of all works. Even in this it is to be understood that the desire is sincere and earnest, and not merely an excuse for lawless conduct. If this is so, even for a beginner, what need be said about those who have practised and failed?

45. Striving with strength the wise man, freed from sins, obtaining perfection because of efforts repeated through many births, then[1] goes to the supreme goal.

By the accumulated spiritual strength of many births the wise man is able to make such strenuous efforts as quickly to acquire that truth which sets him free.

46. The man of meditation[2] is superior to the man of penance, and also to the man of learning; this is my opinion. The man of meditation is superior also to men of action. Therefore, O Arjuna, become a man of meditation.

47. Of all who are in meditation, he who, with heart gone into me, full of faith, worships me, is supremely in meditation; this is my opinion.

In Chapter V. verse 28, it was declared that the last step is the knowledge of God, which bestows the life eternal. Here it is

---

[1] "Then," that is, on acquisition of spiritual wisdom.
[2] "Man of meditation," he who acquires wisdom as described in this chapter.

said that if the God who is known is not the Supreme God spoken of therein, the result is not final emancipation.

> Thus ends chapter the sixth, called "RIGHT KNOWLEDGE OF MEDITATION," in the blessed BHAGAVAD GÎTÂ, the sacred lore, the divine wisdom, the book of divine union, the colloquy between the blessed KRISHNA and ARJUNA, and contained in the Bhîshma Parvan of the blessed MAHÂBHÂRATA, which is a collection of a hundred thousand verses by VYÂSA.

In this chapter the growth of the capacity for renunciation is set as the limit of the right performance of action (v. 4); then yoga is set forth and the means of acquiring it (vv. 5–23); then instructions are given for restraining the mind, without which yoga is unattainable (vv. 23–36); and finally it is declared that the aspirant for spiritual knowledge through yoga, even though unsuccessful, does not suffer from evil results.

With this chapter closes the first hexad of the "Lord's Lay," declaring the nature of the Individual Spirit.

> Salutation to the Supreme Bliss, Mâdhava, adored of all devotees, who declared meditation upon himself as the crest jewel of all meditation in faith.

UNIVERSAL SPIRIT.

CHAPTER VII.

RIGHT KNOWLEDGE OF REALIZATION.

WITH this chapter begins the declaration of the mystery of the being of the Deity. In supreme reality the Deity has no attribute, and no relation to anything. Yet everything outside the Deity is false in the sense of not having the reality it claims. Man's suffering can never cease until this truth is realized. All religion, all philosophy, all mystical practices aim at this realization as their highest end.

Conditioned beings cannot possibly deal with the supreme truth except through symbolism of words which, without defining, indicates it. Hence it is clear that the value of these symbols depends upon the response which the nature of these beings makes to them. Consequently, as the characters of men differ, the symbols must differ also, in order to be of the same service to all.

The method of approaching the inconceivable Deity must therefore vary in order that all men may have the possibility of accepting some scheme of salvation which is synonymous with the knowledge of the Deity.

Mankind is divisible into three classes in relation to spiritual culture.

1. Those who are capable of realizing what the Deity is by the comprehension of verbal symbols which declare the identity of the Deity with the true Ego as the only reality, and all else an incomprehensible mystery called falsehood or illusion, to show its contemptible character.

In the case of devotees of this class no preliminary training is needed for the perception of the truth, symbolized by the words of spiritual philosophy. As an object is seen as soon as the eye turns to it, so these pure souls find the Deity from the indication given by the words that declare Him. With them there is no exercise of the power of action in obtaining *real* knowledge of the Deity, just as the seeing of an object placed before the eye does not involve the thought of actorship, or the sense of producing the object by looking at it. There is a power in the object which compels the recognition of its existence by the observer. So Truth forces upon these highly spiritual beings its own recognition as soon as it is declared. The present chapter is based upon this view of the truth.

2. Those upon whom the compelling power of Truth cannot operate on account of the restlessness of nature produced in them by passion and worldliness, but who yet receive spiritual truths in faith, and are able to meditate upon them with fixed concentration. The man of meditation hears that the Deity is absolute and identical with the true Self. He *believes* it, but does not *realize* it. The method of spiritual culture appropriate to him is the transference of identity to the Deity by successive stages of self-absorbing meditation as given in the eighth chapter.

The distinction between this and the preceding class is that it recognizes the independent agency of the aspirant for Truth, and has a practical end in view; namely, the realization of identity with the attributeless Deity. Those belonging to the first-mentioned class are free even from this desire; they find Truth is Truth and nothing more. It is obvious that this state of divine illumination is not merely the intellectual admission of Truth in words; as the knowledge of the word "chemistry" is not the same as mastery of the chemical science.

3. Those who through carnality of nature are not even able to concentrate their minds on Truth. These devotees worship God in love, — the love that is feeling God to be the innermost Self; they seek for Him in His wondrous works manifested in nature and in man; they live in brotherly love with all fellow-worshippers, admonishing one another and declaring to one another the mystery of the Godhead, wishing well to all creatures, and performing good works for the sake of God alone, — surrendering the personal will to the unsearchable will of God, the mysterious power which rules the universe. In this class there are individuals in different stages of spiritual development. For the sake of these worshippers the ninth and the three succeeding chapters are given.

All these devotees attain Nirvâna, — those of the first class as soon as the truth which they perceive extinguishes the illusive identity of the self-conscious principle and the Ego. This is accomplished by the separation of interest from the mind by repeatedly bringing it to rest in the Truth that is perceived.

Devotees of the two other classes progress through higher and higher spiritual states before attaining final rest.

Those who have thoroughly realized identity with the Deity are not touched by anything said here; there being nothing beyond the Deity, the Scriptures can have no relation to those who are "His very self" (Chap. VII. 18).

Having declared the superiority of the worshipper of the true God in the last verse of the preceding chapter, the Blessed Lord proceeds to show what God is the true God.

1. O son of Prithâ, with heart devoted to me, practising meditation,[1] depending on me, how thou shalt know me completely, — to that listen.

1 John v. 20; 1 Cor. xiii. 12, 13.

"Depending on me" means, recognizing me to be the only hope of attaining the end aspired for. Everything said, done, or thought is of no value; God's will is the only door to salvation. Depend upon that with hope, and while thou hast to work, perform with body, speech, and mind what has been enjoined upon thee through revealed Scriptures.

2. Together with realization,[2] this knowledge I shall fully declare unto thee; knowing which there shall remain nothing else[3] to be known.

John xiv. 17; Col. ii. 3.

3. Among thousands of men, some *one*, perhaps, strives for perfection; among those striving for perfection, some *one*, perhaps, knows me in reality.

Luke vi. 40; 1 Cor. ix. 24.

[1] "Practising meditation" is the means for acquiring exclusive devotion to "me," the Supreme Spirit, whose mysterious nature is declared herein.

[2] "With realization," a new and mysterious consciousness will be given, and not mere information.

[3] "Remain nothing else;" the knower of truth being omniscient, for him there can be no more desire; he reaches the absolute in the only sense in which that is possible, — the Absolute God and I are one.

The difficulty of attaining to real knowledge of God induces the Blessed Lord Himself to declare it. (Cf. John i. 18; Matt. xi. 27.)

4. Earth, water, fire, air, and âkâsa, manas, buddhi, and ahankâra,—thus is my nature eight-fold divided.

The nature of the Deity is the totality of His power. Now this power is, first of all, divided into subject and object,—the conscious knower and what he knows. This universal object is the nature described in this verse, and the subject on whom nature depends is the Logos; the Logos as he is in himself is the Father whom no one has seen, the absolute consciousness.

It is declared that the principle of objectivity or nature is the power of existing in the eight forms mentioned. Care must be taken to guard against the misconception of regarding the principle of objectivity as the synthesis of these eight considered as components. For that which is the synthesis cannot make itself the synthesis, and therefore requires some outside power to support its existence by stringing together the eight components as the synthesis. But as it is the divine nature itself which is to be studied, where is such a synthesizing power to be found except in that nature itself? Otherwise it will be necessary to maintain the existence of more than one God, and also to incur a *regressus in infinitum*.

This divine power called objectivity is the power to assume eight forms; namely:—

EARTH, which does not mean that which is so designated for practical purposes among mankind, but rather that form of the divine power which produces the earth. It may be otherwise looked upon as the subtle principle of smell.

WATER, FIRE, AIR, and ÂKÂSA; these four elements are to be similarly understood as the divine power of producing them respectively, or as the subtle principles of taste, sight, touch, and hearing.

MANAS ordinarily signifies the faculty which makes images, the reflecting power; but here it means the power of producing that which is perceived as "I am this," without defining what "this" is.

BUDDHI usually means the faculty which produces the sense of reality by investing some one among the images produced by manas with the character of certainty. Buddhi is the power which is perceived in the difference between what is called real and what is called imaginary. In regard to the real object, buddhi works with the image-making power; in regard to the imaginary it does not. Here it is to be taken as that element in the totality of the Divine Power which makes all the workings of that Power to appear as *in themselves* real, and hides their true character of being real only by reflecting the Reality which is the Deity.

AHANKÂRA usually signifies the principle of self-consciousness, or egotism. Here it designates the totality of the dynamic energy of the Deity, the power of producing the universe out of the Divine Substance which never changes.

5. This is inferior; different from this know my superior nature, which is the knower; by which, O thou of mighty arms, the universe is upheld.

John. i. 4, 5.

It is "inferior," because unconscious, unable to exist except in connection with consciousness, which it cannot know, and yet works for. The "superior nature," or consciousness, is to be regarded only in relation with the other power, objectivity. The Supreme God of the universe is the Lord of the superior and inferior nature. He is independent of the universe and His own lordly power over it. (Cf. 1 Cor. xv. 28.)

In other words, the ruling power of the universe as related to consciousness is the Logos. This Logos is omnipotent and omniscient. But what is God in Himself as different from His character of ownership of the inferior and superior nature?

The ownership of the superior and inferior natures is the connection between them. For if any relation exists between consciousness and that which is unconscious, it can only be this, "I know It." The object known is not consciousness, and yet in relation to it is as something it knows. This is the ownership of the inferior nature.

Now, the ownership of the superior nature can only be the power of disconnecting it from the inferior nature; for then will cease the power represented by the statement "I know It." The ownership of both these natures is the power of uniting and disuniting them. (Cf. 1 Cor. xv. 27, 28.)

In order to know what the Deity is in Himself, this power is to be included in Power which has no being apart from the Deity. If that is realized, all notions of knower, knowledge, and known are ended. In consequence, Power, or Nature, both superior and inferior, disappears, and what remains is consciousness without its character of being the superior nature, because it is not connected with any object.

This is the FATHER of the New Testament, whose Son, the Word, is the conscious creator, preserver, and destroyer of the universe, and is eternally in the bosom of the Father. Time is the relation between nature and consciousness; how then can time affect God? The relation between nature and consciousness cannot be ended by lapse of time, but by the knowledge that consciousness is not nature, which is unconscious.

This knowledge, being unrelated to time, is not an act of knowing, but a thing called knowledge, and therefore very rightly called the Grace of God, which alone can exercise the power by which the connection between nature and consciousness is severed. Consciousness, in itself, cannot be the object of knowledge; therefore no man at any time hath seen God (the Father); but the Son, or Consciousness, as related to nature, " hath *declared* Him." The Logos, as knowing and dominating nature, knows also his own independence of nature or the self-existence of consciousness, and thus can declare the Father, but not know Him, except as identical with Him, the quality of consciousness which is the Spirit of God being the same wherever found: and this cannot rightly be called knowledge.

6. Know that all creation has these[1] for their source: I am of the whole universe the origin and the end.

Col. i. 15-17; John i. 3.

Through these two powers, "the origin and the end," the Deity is the cause of all things,—the Alpha and Omega of existence. As Himself, the Deity has no attributes; but as the Word, the Lord of the two powers, He is the God of the universe.

7. O conqueror of wealth, there is nothing superior to Me;[2] all this is threaded by Me[3] as gem-beads by string.

Isa. xlv. 6.

---

[1] " These," that is, superior and inferior nature.
[2] " There is nothing . . . me." Absolute consciousness is beyond all things.
[3] " All this is . . . me;" as the string, though unseen, keeps together the

How all things are strung on Nature's Lord is shown by the declaration of His powers as their essence.

8. O son of Kuntî, I am the taste in water, the splendor of Sun and Moon, the Pranava[1] in all the Vedas, sound in space, the humanity in men.

9. I am the sacred smell[2] in the Earth, and the brilliance in the Fire; the life in all creatures and the power of concentration[3] in those whose minds are concentrated in the Spirit.

Heb. xii. 28.

10. Know Me, O son of Prithâ, as the eternal seed[4] of all creatures. I am the wisdom[5] of the wise and the power[6] of the powerful.

11. Of the strong I am that strength[7] which is free from relish[8] and longing;[9] in all creatures I am the desire unopposed to righteousness.[10]

12. Know the moods arising from the qualities of *satva*, *rajas*, and *tamas*, as from Me;[11] they are in Me, but not I in them.[12]

Amos iii. 6.
Rom. ix. 18.

---

gem-beads that it threads, so consciousness, though not perceived, keeps together the universe of objects which are but manifestations of its power.

[1] "Pranava;" this mysterious syllable, Om, is the essence of all the Vedas; to comprehend its import is to comprehend the Truth embodied in the Vedas.

[2] "Sacred smell;" all things are sacred in their natural condition; they become defiled by contact with the impurity of creatures.

[3] "Power of concentration," that by which they are connected with me.

[4] "Seed," that is, final cause.

[5] "Wisdom," that is, manifestation of Truth in the form of Faith, or certainty about Truth.

[6] "Power," that is, the capacity for overcoming opposition.

[7] "Strength," that is, the capacity of not being overcome.

[8] "Relish," that is, the pleasure with which an object is enjoyed.

[9] "Longing," that is, the pleasure with which an absent object of enjoyment is contemplated.

[10] "Desire unopposed to righteousness," for example, eating and drinking for the maintenance of life.

[11] "From me," that is, the "qualities" are contained in the "inferior nature" which is their final cause.

[12] "Not I in them," that is, unlike creatures, the Creator is not bound by Nature; the Divine will is absolutely free, and the Divine substance absolutely unconditioned.

"Moods" are states of mind leading to variety in experience. As affected by *satva*, they are unselfishness, truthfulness, and so on; by *rajas*, they are vanity, self-gratulation, and the like; by *tamas*, they are grief, confusion of mind, and similar attributes. The nature of these "qualities" is fully explained in Chapter XIV.

13. The whole world, deluded by these three moods, born of qualities, knows not Me, the unmodifying,[1] as distinct from these.

The world is "deluded" through spiritual blindness; the world does not know the Deity, the spirit of all creatures, and possessed of eternally pure, wise, and unconditioned nature, as really distinct from the causes which in their totality form the "inferior nature." (Cf. John i. 10, 11.)

The path which leads out of delusion is now declared.

14. Because this,[2] my[3] illusive power,[4] formed of qualities, is so difficult to cross over, — is Divine,[5] — therefore those cross over this illusive power who seek refuge in Me alone.

Ps. lxii. 7, 8.
John i. 12.

The last sentence shows that those who, perceiving through faith that the Deity is independent of nature and is its Master, abandon all desire and dedicate to Him the personal will, attain Nirvâna.

Now follows the reason why all men do not seek refuge in the Deity.

15. The worst among men, deluded, workers of evil, bereft of spiritual perception by the illusive power, and resting in demoniac dispositions,[6] do not seek refuge in Me.

Isa. vi. 9;
John viii. 43,
44, 47.

---

[1] "Unmodifying," that is, simple essence.
[2] "This," that is, known to me in its true character.
[3] "My," that is, I am its Master.
[4] "Illusive power," that is, capable of making one thing appear as another, — forming this wondrous world out of darkness.
[5] "Divine," that is, possessed or dominated by the Deity forming the inferior nature.
[6] "Demoniac dispositions," characterized by cruelty, untruth, and other similar qualities. "Disposition" is a lasting mood.

It may here be added that the holding back of truth from those of "demoniac disposition" is for their own good, because they would cease to be themselves, and in that sense would be destroyed by the reception of truth. Sometimes they would say, "Give us Truth, even if it slay us;" but they say so only because they do not believe that Truth exists; their object is not to obtain Truth, but vainglorious satisfaction in the confirmation of their belief that Truth is not. They get what they seek.

16. Four classes of men, workers of righteousness, worship Me, O Arjuna, — the afflicted,[1] the searchers for Truth,[2] the desirers of possessions,[3] and the wise,[4] O son of Bharata.

1 Kings iii. 11.

It is possible for every worshipper to cross over this life of illusions, but owing to diversity of motives impelling them, the actual result is not the same.

17. Of them the wise man, eternally illuminated,[5] devoted exclusively to Me,[6] is the best. I am, indeed, extremely beloved[7] of the wise man, and he of Me.[8]

1 Kings iii. 10; 1 Cor. xiii. 12.

18. Excellent indeed are all of them, but the wise man is myself — this is my opinion, because the wise man is, with heart in peace, established on the road to the superiorless goal,[9] which is even Myself.

---

[1] "The afflicted" are relieved from their afflictions.
[2] "Searchers for Truth" obtain it.
[3] "Desirers of possessions" gain their desires here or hereafter.
[4] "The wise," those who have realized that the Deity is the true Ego.
[5] "Eternally illuminated," by self-knowledge.
[6] "Exclusively to me;" perceives no other object in the universe worthy of devotion besides the Supreme Spirit. In the universe of falsity the only truth is the Lord, and I and He are one and the same.
[7] "I am ... extremely beloved." It is well known that the most beloved object is the self, and the Lord being the Self is the most beloved of the wise, who knows Him to be the Self.
[8] "He of me." In granting the realization of identity to the wise man, the Deity accepts him as Himself.
[9] "Superiorless goal," or Nirvâna, which is the very Self of the Deity.

It is not true that the other three classes of worshippers are not dear to me, but they are guilty towards me of the offence of ignorance, which prevents the perfect manifestation of my love to them. Yet it is better to worship the Deity for a selfish object than not to worship Him at all; for the selfish worshipper can at any time become a true worshipper by abandoning selfishness.

19. At the end of many births [1] the wise man finds me as the Vâsudeva who is all this;[2] such an one, of great soul, is extremely difficult to find.

The reason for the non-recognition of Vâsudeva as the spirit of all now follows.

20. Bereft of discriminating wisdom[3] by special desires,[4] men worship other gods, adopting peculiar modes of worship,[5] in subordination[6] to their own hearts.

Col. ii. 18.

It is better to worship the true God, even with wrong motives, than to become idolaters; for in the first case a gradual attainment of Nirvâna is possible.

The reason is next given why men do not, through worship of false gods, become fit worshippers of the true God in course of time.

21. Whatever form[7] a devotee desires to worship in faith, in the same unswerving faith I ordain.

By the tendencies generated during one birth the conduct during the next is regulated, and that in its turn strengthens the same tendencies; and thus the wheel rolls on ceaselessly.

---

[1] "At the end of many births." From the beginningless past time the great-souled sage has acquired the tendencies on the maturity of which spiritual knowledge arises.

[2] "Vâsudeva who is all this," or the Supreme Spirit which dwells in all things and yet is apart from all things; it is a name of Krishna.

[3] "Discriminating wisdom" as to the true God.

[4] "Special desires," such as greatness among men, revenge upon enemies, and so on.

[5] "Peculiar modes of worship," that is, fasting, singing hymns, etc.

[6] "In subordination," etc., that is, in adopting peculiar rites and ceremonies they are guided by their own natures, or rather characters, formed by the desires and acts in previous births.

[7] "Form," all gods are the bodies or forms of the true God, who is beyond all form.

Like the tree and the seed, tendencies and acts are perpetuated by the regulating power of the Deity which attaches to each man his previously generated tendencies; this is why idolatry is such an abomination.

22. Joined to that faith, he labors for the worship of the particular god, and gains from him his desires; but really they are ordained by Me.

False gods have no independent power. Whatever power they may seem to possess, it is but the reflection of the almightiness of the true God.

23. The result that comes to them, men of little understanding,[1] is temporary. To the gods the worshippers of the gods go; my worshippers go[2] to Me.

It is true that the false gods are apparently nearer to men than the true God; but here in the Blessed Lord, the true God, is manifested through His mysterious power. Why is it that men still refuse Him worship?

24. These, devoid of understanding, consider Me, the unmanifest, as manifested,[3] not knowing the supreme condition[4] of Me, the exhaustless and superiorless.[5]

John i. 18; 1 Tim. i. 17.

The mystery of the incarnation is misunderstood, and men devoid of understanding think that which is seen of them is God. They know the Christ only in the manner of the flesh.

---

[1] "Of little understanding," because the same amount of labor in the service of the true God would have yielded endless results.

[2] "Go," this verb is quite appropriate, because as the Deity is omnipresent there is no need to break the rhetorical symmetry which is preserved by the repetition of the verb used before.

[3] "Unmanifest as manifested." They think that the God who was unmanifested until the incarnation became changed into the mortal man. Thus the incarnation is made a new ground for idolatry, and the Supreme is degraded to the level of false gods.

[4] "Supreme condition." Where the absolute God is looked upon in relation to His creatures He stands as the other pole of existence, yet really He is

[5] "Exhaustless and Superiorless," that is, absolute.

Those who would hold that there was any change of consciousness in the Deity owing to the birth of the babe in the manger, or that the Logos at any time did not know his own true nature, — or, strictly speaking, independence of nature, — would be "of little understanding," according to the meaning of this last verse.

25. I am not manifest to the world,[1] being wrapped up by the creative power; therefore this deluded world does not recognize Me, the unborn, exhaustless.

John i. 10-12.

26. I know the creatures that are past and that are present as also that are future, O Arjuna, but Me no one[2] knows.

As the magician causes illusion to all but is not affected by it himself, so though the world is deluded by the qualities, yet I am not affected by them; my omniscience is never impaired.

27. O son of Bharata,[3] by the delusion of opposites, arising from attraction and hatred, all creatures at the time of birth[4] fall into delusion, O harasser of thy foes.

The "opposites" are the species contained in the genus "attraction and hatred." As they arise, the tranquillity necessary for wisdom is disturbed by the feeling that "I am undergoing change." The egotism thus strengthened prevents the realization of the true Ego.

28. Men of righteous deeds,[5] whose sins have come

---

[1] "Not manifest to the world," but only to my devotees. (Cf. John xvii. 9; Luke viii. 10.)

[2] "No one," except the wise.

[3] "Son of Bharata" and "harasser of thy foes" are epithets intended to call forth all the energies of Arjuna by the recollection of the greatness of his family and his own prowess, in order to emancipate himself from the power of the opposites, heat and cold.

[4] "At the time of birth;" by attraction towards it, and repulsion from it, the incarnating ego loses its previous knowledge.

[5] "Righteous deeds" purify the heart.

to an end,[1]—they, freed from [2] the pair of opposites, and delusion, worship Me, persevering in faith.

<small>Matt. x. 22; Eph. iii. 17-19.</small>

"Persevering in faith" is having the firm faith that this is the true God whom I worship. He is the nearest and dearest thing to me, being the true Ego; and for His sake I renounce the world and all it contains.

29. Those who for liberation from decay and death strive, depending on Me, they know Brahmă, the whole Adhyâtma, as well as all Karma.

The expression "depending on me" teaches that those devotees who have been spoken of before find me as the attributeless Deity, from scriptural declarations, and in consequence are not under the necessity of any action as means for the attainment of the Supreme Spirit. But those who are unable to do so must depend on divine grace and meditate on me, seeking to realize the declaration contained in the succeeding chapter, to which this last and the concluding verse are the introduction. These are the worshippers described before as belonging to the second-mentioned class.

30. Those who know Me together with Adhibhûta,[3] Adhidaivata, and Adhiyajna, resting with their hearts in Me, know Me even at the time of death.

> Thus ends chapter the seventh, called "REALIZATION OF THE SPIRIT," in the blessed BHAGAVAD GÎTÂ, the sacred lore, the divine wisdom, the book of divine union, the colloquy between the blessed KRISHNA and ARJUNA, and contained in the Bhîshma Parvan of the Blessed MAHÂBHÂRATA, which is a collection of a hundred thousand verses by VYÂSA.

---

[1] "Whose sins have come to an end," that is, well-nigh exhausted; complete sinlessness is Nirvâna.

[2] "Freed from," etc. This is the consequence of deeds of righteousness and exhaustion of sins.

[3] "Adhibhûta" and the other terms are explained in the following chapter.

Those who work out their salvation through mystical meditations, depending on divine grace, not only know that which is mentioned in verse 30, but also those spoken of here, and have no fear of falling away from their state of knowledge at the time of death, when the mind and body are extremely oppressed with agony.

For the highly spiritual this chapter declares the attributeless Deity, who can only be *indicated* by speech.

Salutation to Krishna, whose devotees, striving for liberation, obtain that knowledge which is liberation from this life of bondage.

CHAPTER VIII.

SUPREME SPIRIT NAMED AS OM.

The preceding chapter declares the Supreme Spirit and His two unsearchable powers, called superior and inferior nature, consciousness and unconsciousness, subject and object. Those who can perceive THAT which the words indicate from the words alone, are beings of the highest order of spirituality. The present chapter is meant for those who believe that Truth is embodied in the words but are yet unable to perceive it.

The seven questions with which the last chapter closes are here answered in such a manner that if they are meditated upon in exclusion of every other object the Truth will be perceived. The acme of meditation is to lose self-consciousness in the object of meditation and thus to become it. It is true that no one can ever *become* the Supreme Spirit, for in reality he is never anything else. To know and to become the Supreme Spirit is really the same thing; the difference in expression is due to the difference in the inner peace of the different classes of devotees.

It is also to be borne in mind that the Supreme Spirit is not in Truth liable to be known as an object. Being nothing but pure consciousness, where is to be found anything else to know it? Nor can consciousness know itself. For to be known is to cease to be consciousness. The purpose of spiritual culture is not intellectually to explain Nature and God, but to purge away our humanity and leave divinity as the only Truth and Ego; this is the knowledge of the true God.

Hoping to obtain an explanation of the five words mentioned in the two concluding verses of the last chapter,

Arjuna said:

1. What is that BRAHMĂ, what is ADHYÂTMA, what is KARMA, O Purushottama, what is ADHIBHÛTA spoken of, and what is called Adhidaivata?

2. ADHIYAJNA who is in this body, and how, O Slayer of Madhu; and at the time of death how art thou to be known by souls in meditation fixed?

Brahmă has two aspects; namely, with the totality of nature as attribute, and without all and every attribute, as in supreme reality. The first is the Son, who is eternally in the bosom of the Father, is with God, and, as apart from His attributes, is God. The second is the supreme Brahmă, whom no man hath at any time seen and whom no man can see.

"Adhyâtma" literally means that which dwells in the body, and thus signifies the senses and organs, as well as the Supreme Spirit, by the mysterious power of illusion appearing as the Spirit dwelling in every man.

"Karma" means religious rites and action in general.

"Purushottama" is literally the Supreme Spirit, and as here used refers to the omniscience of the Blessed Lord.

"Adhibhûta" may mean the Supreme Spirit dwelling in earth, water, and the other elements, and in the whole universe of effects, through the mysterious divine power or illusion.

"Adhidaivata" may mean the highest manifested consciousness, dwelling in the solar orb, or the conscious mind as affected by meditation on the nature of celestial beings.

"Adhiyajna" is literally "the director of a sacrificial ceremony;" the ceremony here meant is the life of man. Who performs this sacrifice, and who grants the boon to obtain which the sacrifice is instituted?

The word "how" in the last verse signifies, How does he dwell in the body, inside or outside; always, or at certain times? It may also imply, How is he to be known, as identical with or as an attribute of the Supreme Spirit?

"Madhu" here means honey,—the anticipated pleasure in acts, the fruit of action. He by whom this honey is slain knows all that relates to the nature of action and its consequences.

THE BLESSED LORD *spoke:*

3. The Exhaustless is the supreme Brahmă.[1] Own-ness is called Adhyâtma. By Karma is meant the parting with objects for the birth and prosperity of creatures.

Job xi. 7.

Adhyâtma is the same Brahmă, appearing by its own mysterious power as the individual spirit, the innermost thing in man, the very ownness. If the mind, unfettered by desire or hatred, follows the thing which answers to the word " I," acknowledging and at the same time denying identity with the assemblage of the body and the inner faculties, the pursuit will go on uninterruptedly until it disappears, as appetite disappears by eating. The ultimate reality obtained on the cessation of this pursuit is Adhyâtma, or ownness, which differs from the exhaustless Supreme Brahmă only in name.

"Karma" here means all the rites and ceremonies which involve the giving up of ownership in anything for the sake of the Deity or gods, where no higher conception of Divinity exists. In the fourth chapter the influence of sacrifices on the prosperity of creatures is explained.

4. Adhibhûta[2] is the changeful condition. Adhidaivata is the Purusha. I am the Adhiyajna in this body, O best of those who have a body.

"Purusha" has two meanings, "He who sleeps in the city of nine gates," that is, the body; and "He who is full." Here Purusha is to be taken as the universal consciousness, in relation to which alone exist the power which operates in the senses, organs, mind, egotism, and the power which gives objective reality to mental images. This is the spirit that is said to dwell in the sun, which is the centre of the energy which gives life and activity to the whole system.

5. And at the time of death, whoever goes forth,

---

[1] "The exhaustless ... Brahmă," that is, the attributeless Absolute.

[2] "Adhibhûta," that which becomes; it excludes all effects and is the causing power.

abandoning the body, meditating upon Me indeed, he attains to my state;[1] of this no doubt exists.

The right way of approaching the Deity at the time of death is to meditate upon "Me indeed;" that is, upon the Deity as he is, and not in the various aspects here described.

6. Whoever, in consequence of constant meditation on any particular form,[2] gives up this body, thinking of that form at the time of death, even to the same form he goes, O son of Kuntî.

The influence of the last thought on the future of the soul is a general truth and not confined to the case of the Deity. At the time of death, when the senses, organs, and internal faculties are in excruciating pain, that thought is entertained which by reason of the greatest familiarity comes with the greatest ease.

7. Therefore at all times[3] meditate on Me and fight;[4] thy manas and buddhi being devoted to Me,[5] without doubt thou shalt come to Me.

8. With heart that abides in Me alone, and to nothing else wanders, he, O son of Prithâ, through proper meditation on the Divine Spirit, goes to it.

1 John ii. 15-17.

The thinking self loses its restlessness and becomes engrossed in the perception of a single object, which in this case is the Deity considered as an object of perception. In order to bring the thinking self to this condition, long, continuous, and loving meditation on the Deity is to be practised again and again.

Proper meditation is that in accordance with the teaching of the Scriptures and holy teachers. No religion can be of the highest

---

[1] "My state," that is, Nirvâna.
[2] "Form," for example, some inferior god.
[3] "At all times," that is, frequently, continuously, and lovingly.
[4] "And fight," that is, perform thy duty, but yet remember me.
[5] "Thy manas ... to me," the whole heart being devoted to the Deity, everything is perceived as a manifestation of Him; the actor, action, and the result thereof being realized as the Deity, the goal after death is necessarily the Deity.

value unless it is founded upon a set of Scriptures the full meaning of which is realized by the teachers of that religion.

The "Divine Spirit" is the Supreme Spirit considered as an object of perception. This is the spirit that is said to dwell in the sun as the source of its power of self-luminousness. The Spirit is described in the succeeding verses.

9. Whoever properly meditates upon the all-wise, the eternal, the supreme ruler, the subtlest[1] of the subtle, the supporter of all, of unthinkable form,[2] sun-charactered[3] by being beyond the darkness.[4]

This verse embodies a Vedic text, "I know that great Spirit, sun-charactered by being beyond the darkness."

10. With mind unwavering, and united to love,[5] and the power of meditation,[6] he, at the time of death, perfectly concentrating[7] his vital powers between the eyebrows, attains to that supreme, refulgent Spirit.[8]

Mere devotion and the power of tranquillizing the heart are not sufficient without knowledge.

11. That which those wise in the Vedas[9] call exhaust-

---

[1] "Subtlest," being the cause of all things.

[2] "Of unthinkable form," that is, though eternally present, no adequate form of Him can be imagined.

[3] "Sun-charactered." As the sun requires no extraneous light for its manifestation, so the Divine Spirit, being consciousness, requires nothing to support its existence. The universe, being objective, depends upon consciousness for existence.

[4] "Darkness," that is, false knowledge or illusion, which is the root cause of the universe; true knowledge is to know the universe as no reality. This true knowledge is not the Deity, inasmuch as He is consciousness.

[5] "United to love," that is, absorbed in the love of the Deity, who, being the true and only Self, must be the only and absolute love.

[6] "Power of meditation," that is, the unconscious and irresistible tendency to keep the heart at rest, generated by long-continued and loving practice of meditation.

[7] "Perfectly concentrating;" that is, the self-consciousness being transferred through the fervor of meditation to the Logos in whom the powers of cognition and action are at rest. This is a mystery of the Spirit which is not generally understood.

[8] "Refulgent Spirit." The Divine Spirit is so called on account of the independence of consciousness of all things.

[9] "Wise in the Vedas," those who have realized the truth declared in the Vedas.

less,[1] into which enter those who, free from attachments, labor for salvation, desiring which they lead the Brahmachâri's life, — in short, I shall tell thee what makes that known.

The "Brahmachâri" lives under a spiritual master, vowed to celibacy, mendicancy, and other similar observances. Having cast out of his heart all other desires, he "labors for salvation," realizing more and more perfectly the illusive character of the universe, which rests upon non-perception of identity with the Supreme Spirit.

The Pranava is that which "makes that known." How divine knowledge is obtained by comprehending the mystery of this syllable is the subject of many Vedic treatises. This verse is from the Vedas.

The method of worship through this mysterious syllable is next described.

12. Having controlled all the gates,[2] imprisoned the mind in the heart,[3] and having placed the vital powers in the head, at rest in the fixedness of meditation,[4]

13. Repeating the one, exhaustless OM,[5] whoever departs, abandoning the body,[6] goes to the supreme goal.

The vital powers are not the production of the mind and egotism alone. Consequently, when the mind is absorbed in the egotism the vital powers are not completely absorbed; they are then drawn into the cause of the egotism, the buddhi, which, according to mystics, is seated between the eyebrows.

But what is to be done by those who are unacquainted with the mystical process by which death is brought under control?

---

[1] "Exhaustless," the name of the Deity independent of all relations.

[2] "The gates," that is, senses and organs.

[3] "Imprisoned . . . heart," that is, restrained the mind from assuming the form of any object, and thus made it latent in the heart or egotism from which the mind emanates.

[4] "Meditation;" that is, while the body is engaged in uttering the sound, the mind is in pursuit of its significance.

[5] "Om." This is the name of the one exhaustless Spirit.

[6] "Whoever . . . the body," that is, leaves the body without the sense of losing any object of possession.

14. Whoever, with heart that to nothing else turns, constantly and during the whole of life meditates on Me, — for him, the man of yoga, constant in meditation, I am easy of attainment, O son of Prithâ.

15. On attaining Me,[1] the great-souled ones, reaching the supreme consummation of being, incur not rapidly-revolving[2] re-births, the mansion of woe.[3]

16. All the worlds from the abode of Brahmâ are revolving again and again; but, O son of Kuntî, on attaining Me there is no re-birth.

John iii. 15.

There is no rest in "all the worlds," except in the Deity. Immortality remains a mere word until the identity is fixed on the Supreme Spirit; hence the necessity for man to work out his salvation.

Brahmâ is the Deity considered as the creator of personal creatures, not of the Ego which transcends personality. As the body appears as a personal creature by reason of a false attribution of consciousness — which being no object cannot be legitimately attributed to any object — to the body, similarly the universal power of personality, under the false attribution of consciousness, appears as Brahmâ.

17. The day of Brahmâ is limited by a thousand yugas;[4] his night also ends in a thousand yugas; these the knowers of night and day[5] know.

---

[1] "Attaining me," that is, realizing identity with the Supreme Spirit.

[2] "Rapidly-revolving," the instability of life renders it difficult to perceive its true character as the

[3] "Mansion of woe." Not only things in this life are subject to change, but the change is also from agony to agony.

[4] *Yuga* here stands for four-yugas. This computation of time can be shown thus: —

  1 human year = 1 day and night of the gods.
  12000 celestial years = 4 yugas.
    1000 four-yugas = 1 day of Brahmâ, his night being of equal duration.
    360 days and nights of Brahmâ = 1 year of Brahmâ.
    100 years of Brahmâ = the term of his life.

[5] "Knowers of night and day;" not those who are merely versed in the apparent movements of the heavenly bodies, but who through spiritual perception have realized the nature of time.

18. From the unmanifested all the manifested issue. At the approach of the day, at the approach of night, they merge even in that [1] same called the unmanifested.

"Unmanifested" does not here mean the Deity regarded as the cause of the universe, but the power known as the creator Brahmâ's sleep; because it is only at the end of a hundred years of Brahmâ that the universe is reduced into the First Cause. One of the secondary causes is here meant.

19. This assemblage of entities in this manner having become, is destroyed at the approach of night, O son of Prithâ; the same, resistless,[2] emerges at the coming of day.

Vain are the efforts of man to find any happiness in the world; there is a power which overbears him, and he is chained to the wheel of pain. The powers that constrain him are the consciousness of separateness from the Deity, egotism, attraction and repulsion, and fear of the unknown. These form themselves into the endless stream of cause and effect, which flows on irresistibly; those men alone are wise who perceive this evil and wish not for conditioned existence. The wise must therefore work out their salvation in the way before described.

20. There is yet another unmanifested,[3] dissimilar to the preceding, which is the eternal, and which, all things being destroyed, is not destroyed.

The "one, exhaustless" spirit named by the sacred monosyllable is here declared. The subject is resumed after the necessary and contrasting description of the transitoriness of all things in heaven and on earth except the Deity.

[1] "Even in that;" "even" shows that the unmanifested is the basis upon which waves of manifestation appear and disappear.
[2] "Resistless," because they have not obtained control over nature.
[3] "Another unmanifested." The Supreme Spirit is unmanifest because not perceptible by any sense or faculty; yet it is totally unlike and unrelated to the unconscious, material cause of the universe.

21. That called exhaustless,[1] unmanifested, is the same they[2] term the supreme goal, obtaining which they fall not back, — that is my supreme abode.[3]

These two verses show that the Supreme Spirit, symbolized by the mysterious monosyllable, is different from all that is comprehended by cause and effect.

22. He is the Supreme[4] Purusha, attainable by exclusive love;[5] all creatures are contained within him,[6] and by him all this is pervaded.[7]

Acts xvii. 27, 28.

All are subject to migratory existence except those who attain to the Supreme Spirit (v. 16).

The path of those who depart from hence never again to return, and of those who go but to come back again to this mortal sphere, are next described.

23. The time when, dying, men of yoga enter into revolving existence and when into non-revolving being, — that time I shall declare, O best of Bharata's sons.

"Time" means the powers that cause change; the divinities that guide souls to their proper spheres, — the wise devotees to Nirvâna, and others to their temporary celestial abodes.

The eternal life can only be attained through the realization of identity with the Deity, and therefore has nothing to do with the season in which death occurs.

24. Fire, Light, Day, Fortnight of Waxing Moon, and Six months of the Sun's northern circuit, — going on that path, men knowing the Supreme proceed to the Supreme.

---

[1] "Exhaustless," that is, the Supreme Spirit.

[2] "They," that is, those versed in the Vedas.

[3] "My supreme abode," that is, Nirvâna, which is not a state, but the very self or being of the Deity. This term is similar to "my consciousness;" there is no ego outside the consciousness to possess it.

[4] "Supreme," being the ultimate. The Vedic text declares, "Beyond Purusha there is nothing; he is the ultimate, he is the supreme goal."

[5] "Love," the realization that the whole universe is emptiness except the Supreme Spirit; and I am not different from him.

[6] "Contained within him," as the effect is contained within the cause.

[7] "All this is pervaded," as the knower of all, that within us which feels that he knows is a mere reflection of the Supreme Spirit.

"Knowing the Supreme," not in the way the spiritually illuminated sage knows him, as described in the preceding chapter, but as those who, having heard from sacred authorities what the Supreme Spirit is, engage in worship in the manner here declared.

This is called the "path of the gods."

25. Smoke, Night, also Fortnight of Waning Moon, and Six months of the Sun's southern circuit,—proceeding on this path, the man of action[1] falls back, having obtained the lunar rays.[2]

Performance of religious and other ceremonies for the sake of the Deity alone, leads to gradual liberation, proceeding from higher to higher spheres. When performed with some special object, they secure a residence in a transitory celestial sphere, where the special object is attained. Doing that which is forbidden by the sacred authorities leads to an abode in hell. The performer of no religious ordinances, who is also wanting in faith, devotion, and spiritual wisdom, goes to the land of shadows and then returns to earth.

This is called the "path of ancestors."

26. White[3] and black,[4] indeed,[5] are these two paths for the world[6] eternal, I opine; by one a man goes into non-revolving, by the other he revolves again.

27. Knowing these two paths, O son of Prithâ, the man of meditation is not deluded ; therefore at all times, O Arjuna, be joined to meditation.

---

[1] "Man of action," one who fulfils his religious obligations by the performance of all prescribed rites and ceremonies.

[2] "Lunar rays," that is, celestial abodes of enjoyment terminable by re-birth.

[3] "White" is the path marked by Fire and the Time gods associated with him, the path of gods, so called from the illumination of knowledge which guides the blessed soul to this path.

[4] "Black" is the path of ancestors, which opens itself out to those who perform religious and moral duties with the expectation of personal gain.

[5] "Indeed," that is, the paths called in the Vedas and other sacred writings the white and the black path have here been described.

[6] "For the world," that is, for the worshipper through action and the performer of religious works from selfish desire. All men are not here spoken of ; for by the atheist, sceptic, hypocrite, idolater, magician, and scoffer, neither of these two paths is attainable. These paths are eternal because the world is eternal through alternating periods of activity and rest.

He who through fervor of meditation realizes even the nature of these two paths, goes beyond delusion; because when it is vividly impressed upon the soul that by performance of religious works there is no final escape from suffering, unless the motive be exclusively the love of God, there will be no inducement for performing works with any other motive.

"Therefore" if meditation upon the nature of the paths is productive of such good results, how much more beneficial must it be to be joined to the already described meditation, which is a real spiritual entity!

Now listen to the glory of meditation.

28. Whatever meritorious results have been declared[1] to be in the Vedas,[2] in sacrifices,[3] in austerities,[4] and in gifts,— all that the man of meditation,[5] knowing this,[6] transcends, and attains the supreme,[7] primeval seat.[8]

> Thus ends chapter the eighth called, "SUPREME SPIRIT NAMED AS OM," in the blessed BHAGAVAD GÎTÂ, the sacred lore, the divine wisdom, the book of divine union, the colloquy between the blessed KRISHNA and ARJUNA, and contained in the Bhîshma Parvan of the blessed MAHÂBHÂRATA, which is a collection of a hundred thousand verses by VYÂSA.

Salutation to Krishna, who is the Lord of the right knowledge of all mysteries, and who has declared the knowledge of the path of meditation by answers to the seven questions.

[1] "Declared" by sacred authorities.
[2] "In the Vedas," that is, in their study according to prescribed rules.
[3] "In sacrifices," performing them without deviating from the sacred injunctions relating to them.
[4] "In austerities," performed not merely with the body, but with the inner faculties also.
[5] "Man of meditation," he who worships God in spirit as described before.
[6] "Knowing this," that is, realizing the truth embodied in the answers to the seven questions set forth in verses 1 and 2.
[7] "Supreme," being the ultimate.
[8] "Primeval seat;" because unaffected by the creation and destruction of the world, Nirvâna is so called.

CHAPTER IX.

RIGHT KNOWLEDGE OF THE ROYAL MYSTERY.

In the eighth chapter, those of moderate spirituality are counselled to practise meditation upon the Supreme Spirit in the way described there. The result of such meditation is declared to be the gradual emancipation along the "path of gods." For those whose spiritual condition is lower than that, and who are in consequence unable to restrain the mind to meditate with concentration, what hope is there? The form in which the Deity receives external worship from his faithful devotee is declared in the present chapter.

THE BLESSED LORD *spoke:*

1. To thee, unreviling, I shall declare even this[1] most mysterious knowledge, together with realization, knowing which thou shalt escape from evil.[2]

The use of the superlative degree, "most mysterious," requires at least three objects of the same class. The knowledge regarding physical nature is itself mysterious, more so is the knowledge of the moral nature, and the knowledge of the Spirit is the most mysterious of all.

2. This is the royal knowledge,[3] the royal mystery, the excellent sanctifier,[4] directly realizable,[5] lawful,[6] easy to practise,[7] and exhaustless in result.

---

[1] "This," that is, which thou art able partly to apprehend.
[2] "Evil," the bondage of existence.
[3] "Knowledge," that is, theoretical knowledge; the way to do a thing.
[4] "Excellent sanctifier," that is, capable of removing the accumulated results of acts performed during endless incarnations.
[5] "Directly realizable," like pleasure and pain.
[6] "Lawful," not opposed to the law of righteousness.
[7] "Easy to practise," does not involve great difficulties, or severe asceticism, and yet its result is Nirvâna, which knows no end.

3. Men who have no faith in this righteous truth, O harasser of thy foes, revolve in the way of the death-dealing world,[1] not finding Me.[2]

"This righteous truth" is devotion to spiritual knowledge, leading to Nirvâna. Those who have no faith in it are men who believe this body to be the Ego, and that there is no soul whose welfare need give them the least concern, nor any absolute being to aspire to.

4. By Me,[3] of unmanifest[4] form, all this is pervaded; all creatures are seated in Me,[5] but I am not seated in them.[6]

5. Nor are creatures seated in Me, behold my divine creative power; supporting all creatures, yet not in any creature, my spirit produces creatures.

In the preceding verse the Blessed Lord said that all creatures are seated in Him; now He declares that even that is mere illusion. And indeed it is; for, as the universe is in reality nothing but the Supreme Spirit, so the relation of container and contained between them is illusive; or in other words the Supreme Spirit while supporting the universe by the Divine power is yet independent of the universe.

Some of the mysterious ways in which the Divine power works are now shown.

6. As air existing in space always goes everywhere, and is unlimited, so are all things in Me; understand it to be thus.

---

1 "In the way ... world," that is, revolving through the various births.
2 "Me," that is, they do not acquire that faith in me which would ultimately bring them to Nirvâna.
3 "By me," that is, by my superior nature or power of consciousness.
4 "Unmanifest," that is, not perceptible by the senses nor the understanding.
5 "Seated in me;" I being the Ego.
6 "I am not seated in them," that is, as space appears to change and modify into the form of objects it holds, but in reality remains unconditioned, so is consciousness unmodifiable.

The movements of air do not affect space, which contains it. So in the Spirit are contained all things which appear as separate realities by the Divine power of creation.

7. At the end of a kalpa,[1] O son of Kuntî, all things return into my nature,[2] and then again I project them at the beginning of the kalpa.

8. Dominating my own nature,[3] again and again I emanate this whole asemblage of things, resistless on account of subjugation by nature.[4]

It may appear that by reason of exercising His creative energy the Deity may become subject to laws; but that is impossible, on account of the Divine absoluteness which renders Him independent of everything.

9. O conqueror of wealth, those acts do not bind Me, remaining as one indifferent, unattached to those acts.

If the Deity is perfect, and has no desire, no action, then how does creation take place? Who creates, for whose benefit, and how?

10. By reason of my being the onlooker, nature gives birth[6] to the animate and inanimate universe; for this cause, O son of Kuntî, the universe revolves.

Since nature is unconscious, it is not possible for anything to take place unless there be consciousness somewhere; for things take place only in connection with some "onlooker," or witnessing power. At the same time consciousness has no power of action;

---

[1] "Kalpa," a day of Brahmâ; at the end of a Kalpa comes a Pralaya, or period of rest.

[2] "Nature," that is, "inferior nature" (Chap. VII. v. 4); the assemblage of the three qualities; "my" nature, because it is not independent.

[3] "My own nature," that is, all the powers of the Deity except that power of wisdom by which Nirvâna is reached, — avidyâ.

[4] "By nature," that is, the character of creatures; their beginningless stream of acts and desires.

[6] "Nature gives birth;" that is, the illusive or creative power; avidyâ, not vidyâ.

consequently the Deity cannot be considered as bare consciousness by the inquirer into the mystery of creation. He must take the Deity as possessing the power of witnessing as well as the power of being witnessed. The supervisory power of the Deity is consciousness, — his "sight," or "looking on," — and nature is the other power.

As regards the questions which are before the mind, consideration will show that they can only be proposed under misapprehension; and any answer other than the demonstration of their illegitimacy can only arise in misconception.

Who creates? No one; for nature is unconscious and cannot create; consciousness is incapable of action. Creation is but the fact of the co-existence of nature and consciousness, destruction being another mode of this co-existence. The question assumes that some one conditioned, knowable being has created, of which there can be no proof; and it is thus based upon an error.

For whose benefit? Benefit supposes a conscious enjoyer of the benefit. Now, if there is to be an act (such as creation) for the benefit of some one, one of two conditions must exist, — either the Creator himself is to be benefited, or some other beings are to be so. It is clear, even at first sight, that the latter supposition is untenable, because it supposes the existence of some one not the Creator, who yet exists before creation. On the other hand, if the Creator be the only being in existence, possessing all the powers that are in the universe, it is impossible to imagine a motive for Him to change his condition of inactivity and become active. Hence it is not difficult to see how the question is based upon the erroneous assumption that the universe was created for the benefit of any one. The universe is not a thing, but is the power of the Deity, as burning is the power of fire; in reality the universe is identical with the Deity, but at the same time it must be remembered that the Deity is not the universe.

How was the universe created? The universe never was created; for time is the power of marking change, and therefore is a part of nature in the sense of the totality of Divine powers. Consequently if the universe is supposed to be non-existent (as suppose it we must in order that creation should be possible as a subsequent fact), time itself is non-existent, because no power to mark change can exist where there is no change to be marked. Hence the question is based upon a misconception of the nature of time.

These considerations amply demonstrate that such questions ought not to be entertained, for they are as baseless and irrational as it would be to ask "Why is the human mind made of tin?"

The fact that such questions do arise, and an apparent view of the universe does support them, is to be noted. The cause of this seeming is the creative power of the Deity, which makes a thing appear to be what it is not. To know this affords the only real and legitimate solution of the questions under consideration. Accept it as a mystery, unsearchable by the mind, which is a worthless thing as a guide through the labyrinth of existence. The Vedas therefore say, "Who knows this, who in the universe can speak about it, whence is it come, where is this creation?"

Such is the unsearchableness of the divine mystery, that although the eternally perfect Deity is the only true Ego of all creatures, yet creatures do not know it. The wonder is the greater in this instance, because the mysterious power has manifested a human being on earth who declares what he knows; namely, the identity of the consciousness within us with the Supreme Spirit.

11. The deluded, not knowing my real being, contemn Me, the Supreme Lord of all creatures, connected with this human body.

John i. 10, 11.

Through delusion men do not believe that the Supreme Spirit, perfect and changeless, can, by the mysterious power of creation, produce a human body devoid of egotism and manifesting the realized identity of the Ego with the Deity. What condition can be more pitiable than to be perfectly ignorant of the Self, which is the only object of real importance and interest? Therefore they are

12. Deluded in hopes, deluded in actions, deluded in knowledge,[1] deluded in reason,[2] and subjugated by demoniac and impish[3] nature, which is deluding.[4]

2 Thess. ii. 8–12.

[1] "Deluded in knowledge," that is, scriptural knowledge.

[2] "Deluded in reason," that is, deprived of mere ordinary wisdom.

[3] "Demoniac and impish;" that is, believing the body to be the Ego. "Demoniac" refers to pride, oppression, in fact, Satanic grandeur of evil. "Impish" implies cruelty, and other mean and abject forms of wickedness.

[4] "Deluding," that is, tending to the perpetuation of delusion and its consequent evils.

On the other hand, pure-minded men who worship in action, believing through faith in the mystery of Divine nature, and the essential identity of the Deity with the being within man, find final rest in the Deity; and *never come to an evil end*,— such is the power of faith.

13. But the great-souled ones, united[1] to godlike nature, knowing Me[2] to be the exhaustless origin[3] of all things, worship Me with mind that turns to nothing else.

Eph. iii. 9, 12, 14, 16-19.

The "godlike nature" is characterized by self-restraint, faith, benevolence, etc. The three kinds of nature are due to the predominance of the three qualities of nature; goodness produces godlike nature; passion produces demoniac nature; darkness, impish nature. These qualities and their results are treated of in a succeeding chapter.

How do they worship?

14. Constant[4] in union with faith they worship, always proclaiming Me,[5] striving for Me with fixed vows,[6] and bowing down to Me.[4]

Eph. vi. 18.

The "striving" is in the sense of aspiring with an unswerving faith that the mode of worship adopted is the best in the universe, and then persevering in it to the death. Every other mode of worship is defective, but not evil; because, after all, it is the Deity who is worshipped.

---

[1] "Great-souled ones;" those whose hearts have been purified from violent desires.

[2] "Knowing me." Before the one-pointed faith grows, care must be taken properly to study the Scriptures, lest the heart fall into the worship of false gods.

[3] "Exhaustless origin," that is, unchanged though causing change.

[4] "Constant," believing that without faith in the Deity and His nature as declared all else is valueless.

[5] "Proclaiming Me" as the Supreme Deity revealed to man by the Scriptures.

[6] "Fixed vows," that is, fidelity to the Deity. This consists in withdrawal of senses from objects, mental and bodily restraint, benevolence, inoffensiveness, and so on, as amplified in concluding chapters.

[4] "Bowing down to Me," the bosom's Lord.

15. Other devotees worship me in other modes of worship; by sacrifice through knowledge in many ways, — as secondless,[1] as different,[2] as the Spirit of the universe.[3]

Acts x. 35; Rom. ii. 13-15.

How the various modes of worship through knowledge are all worship of the Supreme Spirit, though in so many forms.

16. I am the Vedic rite, I am the sacrifice, I am the offering to ancestors, I am food, I am the sacred formula, I am the sacrificial butter, I am the fire, and I am the oblation.

Vedic rites are distinguished from sacrifices resting on non-Vedic authorities, such as the sacred laws. There is nothing which can be known as an act, or the result of an act, or the instrument for the performance of an act, which is not the Deity, because they are merely His power, and power without the powerful is nothing in reality.

17. I am the father[4] of this universe, the mother,[5] the regulator,[6] the grandfather,[7] the object of knowledge,[8] the sanctifying syllable Om,[9] Rik, Sâma, Yajur, and the other:[10]

[1] "As secondless," pursuing the knowledge that the Deity is identical with the consciousness within man divested of all attributes that are ascribed to it by Error.

[2] "As different," striving to realize that the One and secondless Deity is life and soul of Sun, Moon, etc.

[3] "As the Spirit of the universe," that is, seeking to realize that the universe is the body, of which God is the Spirit. Arjuna's vision of the Deity as the Spirit of the universe is described in Chapter XI.

[4] "Father," as the consciousness.

[5] "Mother," as Prakriti, or power.

[6] "Regulator" is the preserver of the sequence of cause and effect.

[7] "Grandfather" is the Deity in whom the distinction of subject and object does not exist.

[8] "The object of knowledge," that is, he whom the sages seek to know.

[9] "The ... Om;" according to the four Vedas, the Deity can be known, as far as that is possible, by the proper comprehension of the mystery of this sound.

[10] "The other," that is, Atharva Veda, which completes the quaternity of the Vedas.

18. The goal,¹ the nourisher, the lord, the witness,² the place of dwelling,³ the refuge,⁴ the friend,⁵ the source, the end, the place of continuance,⁶ the storehouse,⁷ the eternal seed.⁸

19. I cause heat⁹ and light; I cause rain; I suck in¹⁰ and I throw out;¹¹ I am immortality,¹² and also death,¹³ — also the latent¹⁴ cause and the manifested effect, O Arjuna.

Isaiah xlv. 7, 8.

Those who worship the Deity in any of the various ways described in verses 13-18 will reach Nirvâna. What happens to those who worship God with some special desire is now declared.

20. Those versed¹⁵ in the Vedas, worshipping Me with sacrifices, sanctified¹⁶ by the drinking of the Soma juice, who desire for passage to celestial abodes, enjoy in heaven heavenly enjoyment,¹⁷ attaining to the abode of Indra¹⁸ as the result of meritorious works.

¹ " The goal " is the final result of all labor and striving.
² " The witness " of all that is done.
³ " The place of dwelling," that is, he comprehends everything.
⁴ " The refuge," that is, the place of safety where no trouble can reach.
⁵ " The friend," the benefactor wishing neither return nor acknowledgment.
⁶ " Place of continuance." As we are now in God, so we were before the world was, and so shall be even when the world has ceased to be.
⁷ " Storehouse," that is, we are preserved in Him during the universal desolation, as seed in a storehouse for future harvest.
⁸ " Eternal seed," that is, the cause, which is the eternal form of all things.
⁹ " I cause heat," as the Spirit of the Sun the Deity does all this through His mysterious power.
¹⁰ " I suck in," that is, evaporate water.
¹¹ " I throw out," that is, precipitate it in rain.
¹² " Immortality," which gods are said to enjoy, and
¹³ " Death," to which men are subject.
¹⁴ " The latent," etc.; when an effect is produced the reality of the cause is manifested, which until that moment was latent.
¹⁵ " Versed," studying the Vedas and performing the rites and ceremonies enjoined by them, but with some personal desire.
¹⁶ " Sanctified ; " it is an act of great merit to drink the Soma juice at the end of a sacrifice.
¹⁷ " Heavenly enjoyment ; " in heaven a man enjoys the whole class containing every individual object of his desire while on earth.
¹⁸ " Abode of Indra," the highest of the celestial spheres.

21. They, having enjoyed that wide celestial realm, enter the sphere of mortals on the exhaustion of their merit; thus those devoted to the law of the three Vedas, and desiring desires, obtain coming and going.[1]

"Those devoted to the law of the three Vedas and" *not* "desiring desires obtain" final rest.

22. Of those men, who thinking of Me in identity,[2] worship Me,—for them, always resting in Me, I bear the burden of acquisition and preservation of possessions.[3]

Matt. vi. 33, 34.

23. Even those, the devotees of other gods, who worship in faith, they, O son of Kuntî, worship Me in ignorance.

Although the worship offered to any god in faith goes to the true God, yet the ignorance in which the worship is offered prevents the worshippers from attaining identity with the Deity. The nature of this ignorance is now shown.

24. I am the lord[4] and enjoyer[5] of all sacrifices, but they do not know Me in truth; therefore they fall.[6]

The fall is due to their ignorance, but this does not affect their title to the reward which they wish for. They receive whatever they wish for; and it is because of ignorance that they do not wish for liberation, which is the highest good.

25. Those devoted to the gods go to the gods; to the ancestors go those devoted to the ancestors. Those

---

[1] "Coming and going," and not independence.
[2] "In identity," that is, recognizing Me as the only Self.
[3] "I bear . . . possessions;" as they wish for nothing but Me, so I, in consequence of identity, provide them with what they need and prevent their loss.
[4] "Lord," as the consciousness in the breast of the sacrificer.
[5] "Enjoyer;" the real enjoyer of them as the consciousness in the gods to whom offerings are made.
[6] "Fall;" that is, they are deprived of the highest fruit of their sacrifices, which is liberation.

that worship the evil spirits go to the evil spirits, and my worshipper also comes to Me.

The result of worshipping the true God is great, yet the mode of worship is not at all difficult. His yoke is light.

26. Whoever in love offers to Me a leaf or flower or fruit,—that, given in love by the pure-hearted, I accept.

Therefore,

27. Whatever thou doest, whatever thou eatest, whatever thou offerest in sacrifice, whatever thou givest away, whatever austerities thou practisest, O son of Kuntî, commit that to Me.

Col iii. 17; 1 Cor. x. 31.

The yoke of God is very light indeed. None need do any special thing for Him; but in the performance of the ordinary acts of life He is fully worshipped if they are performed for His sake alone; the interior spirit is superior to all works.

28. Thus from bondage of action consisting of good and evil experiences shalt thou escape; with thy heart joined to renunciation [1] and action [2] thou shalt come to Me.

Thou shalt attain to liberation, which is the cessation of all suffering and the attainment of absolute bliss.

29. I am equal to all creatures; there is none hated or beloved by Me. But those who worship Me in love, they are in Me and in them I am.

Matt. v. 45; Job xxxv. 6, 7; John xiv. 23.

As the fire warms those who approach it, and not those who are far from it, so God loves those who love Him. He is free from desire Himself. (Cf. James iv. 8.)

---

[1] "Joined to renunciation," because of absence of desire.
[2] "And action," because of performance of action for the sake of the Deity.

30. Even if the most evil-conducted man worships Me with exclusive devotion, he is to be considered even as righteous because he is rightly determined.[1]

<small>Psalm li. 1-10; Isaiah i. 18, 19.</small>

Love of God is the only road to salvation for the sinful man.

31. Such an one quickly becomes righteous-souled, for he[2] comes to perpétual peace. Swear, O son of Kuntî, my devotee never is destroyed.

<small>John v. 24.</small>

32. O son of Prithâ, having taken refuge in Me, even those who are of evil-womb, women, vaisyas, and sudras, proceed to the supreme goal.

<small>Matt. xxi. 31, 32.</small>

No training or qualification is needed for those who seek refuge in God. Love makes all equal.

33. What then is to be said of holy Brâhmans and devoted kingly sages? Having obtained this transitory, joyless world, worship Me.

The life of man is particularly suited for the growth of love for God on account of our joyless lot. Animals, owing to dulness, and gods through contentment, are not privileged to know this love in such purity of perfection as men.

How God is to be worshipped.

34. Be with heart fixed on Me; loving Me, and worshipping Me, bow down to Me; thus at rest, thou shalt come even to Me the Spirit.

<small>Psalm cviii. 1-6; Matt. v. 8.</small>

---

[1] "Rightly determined;" that is, by the acceptance of the true end of life he is established on the right road.

[2] "For he," etc.; because he attains peace, his previous unrighteousness of life soon comes to an end, having no freshly generated impulses in that direction.

Thus ends chapter the ninth, called the "RIGHT KNOWLEDGE OF ROYAL MYSTERY," in the blessed BHAGAVAD GÎTÂ, the sacred lore, the divine wisdom, the book of divine union, the colloquy between the blessed KRISHNA and ARJUNA, and contained in the Bhîshma Parvan of the blessed MAHÂBHÂRATA, which is a collection of one hundred thousand verses by VYÂSA.

In this chapter is declared the supreme attributeless God who is also the God for the adoration of the indifferently spiritual.

Salutation to Krishna, who has declared the wonderful mystery of Divine power as well as the power of love to the Deity.

CHAPTER X.

RIGHT KNOWLEDGE OF DIVINE POWERS.

The mystery of the being of the Deity was declared in the seventh chapter. From the standpoint of pure reality the Deity is absolute and attributeless. But in consequence of the unsearchable power of the Deity there is an apparent relation between the Absolute Deity and conditions and attributes.

The declaration of the Blessed Lord concerning the Divine power, commenced in the seventh chapter, is interrupted in the eighth and resumed in the ninth, and is continued in this chapter.

The power of the Deity comprehends and yet transcends the universe; for the universe is nothing but the power of the Deity, but the Deity is not the universe. If the Deity be the same as the universe, then it is a mere multiplication of words without meaning to speak of universe and Deity. If the universe were different from the Deity, and both real, there would be a higher reality embracing the Deity and the universe.

Pantheism as well as Deism must be rejected. "Moveless and profound, neither light nor darkness, without name and manifestation, a mysterious reality," the Deity is in Himself. The universe is a portion of the Divine power; yet there is another portion, by reason of which the Deity is not the universe. The unsearchable power of the Deity is declared in the present chapter for the devout meditation of the worshipper.

The Blessed Lord *spoke:*

1. Even again, O thou of mighty arms, listen to my supreme [1] words, which to thee, rejoicing,[2] I am going to declare, desiring thy welfare.

---

[1] "Supreme," because relating to the supreme truth.

[2] "Rejoicing;" the reason for my speaking is the great joy with which thou art receiving my words.

The reason for the repetition of the subject by the Blessed Lord himself is given next.

2. My lordly power[1] the godly synod does not know, nor even the great sages;[2] because I am the source[3] of gods and great sages.

<small>Job xxxvi. 22, 26.</small>

3. Whoever knows Me, the unborn,[4] beginningless, supreme lord of the worlds, he among men, undeluded, becomes liberated from all sins.[5]

<small>Rom. viii. 14-21.</small>

4. Subtle perception,[6] spiritual knowledge,[7] right judgment, forgiveness, truth, external and internal self-mastery, pleasure, pain, prosperity and adversity, fear and serenity,

5. Inoffensiveness, even-mindedness, satisfaction, restraint of body and mind, almsgiving, fame for righteousness, and ill-fame for unrighteousness, become from Me the various[8] conditions of creatures.

<small>Rom. ix. 22, 23; 1 Cor. xii. 6-11.</small>

Not only does God possess all that is as His nature, but He is also the knower of all, the ruler of all, and the pervasive influence.

6. The great sages seven, and the ancient Manus four, of whom this world is the offspring, are pervaded by my power and born of my mind.

<small>Acts xvii. 28.</small>

---

[1] "Lordly power" might also mean "origin."

[2] "Great sages;" that is, the seven primeval sages, sons of Brahmâ the creator.

[3] "Source;" that is, causing power, and the material forms, the gods, etc. The Supreme God being the cause of the gods is not known to them.

[4] "Unborn," therefore beginningless.

[5] "All sins;" that is, whether knowingly or unknowingly committed.

[6] "Subtle perception" is the perception of things not comprehended by the ordinary mind.

[7] "Spiritual knowledge" applies to the nature of that which is beyond the reach of internal and external senses.

[8] "Various," that is, different according to the difference in the character of individuals.

The seven sages are the primeval teachers of our race, and whatever spiritual knowledge exists in the world has been and is preserved by the spiritual descendants of these seven, the archetype of teachers, as the ancient Manus, or primeval kings, are the archetype of kings.

According to one authority "four" does not refer to the number of Manus, but to the four sons of Brahmâ, — Sanaka, Sanandana, Sadânanda, and Sanatkumâra. These sons of Brahmâ, in a previous epoch of the world's history, worked for final liberation by identification with the Deity, but did not attain to the supreme goal, and so are, in this epoch, the preservers of the path to Nirvâna.

The powers of these super-human personages exist in consequence of the omnipotence and omniscience of the Deity, as they have no independent power. "Born of my mind" signifies that the unsearchable Deity, as the creator Brahmâ, thought, and the sages and Manus started into being. In the subsequent work of creation the agency fell to these elder-born sons of God.

The fruit of realizing these powers of the Deity is next given.

7. Whoever knows perfectly these manifestations,[1] and the power to cause them, becomes united to unwavering right perception; of this there is no doubt.

The power of the Deity to modify the Divine power into these manifestations is here emphasized. It must not be thought that the Deity is forced by some extraneous powers to produce these, or any other manifestations; it is also a *power* to exercise these powers; the Deity need not create unless He chooses to do so.

The nature of unwavering right perception is described.

8. I am the source[2] of all; owing to Me all things work; knowing this,[3] the wise, full of love,[4] worship Me.

Col. i. 16; iii. 17.

[1] "Manifestations;" that is, various modifications of Divine power, such as the sages and Manus just mentioned.

[2] "Source," is the Maker.

[3] "Knowing this." The conviction of the emptiness of the world without the Deity fits a man to be a real worshipper.

[4] "Full of love;" God is the only joy in existence, but through the darkness which envelops our nature things seem attractive which are not God, and therefore not joy. The worship of God is not an obligation, but a privilege and delight.

"Owing to Me all things work" teaches that the continuance or destruction of creatures depends entirely on the Deity; for although it would appear that these processes require some co-operation on their part, in reality it is not so.

When the worshippers have this above-mentioned conviction, what are they to do?

9. With heart and life gone into Me,[1] enlightening one another[2] and declaring Me[3] always, they want no more[4] and find enjoyment.

<small>Col. iii. 15, 16.</small>

10. To them, ever attached to Me, worshipping Me in love,[5] I give that union to knowledge by which they come to Me.[6]

11. To grant them grace, I, remaining in their hearts,[7] destroy the darkness born of ignorance[8] by the brilliant lamp of knowledge.

The lamp of knowledge is the perception of truth. The lamp is the passionless heart; its oil is Divine grace; the air that keeps it burning is the breeze of love that blows between man and God; and the boisterous wind from which it is protected is the desire for things perceived by sense or mind.

---

[1] "Heart and life gone into me;" that is, the whole nature of man is at rest in the Deity, from absence of desire. Life is of no value without the Deity; this consciousness is described by the expression, "gone into me."

[2] "Enlightening one another;" that is, communicating to one another spiritual knowledge accompanied by faith in the truth declared.

[3] "Declaring Me," that is, instructing one another in the mystery of the Divine Spirit.

[4] "Want no more;" cessation of want may be produced by conviction of the hopelessness of the desire or by its full gratification. Worshippers of the Deity want nothing, because they are full of enjoyment in God.

[5] "Worshipping Me in love;" worshipping for no object that they wish to attain.

[6] "Come to Me;" that is, they recognize the Deity as the Self.

[7] "Remaining in their hearts," that is, the hearts of the devotees being completely at rest in the Deity, He appears in their hearts as the spirit of illumination.

[8] "Darkness born of ignorance;" darkness born of belief in falsehood, which, if true, would make God false. The unsearchable God is true, therefore all this that we now call true is really dark and false.

Having heard of the form with attributes and of the attributeless Absoluteness of the Deity, Arjuna longs to hear more about the first aspect, as the other is incomprehensible.

ARJUNA *said:*

12. The Supreme Brahmă, the Supreme power, Sacred[1] and Supreme Thou, the Spirit Eternal, the Divine,[2] the primeval God,[3] the unborn, the all-pervading,

13. Thee, thus they call, the sages every one, the celestial sage[4] Nârada, Asita, Devala, Vyâsa, and thou sayest the same to me.

14. All that thou sayest to me I believe to be true, O Lord; thy majesty[5] is indeed not known to gods or demons.

15. O thou Supreme Spirit,[6] by thyself thou knowest thyself,[7] thou Creator of all, thou Lord of all, God of gods, and Master of the universe.

16. Thou art worthy to declare fully thy divine powers, by which powers thou art pervading these worlds.

17. How shall I, constantly thinking of thee, know thee,[8] O thou Lord of mysterious powers; in what

---

[1] "Sacred," that is, undefiled by any touch of change.
[2] "The Divine," being seated where the universe is not.
[3] "Primeval God," that is, the only God who remains witness to the birth and dissolution of those whom men call gods.
[4] "Celestial sage," that is, a celestial being who becomes a sage, renouncing all the glory of his state.
[5] "Majesty;" absoluteness.
[6] "Supreme Spirit," the possessor of the acme of wisdom, majesty, and power. The other epithets are marks of great love.
[7] "By thyself ... thyself;" that is, thou art the only instructor about thyself. Therefore "thou art worthy to declare fully thy divine powers."
[8] "How shall I ... know thee," that is, after the purification of my nature is accomplished.

forms[1] art thou, O Lord, to be meditated upon by me?

18. O Janârdana, declare again at length thy powers and manifested forms, since there is no satiety for me in thy ambrosial words.

THE BLESSED LORD *spoke:*

19. Now then shall I declare to thee, the chief among the forms of Divine[2] manifestation, O best of Kuru's sons; there is no end to the variety of my manifested forms.

First is declared what the Deity really is apart from the conceptions of men.

20. O conqueror of sleep,[3] I am the Ego seated in the hearts of all creatures.[4] I am the beginning, middle, and end of all creatures.

21. Among Âdityas[5] I am Vishnu; among those who illuminate I am the Sun, possessed of rays. I am Marichi among the Maruts;[6] among the orbs of heaven I am the Moon.

22. Among the Vedas[7] I am the Sâmaveda, among

---

[1] "In what forms;" for the facility of meditation it is the practice among mystics to concentrate their minds on some emblematic representation of the Divine Spirit, and then gradually to efface the imagined figure from the mind, part by part, until at last the mind can render itself perfectly pure, for the rising of the spirit of illumination in the clear sky.

[2] "Divine;" that is, independent, not produced by any secondary cause.

[3] "O conqueror of sleep" implies that this Supreme Deity is only approachable by one who has awaked from the sleep of delusions.

[4] "I am the Ego . . . creatures;" this is the form in which it is best to meditate on me; but failing that, the forms hereinafter set forth may be meditated on, because "I am the beginning, middle, and end of all creatures," and as such may also be meditated upon.

[5] *Âdityas* are the twelve sun-gods who bring about the universal conflagration by their simultaneous appearance.

[6] *Maruts*, the gods of air.

[7] *Vedas*, the four Vedas, — Rik, Sâma, Yajur, and Atharva.

gods Indra, among senses and organs the manas; of creatures I am the conscious existence.

"Conscious existence" is used here in a peculiar sense; it does not mean the true Ego which being identical with the Deity cannot be classed among his manifested forms, but the peculiar form of Buddhi or intellect which is manifested in the relation of cause and effect, the cognitive faculty.

23. Among Rudras[1] I am Cankara; among Yakshas[2] and Rakshas[3] I am the lord of wealth; among Vasus I am Pâvaka; among high-peaked mountains I am Meru.[4]

24. Among the priests of kings know me, O son of Prithâ, as the highest, Brihaspati; of leaders of hosts I am Skanda;[5] of expanses of water I am the ocean.

25. Among the great sages I am Bhrigu; among words I am the monosyllable Om; among sacrifices I am the sacrifice through the repetition of sacred texts;[6] of things that move not I am the Himalaya.

26. Among all trees I am Asvattha; of celestial sages I am Nârada; among Gandharvas I am Chitraratha; among those perfect from birth I am the sage Kapila.

There are three classes of perfectly illuminated sages: First, those who are born so without any reference to any prior event; second, those who are born perfect in consequence of perfection previously attained; third, those who become perfect after birth in consequence of illumination attained during life. Kapila, the revealer of Sânkhya philosophy, belonged to the first class; with him

---

[1] *Rudras* are the twelve gods of knowledge from whose power the seven great sages are born.
[2] *Yakshas*, an order of spirits not malignant by nature, but extremely sensual.
[3] *Rakshas*, an order of evil spirits.
[4] *Meru*, the celestial mountain where the gods dwell.
[5] *Skanda*, the leader of celestial hosts.
[6] "Sacrifice through . . . texts;" because involving injury to no one.

were innate Knowledge, Power, Virtue, and Dispassion. (See Sânkhya Kârikâ, Aph. XLIII.)

27. Among horses know me to be Uchchaiçravâ, born from ambrosia; among elephant-kings Airâvata; among men as lord of men.

28. Among weapons I am the thunder; among cows, the cow of plenty; among causes of production I am the god of love; among serpents [1] I am Vâsuki.

29. Among nâgas [2] I am Ananta; among things of the sea I am Varuna; among the ancestors I am Aryamâ; among rulers I am Yama.[3]

30. Among daityas [4] I am Prahlâda; among those that reckon I am Time; [5] I am the lion among wild animals; among birds I am Garuda.[6]

31. Among sanctifiers I am the Air; among those that bear arms I am Râma; among fishes I am Makara; among flowing streams I am the Ganges.

32. Among that which is produced I am, O Arjuna, even the beginning, the middle, and the end; among all knowledge I am the knowledge of the Spirit; I am the ascertainment, through discussion, of the meaning of spiritual teachings by those who are free from passion.

The "knowledge of the Spirit" is that form of the perceptive faculties in which no illusion exists, and "ascertainment" denotes the questions and answers by which a pupil learns spiritual philosophy from his master, as opposed to controversy and discussion among ordinary people.

[1] "Serpents," that is, poisonous reptiles.
[2] *Nâgas* are serpents without poison.
[3] *Yama* is the ruler of the dead, the judge of all judges.
[4] *Daityas* are an order of super-human beings.
[5] "Time," the great reckoner of all.
[6] *Garuda*, the celestial bird attending upon Vishnu.

33. Among letters I am the vowel A;[1] among compound words I am Dvandva;[2] I am the endless Time;[3] I am the all-faced regulator.[4]

34. I am the all-snatching Death,[5] and the causer of well-being of future creatures;[6] among women I am Fame,[7] Fortune, Speech, Memory, Intelligence,[8] Patience, and Forgiveness.

35. Among the hymns of the Sâmaveda, again, I am the Brihat Sâman;[9] among metres [10] I am the Gâyatri; among months I am Mârgaçîrsha;[11] among seasons I am Spring, the source of flowers.

36. Of the deceitful I am the dice; I am the power [12] of the powerful; I am victory, I am determination, I am the goodness in the good.[13]

37. Among the sons of Vrishni I am Vâsudeva; among the Pândavas I am the conqueror of wealth;[14] among

---

[1] "The vowel A," because according to the sacred authorities this sound is the basis of all others, which are but its modifications.

[2] *Dvandva*, a peculiar form of compound words in Sanskrit, such as Râma-Krishnauh, meaning Râma and Krishna. It is superior to all others because it preserves the independent meaning of both the words entering into the compound.

[3] "Endless Time;" not time that is counted by months, years, centuries, etc., but the power of causing succession.

[4] "All-faced regulator;" I attach the legitimate effect to all causes that are produced in the universe.

[5] "All-snatching Death," which produces universal dissolution.

[6] "Future creatures," that is, those who will deserve well-being in future periods of creation.

[7] "Fame," the goddess presiding over great deeds of righteousness.

[8] "Intelligence," the goddess presiding over the right understanding of sacred writings.

[9] *Brihat Sâman* reveals the path to Nirvâna.

[10] "Metres," that is, the Vedic *mantras* or hymns; among these the Gâyatri is the best because it confers Brahmanhood

[11] *Margaçîrsha* is the month consisting of parts of November and December. It is the best of months because in it the harvest ripens.

[12] "Power," that is, absence of the liability to have one's commands successfully opposed.

[13] "Good," possessed of the quality of *Sattva*, or goodness, which is manifested as righteousness, wisdom, dispassion, and other similar forms.

[14] "Conqueror of wealth" is Arjuna.

those who understand the meaning of the Vedas I am Vyâsa;[1] among the end-seeing I am the seer Uçanâ.[2]

38. I am the sanction of the representatives of the law;[3] I am the policy of those desiring to conquer; I am the silence of the secret,[4] I am the wisdom of the wise.

39. That am I which also is the seed[5] of all things, O Arjuna; that thing, animate or inanimate, is not, which is without Me.

40. O harasser of thy foes, no end there is of my divine manifestations; a part only of the infinite manifestations is thus declared by Me.

Job xxvi. 14.

41. Whatever creature there is, possessed of lordly power, of good fortune, or of power of determination, know all such as born of a portion[6] of my power.

Isa. xlv. 1-6.

42. Or, O Arjuna, of what avail is it for thee to know much like this? I hold with one portion[7] all this universe.

The powers of the Deity are beyond description and enumeration; yet both description and enumeration are needed for the benefit of the devotee. For that devotee, however, who can conceive of the infinite universe as though it were only a portion of the power of the Deity, no such helps to the budding spiritual perception are needed.

[1] *Vyâsa*, the author of the Mahâbhârata, of which the Bhagavad Gîtâ is a part.
[2] *Uçanâ*, the first teacher of ethics and politics.
[3] "Representatives of the law;" that is, those whose duty it is to keep men straight on the path of the law, and by punishment bring back those who go astray.
[4] "The secret," those who through maturity of spiritual knowledge have gone beyond the need of speech; and "silence" is the wisdom of such beings.
[5] "Seed," the first cause; the reflection of consciousness on objectivity.
[6] "Portion;" it must not be supposed that the Divine Power is liable to be portioned, but it seems as though it were portioned.
[7] "Hold with one portion;" because the universe does not manifest the divine power by which it can be destroyed.

Thus ends chapter the tenth, called the "RIGHT KNOWLEDGE OF DIVINE POWERS," in the blessed BHAGAVAD GÎTÂ, the sacred lore, the divine wisdom, the book of divine union, the colloquy between the blessed KRISHNA and ARJUNA, and contained in the Bhîshma Parvan of the blessed MAHÂBHÂRATA, which is a collection of one hundred thousand verses by VYÂSA.

Having declared the manifestations of the Deity which the mind can grasp, it is finally shown that the infinite Majesty of the Deity is infinitely beyond the manifestation called the universe. If from infinity, infinity is taken, infinity still remains.

Salutation to Krishna, who, for the benefit of those whose minds still wander out through the gates of sense, has declared his divine manifestations for the meditation of the devotee.

CHAPTER XI.

VISION OF THE DEITY AS THE SOUL OF THE UNIVERSE.

THE Blessed Lord having declared, in the last chapter, that he holds the whole universe by one portion of his power, Arjuna begs to be favored with a vision of the way in which the Deity by His unsearchable power supports the whole universe; and his prayer is granted. In reality the Deity has no form; what prophets and pure-souled devotees see is the reflection, so to speak, of the incomprehensible Divine Majesty on the spiritual perception of man. Arjuna's vision recalls the visions of Moses, Isaiah, Ezekiel, and Saint John. The mysterious and symbolical import of these spiritual experiences is not perceived by the spiritually blind, who in consequence fall into the most degrading superstitions.

ARJUNA *said:*

1. By the words supreme,[1] and relating to the mystery of the Spirit,[2] by thee spoken, has this, my delusion,[3] been removed.

2. By me have been heard from thee in full[4] the origin and end of things,[5] O thou with eyes like the lotus-leaf,[6] as also the exhaustless majesty.[7]

---

[1] "Supreme," because showing the path to Nirvâna.
[2] "Mystery of the Spirit;" that is, discrimination between Ego and non-Ego. The words of the Lord beginning with Chapter II. verse 11, are here referred to.
[3] "My delusion," about the slayer and the slain.
[4] "Heard from thee in full," in Chapters VII. to X.
[5] "Origin and end of things;" that is, I have heard from thee that the inscrutable divine power causes the origin and end of things (Chap. VII. v. 6).
[6] "Eyes like the lotus-leaf;" that is, as peaceful as the lotus-leaf.
[7] "Exhaustless majesty." See Chapter IX. verses 7–9.

3. O Supreme God, it is even as thou sayest of thyself. I long to see thy Divine form, O Supreme Spirit.

The first epithet here is intended to show that Arjuna has no doubt of the absolute truth of what the Blessed Lord has said, and that it is not as a test of His authority, but for the satisfaction of his own spiritual aspiration, that he wishes to see the universe-form of the Deity.

Arjuna uses the final epithet to express his eagerness to see the highest form of the Deity, and not any of the other forms.

4. O Lord,[1] if thou thinkest it possible to be seen by me, then show me, O King of all mystics,[2] thy exhaustless Self.

THE BLESSED LORD *spoke:*

5. O son of Prithâ, behold my forms, by hundreds and by thousands, of many varieties, divine,[3] and of many colors, and with many limbs.

6. Behold the Vasus, the Rudras, the Açvins, and also the Maruts, O son of Bharata; behold many and wonderful things never seen before.[4]

7. Here, in my body, behold to-day, O Gudâkeça, the whole universe, animate and inanimate, in one place contained, and every other thing that thou wishest to see.[5]

8. But[6] thou art not able to see Me[7] with these thine own eyes. I shall give thee the eye divine;[8] behold my power as God.

Matt. xi. 27.

---

[1] "O Lord," receiver of my prayer, in whom I put all my trust.

[2] "O King of all mystics;" that is, if mystics can exercise superhuman powers, then who can tell the extent of thy powers, since all other powers are but the reflection of thine? If in thy eyes I am fit (I know I am not in mine) for this favor, may it be granted to me.

[3] "Divine," that is, produced by no temporal or secondary cause.

[4] "Seen before;" that is, by thee or any other mere mortal man.

[5] "That thou wishest to see;" that is, the uncertainty that thou hast felt as to the issue of the battle will be dispelled by this vision (Chap. II. v. 6).

[6] "But," in reply to verse 4.   [7] "Me," as the soul of the universe.

[8] "Eye divine;" that is, the spiritual illumination which a man cannot get from within his self-conscious nature.

SANJAYA *said:*

9. O King, having said this, Hari,[1] the lord of great and mysterious power, showed to the son of Prithâ the Supreme form Divine.

The Deity has no form in reality, but by reason of His unsearchable powers He appears to have infinity of forms and attributes. Among such forms, that seen by Arjuna is the highest.

10. With many mouths and eyes, with many marvels, with many divine ornaments, with many divine weapons raised,

11. Wearing divine garlands, and garments, with divine perfumes and ornaments, full of what is wonderful to all, the universe-faced infinite Lord.[2]

12. The splendor of that great Soul may haply be likened to the radiance of a thousand suns risen at once in the heavens.

13. Then Pându's son beheld, seated in one place, in the body of the God of gods, the whole universe, in many forms varied.

14. Then Dhananjaya, overcome with wonder, and hair standing on end with joy, bowing down with his head to the Deity, spoke with joined palms.

ARJUNA *said:*

15. O God, in thy body I behold all the gods, the assemblage of things of every kind, the lord Brahmâ

---

[1] *Hari* literally means the remover. Krishna is so called because he removes ignorance with all its powers.

[2] "Universe-faced;" that is, having equal power over every part of the universe.

seated on his lotus-seat,[1] and all the sages[2] and uragas[3] divine.

16. I behold thee on all sides, with infinite forms, with many arms, stomachs, mouths, and eyes. O Lord of the universe, O Universe-formed, thy end, nor middle, nor again thy beginning do I see.

17. Thee, with diadem, mace, and discus, the mass of splendor, on all sides refulgent, do I behold, so difficult to behold,[4] immeasurable, on all thy sides the majesty of burning fire and sun.

18. Thou art the exhaustless, supreme goal of knowledge; thou art the supreme support of this universe; thou art changeless, the protector of the unchanging law of righteousness; thou art the Eternal Spirit, — this is my faith.

Arjuna in his vision sees the Deity as possessed of the infinity of attributes; consequently the attributeless Deity referred to in this verse could be perceived by him only through faith.

19. Devoid of beginning, middle, and end, with power infinite, with infinite numbers of arms, with sun and moon as eyes, I behold thee, with burning-fire-mouth, and with thy majesty oppressing[5] the universe.

20. Heaven and earth and space between are filled by thee alone, as also the sides, every one. Seeing this thy marvellous form of terror, the worlds three[6] are afflicted, O thou great Soul.

---

[1] "Lotus-seat." The lotus is the emblem of the universe. The Supreme Deity, as the creator Brahmâ, is seated in the centre of the infinite universe; this is his lotus-seat.

[2] "Sages," that is, the seven sages.

[3] "Uragas" are an order of celestial beings who possess great wisdom, usually understood to be in some way connected with serpents.

[4] "So difficult to behold," for those not favored by Divine grace.

[5] "Oppressing," that is, the universe seems unable to bear the majesty of the Deity.

[6] "Worlds three," that is, "heaven and earth and the space between."

21. This concourse of gods[1] enters into thee, and some in fear[2] chant praise with joined palms, the assemblage of great sages and perfect beings,[3] saying "Svasti,"[4] behold and glorify thee with perfect hymns.

22. The Rudras, the Adityas, the Vasus, and they called the Sâdhyas,[5] the Viçvadevas,[6] the Açvins,[7] the Maruts, and the Ushmapâs,[8] the Gandharvas,[9] the Yakshas, the Asuras,[10] and the assemblage of the Siddhas all behold thee in wonder.

23. O Thou of mighty arms, beholding thy form immense, with many mouths and eyes, with many arms, thighs, and feet, many stomachs and many twisted tusks, all beings are trembling with fear, and so am I.

24. Seeing thee, sky-touching, with many resplendent limbs,[11] with gaping mouths, my heart oppressed with terror, I know not self-possession, nor can I gain calmness of spirit, O Vishnu.[12]

25. Beholding thy faces like the fire of destruction, and frightful to behold, owing to tusks, neither do I

---

[1] "Concourse of gods," that is, the heroes gifted with godly powers, who are about to fight this great battle.

[2] "In fear," that is, overcome with fear of the divine wrath. Those among the warriors who are filled with diabolical powers can neither fight nor flee; humbled, they cry, "Glory, glory to the Lord, destroy us not."

[3] "Perfect beings;" such as Kapila. (See Chap. X. v. 5.)

[4] "Saying 'Svasti;'" dreading the untimely destruction of the universe, the sages cry "Svasti," — "good be the world."

[5] *Sâdhyas*, a celestial order.

[6] *Viçvadevas*, a class of gods connected with funeral ceremonies.

[7] *Açvins* are two brothers, physicians to the gods. The name literally signifies "horsemen."

[8] *Ushmapâs*, literally the "feeders on warmth." This celestial order is composed of the pious dead raised to superhuman life.

[9] *Gandharvas* are celestial musicians.

[10] *Asuras*, that is, those among them who are not rebels, but worshippers of the Deity.

[11] "Resplendent limbs;" strictly, the word translated "limbs" means the rise and fall in the body in consequence of the distribution of limbs.

[12] *Vishnu*, the Pervading Spirit.

know the points of heaven, nor can I gain peace. Be gracious, O Lord of gods, O Support of the universe.

26. All these sons of Dhritarâshtra, together with this assemblage of the rulers of earth, Bhîshma, Drona, as also Karna, together with the chief among warriors on our side,

27. Impetuously are rushing into thy mouths, terrible and preternatural owing to the tusks. Some are seen, caught between thy teeth, with their heads crushed.

28. As the many-watered rush of rivers flows ever towards the ocean, so these heroes of this mortal sphere enter into thy mouths, on all sides burning.

29. As moths, with impetuosity excited, enter for destruction into the flaming fire, even so do these creatures, for destruction, enter into thy mouths with collected impetuosity.

30. Whilst swallowing on all sides, with flaming mouths, thou relishest all these creatures assembled; filling the whole universe with thy splendor, thy cruel flames oppress with heat, O Vishnu.

31. Declare unto me who is this terrible form of thine. Salutation to thee, O Greatest of gods! Be gracious! I seek to know thee, the primeval; I know not thy doing.

THE BLESSED LORD *spoke:*

32. Time[1] I am, in fulness, the consumer of creatures, here at work for the destruction of creatures. Besides thee, the warriors in these divisions[2] shall not be.

33. Therefore stand thou up, gain fame; conquering enemies, enjoy foeless empire; even before, by me they

---

[1] "Time;" the divine power of causing change.
[2] "These divisions;" that is, opposed to thee. Bhîshma, Drona, Karna, Duryodhana, and all the others of whom thou hast spoken, must perish.

have been slain; be thou but the instrument, O thou both-handed.[1]

34. Drona, Bhîsma and Jayadratha, Karna, as well as the other heroic warriors, by me slain, conquer thou; lose not heart, fight; thou art[2] the conqueror of enemies in war.

Sanjaya *said:*

35. Hearing these words of Keçava, with palms joined and in tremor, bowing down to Krishna, again spoke the diademed hero[3] with faltering voice, again and again frightened and bowing down.

Arjuna *said:*

36. Verily it is so, O Hrishikeça; by thy glorification the universe rejoices and shows love to thee;[4] the evil spirits, frightened, flee in all directions, and all the assembled perfect men bow down to thee.

37. O Great soul, why should they not bow down to thee, greater even than Brahmâ, the first maker,[5] O Eternal, O Lord of gods, O Abode of the universe. Thou art the aught and naught, the exhaustless essence that is beyond.[6]

---

[1] "Both-handed." Arjuna could draw the bow with either hand with equal skill. His great proficiency in warfare renders him the proper instrument in the hand of Time.

[2] "Thou art," etc., that is, thy future success can be foreseen from the vision vouchsafed to thee.

[3] "Diademed hero." Arjuna is so called on account of the great splendor of his diadem.

[4] "Shows love to thee," that is, the Deity, being the true Self in all creatures, is the most beloved of all; in fact, is Love.

[5] *Brahmâ.* In Brahmanical theology he is not the maker of the plan or idea of the world; his own being is limited by the Divine idea, in obedience to which he makes perceptible and sensuous what the idea contained in an imperceptible and super-sensuous state.

[6] "Thou art," etc. "Aught" is the apparently real existence, and "naught" is what does not exist. The Reality in itself being incomprehensible cannot fall under either of these two classes, which but for the Reality could not exist.

38. Thou art the primeval God, the ancient Spirit; thou art the supreme place of extinction[1] of this universe; thou art the knower, thou art the known, as also the supreme abode;[2] O thou infinite-formed, by thee this universe is filled.

39. The gods Wind, Death, Fire, Water, and Moon, the ancient progenitor thou art, as also the great-grandfather.[3] Salutation, salutation be unto thee, thousandfold and again and again salutation, salutation unto thee!

40. Salutation in the east,[4] and salutation also behind, O thou All; salutation in all directions; thou art of infinite valor and immeasurable power; thou pervadest all things and hence art All.[5]

41. By me, not knowing this thy majesty, whatever lowering to thee has been said, either in thoughtlessness or in love, — such as, "O Krishna, O Yadu's son, O friend,"

42. And whatever unmeet treatment thou hast received in walking, bed, seat, and eating, for the purpose of jest, whether in thy presence or absence, — this I beg thee, the immeasurable,[6] to forgive.

43. Of this universe, animate and inanimate, thou art

---

[1] "Place of extinction," that is, at the season of universal dissolution the Deity is the only being that remains.

[2] "Knower... known... supreme abode," that is, the spirit within us, the God towards which all things turn, their union also is comprehended in this Absolute Deity.

[3] "Great-grandfather," being the Creator of Brahmâ the grandfather, through whose agency the visible universe is formed.

[4] "In the east." Feeling the Divine all-pervasiveness, Arjuna speaks of it by saluting the Deity in all directions; he begins with the east as being the direction in which the sun rises.

[5] "Hence art All." Nothing is of which the substance and form and function is not the Divine Will; and the Will itself is not a co-ordinate reality with the Divine Spirit. Hence the Deity is all things, and yet nothing is the Deity, who is incomprehensible.

[6] "Immeasurable." Being immeasurable, who can give thee meet honor?

the father and the object of adoration, the greatest of the great. There is none equal unto thee, how can there be a superior, O Thou with majesty unimaged in the three worlds?

44. Therefore, bowing down, and holding the body so low, thee, O Lord, I pray for grace; forgive, O Lord, as forgives the father the son, the friend the friend, and the lover the beloved.

45. Having seen what was never seen before, I am joyful, and yet my heart is afflicted with terror; show me that form, O God, be gracious, O Lord of gods and abode of the universe.

46. With diadem and mace in thy hand, I desire to see thee as before. O Thou of a thousand arms, of that form with four arms become Thou, O Universe-formed.

The Supreme Spirit is the Self in the Blessed Lord, and therefore as the Supreme Spirit (in Biblical language "in the name of God") he receives the worship of Arjuna. "He that honoreth not the Son honoreth not the Father which hath sent him" (John v. 23). Neither can there be a second Supreme Spirit, nor can any one see or know Him as an object of consciousness. The Blessed Lord knew Him as the true and only Ego, and hence incomprehensible.

THE BLESSED LORD *spoke:*

47. By me, full of grace, this my supreme form, all-refulgent, all-embracing, infinite, primeval, that has been shown to thee by my mysterious power, has not before been seen by any other.

48. Neither by study of Vedas, nor the practical knowledge of sacrifices, nor through gifts, nor works, nor frightful austerities, I, thus in form, am able to be seen by any but thee, O best of Kuru's sons.

Matt. xiii. 16, 17.

Thou hast seen me in this form only through my grace, and no one not similarly favored can ever see this form.

49. Let there be no affliction for thee, nor down-heartedness; having thus seen this, my form of terror, this my previous form, behold again, with fear departed and joyous in heart.

<small>Matt. xvii. 6, 7.</small>

SANJAYA *said:*

50. Then Vâsudeva, who thus speaking showed again his proper form[1] to Arjuna. The great soul comforted him, the frightened one, by again becoming gentle-formed.

ARJUNA *said:*

51. O Janârdana, having seen this thy gentle and human form, I am now become peaceful at heart and self-possessed.

THE BLESSED LORD *spoke:*

52. This my form, whose sight is so hard to obtain, that thou hast seen, even the gods are ever desirous of the sight of this form.

53. As seen by thee, I may not thus be seen by the study of the Vedas, nor by austere practices, nor by the making of gifts, nor by acts of worship.

54. By self-identifying devotion, indeed, as thus I may be known[2] and seen[3] in truth and entered into.

55. He that works but for me,[4] for whom I am the

---

[1] "Proper form," that is, as the Son of Vasudeva, the mortal father of Krishna.
[2] "Known," that is, from others.
[3] "Seen," that is, by one's self.
[4] "But for me." As the slave works for the master without expectation of personal advantage, so the aspirant for eternal life must perform all acts, enjoyable and painful, for the sake of the Deity, who is his true Self and therefore his absolute joy.

supreme goal, who is devoted to me, devoid of zest in things,[1] and devoid of hostility,[2] comes to me, O Pându's son.

> Thus ends chapter the eleventh, called the "VISION OF THE DEITY AS THE SOUL OF THE UNIVERSE" in the blessed BHAGAVAD GÎTÂ, the sacred lore, the divine wisdom, the book of divine union, the colloquy between the blessed KRISHNA and ARJUNA, and contained in the Bhîshma Parvan of the blessed MAHÂBHÂRATA, which is a collection of one hundred thousand verses by VYÂSA.

The final verse contains the essence of the whole Bhagavad Gîtâ, which in its turn is the essence of all the Vedas. This verse is therefore the very jewel of knowledge, the very pearl of price.

"But what things were gain to me, those I counted loss for Christ. Yea, doubtless, and I count all things but loss for the excellency of the knowledge of Christ Jesus my Lord; for whom I have suffered the loss of all things, and do count them but dung, that I may win Christ" (Phil. iii. 7, 8).

> Salutation to Krishna by devotion to whom is attainable the vision of his universe-form, which even the gods long in vain to see.

---

[1] "Devoid of zest in things," that is, being ready at every moment to part with wife, children, friends, relatives, and wealth, for the sake of the Lord.

[2] "Devoid of hostility," that is, free from the least tendency to injure any creature, even such as are engaged in doing the greatest harm to himself. Such a devotee, on departing from the sphere of mortals, goes nowhere but to the Deity, the soul of the universe, omnipotent and omniscient.

CHAPTER XII.

RIGHT KNOWLEDGE OF DEVOTION.

From the eleventh verse of the second chapter to the end of the tenth chapter the Blessed Lord declared the worship of the attributeless, unsearchable Deity by the acquisition of spiritual knowledge; and also the worship through right meditation on the attributes of the Deity, as declared by the Scriptures.

In the eleventh chapter the worship of the Deity as the soul of the universe is set forth as the road to salvation. The question of the relative merit of these different paths is solved in this chapter by removing the apparent contradiction of the following texts, and manifesting their underlying harmony:—

"Swear, O son of Kuntî, my devotee never is destroyed" (IX. 31).

"He that works but for me, for whom I am the supreme goal, who is devoted to me, is devoid of zest in things, devoid of hostility, comes to me, O Pându's son" (XI. 55).

These texts establish the supreme excellence of devotion to the Great Ruler of the universe. Again, we have such texts as these which declare with equal authority the unparalleled greatness of knowledge:—

"Of them the wise man . . . is the best" (VII. 17).

"If thou wert the greatest evil-doer among all the unrighteous, thou shalt cross over all sins, even by the bark of knowledge" (IV. 36). Therefore,

Arjuna *said:*

1. Among those devotees who thus[1] worship thee, with heart ever at rest, and those that worship the

---

[1] "Thus," that is, as described in Chapter XI. verse 55; working for the Deity alone and loving Him as being the very Self.

unmanifested, exhaustless,[1] who know the knowledge best.[2]

The Blessed Lord, in His reply, divides the subject into two parts, — the path which is most easy to follow, and that which leads immediately to Nirvâna.

The Blessed Lord *spoke:*

2. Those who, with hearts entered into me, constant in devotion, joined to excellent faith, perfectly worship me, are, in my sight, supremely illuminated.

Among those who are not worshippers of the unmanifested, exhaustless essence, the most illuminated are those whose hearts are never void of me.

3. But [3] those who perfectly worship the exhaustless, incapable of being pointed out,[4] unmanifest, all-pervading, unthinkable,[5] the witness of illusion,[6] unmoving,[7] eternal,

4. Withdrawing [8] the assemblage of senses and organs, they, at all times the same in heart, and enjoying benevolence towards all creatures, find even Me.[9]

---

[1] "Unmanifested, exhaustless," those who, having renounced all desires, become attached to knowledge leading to the realization of the attributeless Divine essence.

[2] "Know the knowledge," that is, receive higher illumination.

[3] "But" is used here to exclude the notion of comparison between those declared "supremely illuminated" in verse 2, and those described in the succeeding verses.

[4] "Incapable of being pointed out," that is, being unmanifest, cannot be pointed out as "this" or "that."

[5] "Unthinkable," that is, not representable by the symbolism of words or any intellectual form.

[6] "The witness of illusion;" that is, the consciousness, which appears as though affected by the workings of the unsearchable Divine power, but in reality is only the witness.

[7] "Unmoving;" because consciousness is beyond the illusive power, the universal dynamic energy, and therefore eternal.

[8] "Withdrawing," etc., that is, depriving them of power to adhere to objects through relish of them.

[9] "Find even Me," and are thus identical with Me, and hence cannot be called supremely or otherwise illuminated. This is why there can be no such comparison as is implied in the question of Arjuna.

The perfect worship of the attributeless consists in gaining through study of the Scriptures a direct perception of the truth they contain, continuous and unbroken like the line formed by the closely adhering drops of oil when it is poured out.

5. Greater is the difficulty for those whose hearts are fixed[1] on the unmanifest. Verily, firm devotion[2] to the unmanifest is obtained with great suffering by embodied creatures.[3]

6. On the other hand, who worship Me, committing to Me[4] all actions, regarding Me as the supreme end,[5] and meditating on Me,[6] to nothing else turning,

7. For them, with hearts entered into Me, I become, O son of Prithâ, without delay, the rescuer from the ocean of death-bearing, migratory existence.

Isaiah xlv. 22.

Therefore,

8. Fix thy thoughts[7] upon Me alone; in Me let thy faith[8] dwell, and thou shalt hereafter[9] abide in Me without doubt.

1 John iii. 23, 24.

In his great mercy the Blessed Lord proceeds to smooth the path for every earnest aspirant, however low his state may be.

[1] "Hearts are fixed;" these are such as do not find the worship of a Deity with attributes satisfactory, and only desire to obtain a realization of the attributeless Divine essence.

[2] "Firm devotion;" an all-excluding pursuit of spiritual knowledge. The difficulty of unbroken perception of the mysterious identity between the individual and universal spirit is wellnigh insurmountable to ordinary men.

[3] "By embodied creatures;" those not conscious of connection with the body are not embodied in the present sense. The reason of this great difficulty lies in the abandonment of the identification of the Ego with the body.

[4] "Committing to Me," feeling that they have nothing to do for themselves, but certain charges are laid upon them by the Deity which they must fulfil.

[5] "As the supreme end," desiring God, and not anything that He can give.

[6] "Meditating on Me," the soul of the universe.

[7] "Thoughts," that is, the manas, or reflective self.

[8] "Faith," that is, buddhi, or the conviction of reality attaching to any desire; the "substance of hope" in the God-aspiring; the belief in the reality of the world and its ways in ordinary people.

[9] "Hereafter," that is, after death.

9. If, again, thou art not able to fix thy heart[1] on Me, seek, O Dhananjaya, to obtain Me by devotion through repeated endeavors.

Whenever the heart wanders in search of pleasure in worldly things, bring it back to me by the conviction that of all joys the highest joy is the Deity. The supreme bliss is the Supreme Spirit; of this bliss that which the infinity of creatures enjoy is but an atom.

10. If thou art unable even to practise devotion through repeated endeavors, then regard as supreme, special works[2] for Me. Even performing works for Me thou shalt obtain perfection.[3]

James ii. 24, 25.

11. If thou art unable to do even this, then resting in devotion to Me, and being self-controlled, abandon the fruit of all actions.

Luke xvii. 10.

Knowing that all things come from the Deity, do not believe that any result can come from our efforts except by Divine grace. Therefore the foreseen and unforeseen consequences of our acts are only apparently their effects; in reality, they are sent by God for our perfection. Living this life of faith, perfection becomes attainable. In short, we can, this very minute, put our feet upon the upward path by leading a life of righteousness in obedience to the will of God, and depending upon Him in faith; rejoicing when smitten by the just sentence of the Deity, and gratefully receiving the good that He grants.

But it must never be forgotten that this dependence on the Deity does not imply recklessness of conduct. With self-control and thought we are to do the duties pertaining to our condition in life, with the firm conviction that whatever comes to us, joy or suffering, is from the Deity, who is absolutely righteous and merciful.

---

[1] "Heart," that is, thoughts and faith.

[2] "Special works," such as singing hymns, keeping fasts and feasts, building places of worship, giving alms when performed in faith and for the love of God alone.

[3] "Obtain perfection," by the reception of knowledge for which natures purified in the way described become fit.

The ninth chapter is for the indifferently spiritual, who can only worship the Deity by act, speech, or thought, and not by all-excluding communion in meditation, nor by perception of the full truth. The various sub-divisions of that class appear before the Blessed Lord to receive his commandments in verses 8–11. In conclusion He commands the renunciation of the fruit of all action, and then goes on to impress upon the hearers the benefit of such renunciation by bestowing upon it excessive praise.

12. Better is knowledge[1] than repeated endeavors;[2] superior to knowledge is meditation;[3] to meditation renunciation of the fruit of action is superior; from renunciation immediately comes peace.

Matt. x. 37–39; xix. 28, 29.

"Peace" is Nirvâna. Because from the renunciation of all desires the supreme end is attained, therefore even the renunciation of the ordinarily spiritual aspirant, although of a different order, is yet possessed of the merit of the general class to which it belongs; hence its praiseworthiness.

Although the duty to the Deity is suited to the state of the aspirant's development, yet it is true that the worship of the attributeless God marks the highest spiritual condition.

13. Hating no creature,[4] full of brotherly love, and compassionate,[5] devoid of my-ness,[6] devoid of egotism,[7] equal towards suffering and enjoyment, forgiving,

14. Ever content,[8] of tranquil heart, with nature[9]

---

[1] "Knowledge," intellectual apprehension of spiritual truth.

[2] "Repeated endeavors," accompanied by ignorance of the nature of the goal.

[3] "Meditation," combined with knowledge.

[4] "No creature," not even those which do one harm, because such a devotee regards all creatures as his own self.

[5] "Compassionate," of whom no creature will ever know fear.

[6] "My-ness," consciousness of ownership in anything.

[7] "Egotism," consciousness of being the doer of anything.

[8] "Ever content;" that is, does not think of gain beyond what the body needs in order to be kept alive.

[9] "Nature," that is, the assemblage of cause and effect forming one's personality or individual character.

subjugated, firm in intent, and with thought and faith given up to Me; whoso is my devotee[1] is dear unto Me.

<small>Psalm cxii. 7.</small>

He then goes on to amplify what is said in Chapter VII. verse 17: "I am excessively beloved of the wise man, and he is also beloved of Me."

15. He from whom no one feels perturbation, also whom no one perturbs, who is free from the agitation arising from exultation,[2] despondency,[3] and fear, is beloved of Me.

16. Unexpecting,[4] pure, capable,[5] neutral,[6] devoid of fear,[7] giving up initiation of action, whoso is my devotee is beloved of Me.

17. He who does not feel exultant, nor hates, nor mourns, nor longs, giving up good as well as evil,[8] whoso is possessed of devotion is beloved of Me.

18. Equal towards friend and enemy and also towards honor and disgrace, equal towards heat and cold, towards enjoyment and suffering, and devoid of attachment,

<small>Matt. v. 44-48; vi. 25.</small>

19. Equal to whom are abuse and adulation, silent, content with any and every thing, without fixed habitation, firm in heart, possessed of devotion, — such a man is beloved of Me.

<small>Matt. viii. 20; x. 9, 10.</small>

---

1 "Whoso is my devotee;" that is, a wise man.
2 "Exultation," from the fulfilment of wishes, and
3 "Despondency," from the opposite.
4 "Unexpecting," that is, neither body nor mind craving gratification.
5 "Capable," possessed of presence of mind and sound judgment.
6 "Neutral," not espousing any cause.
7 "Devoid of fear;" this neutrality is not on account of fear of probable consequences.
8 "Giving up good," etc.; that is, having given up all works of merit and demerit, rests in that perfect love which casts out fear.

20. Those who worship this immortality-bearing law[1] as declared, full of faith, regarding Me[2] as the supreme end, and devoted[3] — are excessively beloved of Me.[4]

<small>Matt. xii. 50; John xiv. 22-24.</small>

With this chapter ends the second hexad, containing the declaration of the being of the Deity in His character of the supreme paradox, — the attributeless, unknowable God of the wise, and the infinitely attributed God of goodness to His devotee. The former (the wise) are identical with the Deity by realizing the truth that the innermost-reality in man is the spirit of God, and therefore not dependent upon Him; for the latter He is the only door to salvation.

God is to be known as attributeless where separated from Nature and attributed as possessing her. By the will of God the consciousness in Nature is one with Him, and like oil in the sessamun seed, at the start of creation pervades all things. Those who know the reality call that which is anotherless consciousness by the word Brahmă, the Supreme Spirit, the Lord.

Thus ends chapter the twelfth, called "RIGHT KNOWLEDGE OF DEVOTION TO THE DEITY," in the blessed BHAGAVAD GÎTÂ, the sacred lore, the divine wisdom, the book of divine union, the colloquy between the blessed KRISHNA and ARJUNA, and contained in the Bhîshma Parvan of the blessed MAHÂBHÂRATA, which is a collection of one hundred thousand verses by VYÂSA.

Salutation to Krishna, by devotion to whom the rugged path of devotion to the attributeless becomes smooth, and salvation easy of attainment.

---

[1] "Law," as declared in verses 13-19.
[2] "Me," the attributeless.
[3] "Devoted," resting in that supreme love which is identification with the Deity.
[4] "Excessively beloved of me." This concludes the full exposition of the thought contained in Chapter VII. verse 17.

IDENTITY.

CHAPTER XIII.

THE RIGHT KNOWLEDGE OF THE DISCRIMINATION BETWEEN KSHETRA AND KSHETRAJNA.

THE first six chapters of this book declared the nature of the individual spirit; the six succeeding chapters dealt with the nature of the universal spirit; with this chapter begins the final hexad, which declares the relation between the two to be identity, — the Spirit or Consciousness as itself being one and indivisible.

In the seventh chapter (vv. 4, 5) it is shown that the nature of the Deity is twofold, — that which is composed of the three qualities, the eight-fold divided inferior nature, the cause of bondage; and that which is Consciousness, which is the Spirit of God. By teaching the truth in respect to this twofold nature, the Blessed Lord illuminates the great mystery of the being of the Deity, since the creation, preservation, and destruction of the universe is due to the union and disunion of the superior and inferior nature of the Deity. Further he shows forth the nature of that spiritual knowledge which, joined to the performance of the law declared in the previous chapter (vv. 13-20), makes the devotee eminently dear unto the Lord. It is to be borne in mind that in verse 7 the Blessed Lord said: "For them, with hearts entered into Me, I become, O son of Prithâ, without delay, the rescuer from death-bearing, migratory existence."

How is this done? The Deity, as Himself, is not liable to act. He acts through the mysterious plenitude of power, and salvation from the conditioned life of change is not possible without spiritual knowledge. (Cf. John xvii. 3; 1 Cor. xiii. 12.) Hence in the present chapter the Blessed Lord declares the knowledge of the being of God, who is beyond all comprehension.

THE BLESSED LORD *spoke:*

1. This body,[1] O son of Kuntî, is named Kshetra:[2] who knows it,[3] him, those acquainted with both, call the Kshetrajna.[4]

It is not perfect wisdom merely to know the Ego as different from the body.

2. Know me even as the Kshetrajna in every Kshetra, O son of Bharata; that knowledge which realizes the Kshetra and the Kshetrajna is knowledge in my sight.

The Ego is to be known as different from the body, as being the same in all the infinitude of bodies, and also as being identical with the Supreme Spirit. This does not mean by three different chronological manifestations of the Ego, but as being true once and forever. They are three co-inhering identities which, when realized, show that the real nature of God, Consciousness, is incomprehensible, but by the operation of a mysterious power it seems to be dwelling in all creatures as that which they call the self.

3. That Kshetra,[5] what it is,[6] how it is,[7] what it

---

[1] "This body;" the inferior nature of the Deity transforms itself, for the purpose of the enjoyment and experience of the spirit, or the conscious, superior nature, into the inner faculties, external senses, and the material of the body: this assemblage is "this body."

[2] "Kshetra" literally means "the perishable," "subject to decay." It also signifies "a field," and in this sense is a fitting name for the body, as the seeds of good and evil sown in the body germinate into new forms of good and evil experiences.

[3] "Who knows it;" that is, knows the body completely, and is now receiving instructions about its nature from the Blessed Lord; the Ego in its two aspects, bound and liberated.

[4] "Kshetrajna;" the knower of Kshetra enjoys it as the owner of a field enjoys the fruit thereof.

[5] "That Kshetra." The body is called Kshetra, because to an ordinary man it represents the whole of nature; a man knows everything only in relation to his own body. To understand the truth represented by the usual division into body and soul, it is necessary to comprehend Prakriti (or Power), together with its twenty-three products, and the manner of their production.

[6] "What it is;" that is, it is in essential reality unconscious and objective.

[7] "How it is;" that is, it has the power of producing.

produces,¹ and what is from what derived,² also who he is,³ what is his power,⁴ — all this hear from Me in brief.

Praises of this knowledge of body and soul, object and subject, now follow.

4. By the Rishis⁵ has it⁶ been fully⁷ sung with discrimination⁸ in the Vedic hymns of many kinds,⁹ and by words that indicate the Supreme Spirit, and are certain and full of reason.¹⁰

According to the practice of spiritual teachers, having removed from the mind of the hearer all other things, by declaring that which forms the highest importance of the teachings, the Blessed Lord proceeds to declare the natures of the Kshetra and Kshetrajna. It should here be explained that when the reward of spiritual living is spoken of, the object is not to encourage selfishness, but to remove obstacles from the path of the disciple by quieting the unrest which comes from manifold desires.

---

1 "What it produces;" that is, all that appears to be comes from it.
2 "What is from what derived;" that is, the relation between the primary and secondary causes.
3 "Who he is;" that is, what, in reality, the Ego or Purusha is.
4 "His power;" that is, through reflection in various objective bases.
5 "By the Rishis;" not only is the sufficiency of the right knowledge of object and subject established by authoritative opinion, but also by the eternal revelation of the Vedas.
6 "It;" that is, the knowledge which the Blessed Lord is about to declare in brief.
7 "Fully;" that is, in many ways, and with greater fulness than is to be found in this chapter.
8 "With discrimination;" the cause of bondage is the want of discrimination between the ego and the non-ego, while the realization of this distinction is liberation.
9 "Vedic hymns of many kinds;" many, because of various schools (çâkhâs) of the Vedas, and also, as one authority says, owing to the various names by which the Kshetrajna is called in the hymns.
10 "Words that indicate . . . full of reason;" that is, not only in the hymns, but also in texts where arguments are used to increase the aspirant's receptive power; such as, "approach the âtmâ;" "he that knows the Supreme Spirit attains the supreme goal;" "he who worships another God, and considers his Ego as one and God another, is like a beast of burden to the gods;" "How can that which is come from that which is not?"

5. The great elements,[1] ahankâra,[2] buddhi,[3] and the unmanifest,[4] — it is even this;[5] the ten indriyas,[6] the one,[7] and the five objects of sense,[8]

Then is declared that which is produced by Prakriti.

6. Desire[9] and aversion,[10] pleasure and pain, coherence,[11] conscious life,[12] recuperative power,[13] — thus has been declared the Kshetra,[14] together with its products.

[1] "Great elements;" great because pervading all the products; namely, the ten indriyas, the manas, and the five gross elements.

[2] "Ahankâra;" that is, egotism or the Ego, through false knowledge considered as an object of cognition, — the power represented by "I am this."

[3] "Buddhi" is the producing or determining power of Nature; in individuals it is the intellect or power of judgment.

[4] "Unmanifest," is the root-cause, Prakriti, the unseen power of God. "My illusive power, difficult to cross over" (Chap. VII. 14).

[5] "It is even this;" that is, my eight-fold, differentiated, inferior nature (mentioned, VII. 4) is thus described here.

[6] "Indriyas;" the five senses and the five powers or organs of action. Organs do not here mean the different parts of the body, but the powers which manifest themselves through these various portions of the body, — as walking through the feet, and so on.

[7] "The one;" that is, the manas, or reflecting self.

[8] "Objects of sense;" that is, the gross elements. The assemblage of all these powers is the Kshetra.

[9] "Desire" is the attraction towards an object belonging to the same class as one previously experienced; the concomitant of such attraction is pleasure.

[10] "Aversion," with its concomitant pain, is the opposite of desire.

[11] "Coherence" is the power by which the senses, organs, limbs, and internal faculties are held together as one.

[12] "Conscious life" is not consciousness, which is identical with the Ego, and therefore with the Deity. Conscious life appears to pervade the body as force may be said to pervade matter in which it resides. The buddhi is described as transparent to consciousness, and thus able to produce an image or simulation of consciousness in a being.

[13] "Recuperative power" is the energy supplied from within a creature for the purpose of maintaining the organism and its functions. This power revives the senses when weakened by fatigue; it also shows itself as mental and physical endurance. No amount of food could invigorate a man if this power did not exist before eating. Authority and argument prove these powers to be properties of matter, and not spirit. The Vedic text says: "Desire, intention, effort, belief, non-belief, recuperative power and its opposite, shame, intelligence, fear, — all this is but the mind." The Ego not being an object cannot be related to any of these things, which can be experienced and are therefore objects.

[14] "Kshetra;" the individual body is one of the groups into which these objects are divided.

This explains the nature of the Kshetra, which is the first of the three topics of this chapter. The others are knowledge and the Kshetrajna, in revealing whom knowledge reaches its consummation and ceases to have further use.

The powers enumerated are products of Prakriti and not properties of the Ego which, united to Prakriti, is declared to be omniscient, almighty, etc. By this distinct statement the philosophy of the Atomist and the Logician are rejected. Sânkhya and Yoga philosophers do not completely follow the Blessed Lord, who is declaring the teaching of the Vedânta, the orthodox philosophy of the Brâhmans.

The Blessed Lord proceeds to declare what knowledge is. Although in the third verse knowledge is not distinctly mentioned as one of the subjects, it is yet impossible to describe the object to be known without giving some idea of the knowledge, or the knower. The true Ego being the object to be known, or realized, the apparent knower is really the knowledge. The buddhi, in connection with the body which answered to the name forming the subject of the statement made by another, "He has attained Nirvâna," is the knowledge.

Spiritual knowledge, in short, is that simple reality which is represented by the instructor, the instruction, and the pupil who receives it. This knowledge is an interior or transcendental reality, while the practical meaning of these three words is included in the Kshetra. Spiritual knowledge is not the product of effort, for no effort can produce that which is absolutely nothing before the effort is made. Nor is it a thing which pre-exists the effort which can be said to establish a new relation between it and the maker of the effort, as is the case with any object of possession, where ownership results from the action of the owner; for spiritual knowledge cannot co-exist with the sense of proprietorship or any other form of egotism.

The question as to who gains the knowledge is based upon ignorance of what the knowledge is. Such questions can only arise in regard to the false nature of the Ego as opposed to its true nature. The traditional reply to such questions as "Who is bound by ignorance, and who is liberated by spiritual knowledge?" is the demonstration of their irrationality. Nothing else so clearly discloses the want of humility which prompts questions on a subject which is denied care and thought, as is shown by these questions.

This universe is the false nature of the Ego, and appears as true by the illegitimate ascription to it of the property of Truth. In fact, it is the illegitimacy of the ascription that makes this nature false. The ascriber is also that false nature and no other. As an actor may personate a king without being a king, so the false nature personates the Ego without being it. The actor may pretend to die on the stage and yet his real personality suffers no injury; he remains unchanged when his part is finished. So when the false nature shall finish its pretences the Ego will be itself,—that is, the same it was in the beginning and is now,—having no more parts to play forever and forever. This is the last thought on the stage of the world before the false Ego, or, more strictly speaking, the falsehood about the Ego, finally disappears as the baseless fabric of a dream. "I have done all that is to be done, obtained all that is to be obtained, known all that is to be known,—it is finished." Thus ends the working of the false nature, not indeed by mere lapse of time. As a play does not end from this cause, but by the consummation of the purpose of the play, so by the realization of the purpose of existence, namely, the perception of all that exists, man's destiny is fulfilled; then comes the disappearance of that perception because all things have been perceived, as appetite ceases when a satisfying meal is eaten. Spiritual knowledge is the revelation of this purpose, the completion of the destiny of man. A man hears from those who know what the destiny of man is, and then realizes his own destiny, the purpose of his being. This is spiritual knowledge, to exist no more as a man.

In reality the Ego is as independent of spiritual knowledge as it is of false knowledge. It requires no knowledge, true or false, for a thing to be itself.

7. Want of conceit,[1] want of ostentation,[2] inoffensiveness,[3] forgivingness,[4] sincerity,[5] devotion to spir-

---

[1] "Conceit" is here used for the conscious attributing of merit to one's self.

[2] "Ostentation" is the disclosure of one's spiritual condition.

[3] "Inoffensiveness," causing pain to no creature by mind, speech, or body.

[4] "Forgivingness," want of perturbation in the mind on being injured.

[5] "Sincerity," harmony between act and feeling; the sage having no personal motive has no thought as to how he acts.

itual instructors, cleanliness,[1] firmness,[2] restraint of self.[3]

8. Dispassion about objects of sense,[4] absence of pride, and meditation upon the evils[5] of birth, death,[6] decrepitude, disease, and suffering.

9. Want of attachment to objects and self-identifying interest[7] in son, wife, house, and so forth, and unchanging equal-heartedness on the occurrence of what is favorable and what is unfavorable.

10. Love unfaltering to Me through self-effacement[8] in non-separateness[9] from Me, fondness for secluded spots,[10] and want of pleasure in congregations of men.[11]

---

[1] "Cleanliness," external and internal; the latter is freedom from attachment and aversion, and is gained by impressing upon the mind the unclean character of these qualities.

[2] "Firmness," perseverance in working out one's salvation.

[3] "Restraint of self." "Self" is here the union of body and the faculties, which produces our present being. Its restraint is in the power to end their natural union, which is manifested as the tendencies of the natural man.

[4] "Dispassion ... sense," that is, want of attraction towards any sensuous object, experienced or unexperienced. This comes by

[5] "Meditation upon the evils," etc. "The moment thou art born thou art fated to die; the moment thou diest thou art fated to be again imprisoned in the dark dungeon of the womb, sunk in the foulest impurities, and even while thou livest the body is liable to be afflicted by the most loathsome diseases, and the mind by the intensest sufferings from passions and the uncertainties of life."

[6] "Death." The agonies of death are produced by the violent wrenching of the senses and faculties from their normal operations.

[7] "Self-identifying interest," etc. The thought that their life is my life, their suffering mine, and so on. This natural force has the effect of making the working out of salvation appear to be an act of personal interest to be compared with the interests of son, wife, etc. A man is thus blinded into the belief that it is unselfish to give up working out his salvation for the worldly well-being of his family and relations. (Cf. Matt. x. 37.)

[8] "Self-effacement," or Samâdhi; a state of spiritual exaltation in which consciousness of the present self is completely obliterated.

[9] "Non-separateness." There is nothing beside my God, Vâsudeva, and He is my supreme goal.

[10] "Fondness for secluded spots;" perception of the Spirit is obtained in such places.

[11] "Congregations of men;" in the midst of unregenerate men the eye of the spirit is blinded.

11. Constancy in the pursuit of spiritual knowledge, meditation as to the end of the knowledge of truth,[1] — these[2] are said to be knowledge; ignorance is that which is opposite to this.

The question arises as to how these attributes can be called knowledge of the Supreme Spirit, since they do not define and condition consciousness. It can be observed everywhere that knowledge conditions the object known. This involves reasoning in a circle. It conditions the object known because it is knowledge, it is knowledge because it conditions the object. The truth is, that when knowledge is said to condition the object known, the meaning is that the object is different from other objects not connected with that knowledge; as, for example, the knowledge that reveals a baked earthen jar does not manifest fire.

Hence it is not unjustifiable to speak of these attributes as knowledge of which the object is the Supreme Spirit, meaning by knowledge the concomitant indications of knowledge which is indefinable. The knowledge of the Supreme Spirit is the knowledge "I am He." None can know the "I" as an object; no more can the Supreme Spirit be known as an object. This knowledge in its consummation is Nirvâna.

12. That which is to be known I shall declare, knowing which a man attains immortality, — the beginningless, Supreme Brahmă that is said to be neither Aught nor Naught.

Although the Absolute Deity is so difficult to be known, yet the pursuit of spiritual knowledge is worthy of unfaltering devotion, because the consummation of it is beyond description glorious, — identity with the Supreme Spirit. In order to declare the Absolute Deity, the beginning is made at the highest point of conditioned existence; namely, the cause of creation, preservation, and destruction

---

[1] "End of the knowledge of truth;" that is, liberation. "The truth shall make you free" (John viii. 32). By constant thought about Nirvâna, or eternal life, the mind begins to believe that of all things this is the best, and acquires strength to work for it.

[2] "These;" all that has been said in verses 7–11. "These" are called knowledge because they fit one for the reception of knowledge.

of the universe, which is beginningless for all, and unending for those who do not attain Nirvâna, where the attribute of being the cause no longer illusively conditions consciousness. The Supreme Spirit is beginningless and yet itself.

It might at first sight appear that after the promise to declare what is to be known for the purpose of attaining immortality, it is inadequate to say that the Supreme is "neither Aught nor Naught." But it is not so, and is in perfect agreement with all teachings of the Vedânta. It being impossible to make any affirmation about the Deity, — since all that is, is but falsely imputed to Him as His attributes, — negation is the only right method of declaring Him, who cannot be found out by searching.

The Vedas declare, " Now then this commandment, not this, not that, not great, not small, not short, not long, not within, not without, not before, not behind, not sound, not touch, not form, not changing, also not taste ; " because a legitimate application of the demonstrative pronoun is not possible in respect of the Deity. How is this different from universal negation ? In this ; that about which the verb " to be " is used in an affirmative sense exists, and the reverse does not. But the employment of the verb for affirmation or negation is an act of mental operation, which cannot extend to the Supreme Spirit, who is not an object limited by the mind.

Let us take an example in the phrase, "The barren woman's son." The difference between the two cases is this : In so far as the " barren woman's son " can have any importance he must be perceptible by ordinary physical means. When we reject the figment of the barren woman's son, we mean nothing more than this, that our conscious existence, as well as the happiness which existence implies, is in no way affected by that figment. In other words, it is the implied perceptibility of the barren woman's son that gives the mind the feeling of rest in certitude when we negative his existence.

Not so in the case of the Absolute Deity, in regard to whom there is no implication of perceptibility. Being beyond the possibility of experience by the mind, the Deity cannot be the object of the mental function of negation. Therefore the being of the Deity is proved by the word, that is, by the mystery of revelation. That which is not of any advantage to any man (as is an object declared to be beyond the power to experience), no man can or will invent.

Here another doubt arises. Granted that Absolute Deity is not subject to negation, how is it possible to know Him from whom alone eternal life can be inherited? The very consideration of the impossibility of perceiving the Deity through the mind and the senses, which establishes His being, establishes the other truth that immortality is impossible, because we have no means of knowing the Deity. This doubt is not well founded; for the same authority which establishes the being of the Deity as an absolute truth, and therefore not amenable to sense perception or inference, also declares that there is a power called divine grace or spiritual illumination, which makes the Deity known, not indeed as an object, but as the consciousness within us (Cf. Matt. x. 27; John v. 21, 26). Consciousness alone is life in itself, or is self-existent; and the moment it is perceived that I, the Self, am the Spirit or pure consciousness, immortality is achieved.

The Supreme Spirit is proved by the word but not made known. For words can cause us to realize four categories only; namely, class, action, attribute, and relation. The Supreme Spirit is none of these. How then can He be called reality, which is a class containing many members? This use of reality is a mere figure of speech, and has no scientific precision; for the revealed authority, the Vedas, declares, "For Brahmā there is neither clan nor caste." Respecting action it is said, "Without action, peace;" as regards attributes, "He is one only and attributeless;" touching relation it is explicitly declared, "One without a second." In brief, words can only deal with quality and their co-inherence, usually called substance; but the Supreme Spirit is different from all of them, and consequently beyond all words.

From the rejection of the attribution of reality or being to the Deity, it may seem as though He were nothing. To remove this fear it is shown that the existence itself of the limbs, organs, senses, and faculties of creatures affords the proof that they are the powers of consciousness. Disconnected with consciousness they cannot for a moment be, and yet they are not disconnected. Consequently their apparent non-identity with consciousness is not due to any power in them. Nor is it possible to say that they are self-existent. Hence they are and are not identical with consciousness, without any power of their own. This is the same thing as to say that they are the powers of consciousness with which they are identical or not, according to another power which must be regarded as absolute free-will, or independence of consciousness, — a power not liable to be described. The conclusion is undeniable that the point of view from which reality is attributed to powers cannot admit of the same epithet being applied to the Powerful, but without the Powerful neither attribute nor attribution can be.

The knowledge of the Deity is the realization that the Deity is unknowable by reason of His absoluteness, but being Consciousness, He is that which every creature feels after as the " I." The world being His power is in reality nothing but Himself. The apparent non-identity which gives an apparent reality to the world is an indescribable, unessential something, — a falsehood to be avoided with contempt. Consciousness cannot be known except as that by which and through which all things are known; and no thing can exist that is not known. Consciousness is independent and self-existent, while all things can and do exist only through it. Hence the whole universe is the power of consciousness; in other words, the universe is, and can cease to be, only by the power of consciousness; the power which destroys the universe would itself be destroyed if rejected by consciounesss.

Fully to realize this is to know God with true knowledge. No being can thus know God except those who, thoroughly purified by complete renunciation and perfect resignation, know Him as the Self, — know Him by the knowledge " I am He."

13. That has hands and feet everywhere, everywhere eyes, heads, and mouths, ears everywhere, he remains in the world, covering all.

The bodies and minds of different creatures are really presided over by one consciousness, the Kshetrajna, who appears as though distinct in each creature. But if these illusive forms are rejected, the consciousness which is man, and God, and all beings at the same time, and at all times, remains.

14. Reflected[1] by the functions of all senses and fac-

[1] " Reflected;" that is, nothing can exist without consciousness, yet nothing is consciousness; therefore it is said to be reflected, — consciousness appears as though acting. " He seems to rest, he seems to move," says a sacred text. The revered commentator says, " For those devoid of right discrimination when the senses and faculties act, the Ego appears as though the actor; as, when clouds move about, the moon seems as though in motion."

ulties, yet devoid of all senses[1] and faculties, unattached, yet all-supporting;[2] devoid of qualities, yet witnessing all qualities.[3]

15. That is the within[4] and without[5] of creatures, animate and inanimate; it is unrealizable on account of subtlety, and is distant[6] as well as near.[7]

16. That which is to be known, though undistributed is distributed in creatures,[8] and is the support of creatures,[9] as also destroyer and creator.

17. That is the light of all lights,[10] is said to be beyond darkness;[11] the knowledge,[12] that to be known,[13] and that which is known,[14] seated in specialty[15] in the hearts of all.

[1] "Devoid of all senses;" that is, in reality the Ego is unconditioned by any organ, limb, or faculty. The Scriptures say, "He, devoid of hands and feet, moves and grasps; sees, though without eyes; hears, though without ears."

[2] "Unattached yet all-supporting;" that is, though the Spirit is without relation to anything, yet if it were not, nothing would be. Even the seeming reality of the world requires The Reality to be simulated.

[3] "Qualities," here used in the technical sense of the Sânkhya philosophy, means the three components of nature, fully described in the succeeding chapter.

[4] "Within;" to the wise the innermost thing, the Ego, is the Supreme Spirit.

[5] "Without;" that is, for those who, being in delusion, take the body as the Ego, the Spirit is the external body from the skin to the marrow. Such is their delusion.

[6] "Distant," for the unwise, who search the whole world for it in vain.

[7] "Near," for the wise who know it to be the Self. The holy text says, "It moves, it does not move, it is distant, it is near, it is the innermost of all this as well as the outermost of all this."

[8] "Distributed in creatures;" in consequence of being considered in reference to each body. As the cause, the Spirit is but One, while in regard to effects it is many.

[9] "Support of creatures" during the life of the Kosmos, and at other seasons destroyer and creator.

[10] "Light of all lights;" as without the sun nothing can be seen, so the sun himself cannot be seen except through the majestic, self-sustained splendor of the Spirit.

[11] "Is said to be beyond darkness;" beyond the reach of false knowledge; "said" by the Vedas. (See comment, Chapter VIII. verse 9.)

[12] "Knowledge." (See verses 7-11.)

[13] "To be known." (See verses 12-17.)

[14] "That which is known;" when the truth is realized in a heart purified by the virtues called knowledge in verses 7-11.

[15] "Seated in specialty;" as the rays of the sun fall everywhere but are peculiarly seated in transparent media, so these three realities, though all-pervading, are in the heart or buddhi.

The real nature of the Supreme Spirit is incomprehensible. Whoever, knowing this, knows Him as declared in verses 13-16, and perceives that the real nature of the Deity is identical with the true Self in us, knows truly indeed and is immortal.

18. Thus has been declared in brief the Kshetra,[1] knowledge,[2] and that to be known;[3] my devotee,[4] realizing this, attains to my state.[5]

From the practical point of view the last verse of Chapter XI. is the most important in the book; as regards philosophy, the foregoing verses of this chapter are incomparably the most important. The truth fully sung by Vaçishtha and the other divinely illuminated sages in the Vedas, and illustrated by well-reasoned arguments, has been thus briefly declared by the Blessed Lord. Whoever realizes this truth is set free.

The twofold nature of the Deity is declared in Chapter VII. verses 4, 5, and it is also said that these two form the source from which all things come. The subject is resumed here.

19. Know Prakriti[6] and Purusha[7] as both beginningless. Know the emanations[8] and qualities[9] as born of Prakriti.

Prakriti and Purusha are co-eternal and are the power of the Deity by which creation, preservation, and destruction take place. Prakriti is the power by which all work is done, while Purusha looks on. If he did not oversee she would not work; and if she did not work he could not look on, in the absence of anything to be looked at. But yet essentially consciousness is different from the objective; therefore their union, as described, is due to the fact of

---

[1] "Kshetra;" described in verses 5, 6, for the purpose of giving the right knowledge of the individual ego.
[2] "Knowledge;" that is, the relation between the Kshetra and the Supreme Spirit.
[3] "Known;" that is, the Supreme Spirit.
[4] "My devotee;" he who having firmly placed his entire heart in the Supreme Spirit sees nothing but the Supreme everywhere and in everything.
[5] "My state;" identity with the Supreme Spirit or liberation.
[6] "Prakriti;" that is, the inferior nature of the Deity (Chap. VII. v. 4).
[7] "Purusha;" the superior nature of the Deity, or consciousness.
[8] "Emanations," such as buddhi and the rest.
[9] "Qualities," modifications of nature appearing as pleasure, pain, and delusion.

their being both the nature of the Deity, and is the manifestation of His will. This is the most important thing to impress upon the mind.

The beginningless union of consciousness with matter is due to the free and absolutely unconditioned will of God alone; it is otherwise called illusion or false knowledge, because it is not an object to which the proncun "this" can be applied, and because it is extinguished on attainment of liberation. The essential nature of will being independence of conditions, the dissolution of the illegitimate union between matter and spirit is also the outcome of the Divine will. This union and disunion do not show any changeableness in the will of God, for the very essence of change, which is Time, does not exist except by the union of Prakriti and Purusha. Hence it is clear that no one can attain liberation or true knowledge of the Deity by mere lapse of time. To accept the doctrine of a progressive development for the immortal Ego is to accept death in preference to life. The Ego is essentially immortal, and therefore at every instant free from the conditions of time. The free growth of this faith is the attainment of the eternal life. This, however, can never take place so long as the lie is given to it openly by unrighteousness of conduct and want of resignation, which has its origin in the belief that the Ego is transitory and limited by personal desires.

Bondage and liberation are really nothing but the two aspects of the Divine will, uniting and disuniting Prakriti and Purusha. The difference between the Sânkhya philosophers and the orthodox Brâhmanical teachers lies in the fact that the former ascribe to Prakriti the power of uniting with and disuniting from Purusha; and although she is unconscious, she appears as though conscious by reason of this power of uniting herself with Purusha.

The orthodox sages attach a different meaning to the term Prakriti. The revered commentator says, "Prakriti is the power of the Deity to create objects; the illusive power consisting of the three qualities." And as no creation can take place except by the union of Prakriti and Purusha, therefore Prakriti is not independent, but is subject to the will of God. The Sânkhya philosophers demur to this, and say that Prakriti is "the rootless root."

The others say that Prakriti, being unconscious, cannot be the First Cause, because such a tenet would be opposed to such Vedic texts as declare creation to be caused by a conscious power.

The Sânkhya philosophers reply that such texts do not impugn the truth of their doctrines, because by union with Purusha, Prakriti appears as conscious.

The orthodox school rejects this exposition as being too cumbrous and roundabout. But the seeming difference on this point between these two schools altogether disappears when we reflect over the teaching of the Sânkhya school on this point. It holds that the union between Prakriti and Purusha is due to ignorance, which is destroyed by right knowledge, and that, as a great Sânkhya authority declares, "Verily, no one is bound, nor is released, nor migrates: but resting in many forms, Prakriti herself migrates, is bound, and is freed" (Sânkhya Kârikâ, Aph. LXII).

This aphorism removes the apparent conflict between these two schools upon a very important point, — the real nature of the Ego. On a cursory view of the Sânkhya system, it would appear as if it held that the Ego is essentially possessed of the three attributes, cognition, will, and action, at one time, but that at another time, that is to say, on liberation, it is divested of these attributes. It also seems to hold that the distinctness of personalities is due to real distinctness of egos.

But upon a careful examination of this system as a whole, these apparent tenets give way before very different conclusions. It then becomes plain that this school, in common with orthodox Brâhmanism, admits the indescribableness of ignorance, and does not understand it as mere negation of knowledge; it also teaches the essential attributelessness of the Ego, and the consciousness of the First Cause. Nor does it leave any doubt that in truth the Sânkhya school does not maintain the apparent multiplicity of Purushas to be an ultimate reality. (See Sânkhya Kârikâ, Aphs. XVII. and XX.) The difference of teaching as to the order of the evolution of principles is immaterial, since both lead to precisely the same final result.

The school usually called Theistic Sânkhya differs from the orthodox philosophy as to the nature of the First Cause. It maintains that although the Supreme Spirit is the Creator, and has other functions, he is yet eternally pure and unconditioned; while the Blessed Lord teaches that the Supreme Spirit is really actionless and absolute, — the phenomenal manifestations being the outcome of the relation between the two natures or powers.

Here, also, on reflection, it will be seen that the difference is formal and non-essential. This difference may also be found between the Old Testament and the New. Jehovah the Creator is

Absolute, — "I am that I am," — while in the New Testament the Deity does not create except through His Son, who is not included in the procession of beings. As the union of Prakriti and Purusha is not caused in time, the Son is eternally in the bosom of the Father, "whom no one can see" on account of His absolute majesty.

This last conception is in perfect accord with orthodox Brâhmanism, in which Içvara stands for the Son. Içvara is possessed of all powers, yet is not absolute; because whenever any power is exercised he is the exerciser of that power, and is thus conditioned by it, while the Father "judges no man." Light will be thrown on the limitations of the Son by the will of the Father through such declarations as these: "Verily, verily I say unto you, the Son can do nothing of himself, but what he seeth the Father do; for what things soever He doeth, these also doeth the Son likewise. For the Father loveth the Son and showeth him all things that Himself doeth, and He will show him greater works than these, that ye may marvel. . . . For the Father judgeth no man, but hath committed all judgment unto the Son" (John v. 19, 20, 22).

"I can of mine own self do nothing; as I hear, I judge: my judgment is just, because I seek not mine own will, but the will of the Father that has sent me" (John v. 32).

"And when all things shall be subdued unto Him, then shall the Son also himself be subject unto him that put all things under him, that God may be all in all" (1 Cor. xx. 28).

It is to be noted here that the word Son is expressly rejected by the father of orthodox Brâhmanism of modern times — the revered Sankarâchârya — owing to its implication of a derived and yet independent reality. The Spirit of God, consciousness, is the real nature of the Son as of all creatures. The only real nature of the universe, animate and inanimate, is the Supreme Spirit.

In so far as the Father of the universe is said to do anything, it is done by His mere being, and without even the least liability to being conditioned as the exerciser of power. In order to indicate the absoluteness of the Deity, it is often said that all things are done by His Word. The Word of God eternally uttered contains within itself the totality of phenomenal manifestations. The universe is nothing but the meaning of this Word.

There is a class of interpreters who put a different construction on this nineteenth verse by rendering the original word for beginningless as "not the beginning," in the sense of the ultimate; but this is not to be accepted. Because if God, as Himself, is taken as the First Cause of all things, then Prakriti and Purusha must have been created by Him. Consequently, before their creation God's lordly power would have been absent, and this power being absent, He could not have been the Lord. If the Deity creates, as Himself, without these two instruments, then this universe would have been as real as Himself, and eternal life would have been a mere alternative expression for annihilation; there would have been no bondage or liberation, and all revealed Scriptures and doctrines would have been purposeless and void.

By admitting the co-eternity of Prakriti and Purusha, and the independence of the Absolute Deity, and His identity with consciousness under whatever apparent conditions manifested, all this is avoided. The same truth may be stated by saying that the will of God is the mysterious union between matter and spirit, which are respectively His false or exterior and real or interior nature. The wise words of the great commentator are: "God being eternal, His two natures must also be eternal, because they form His divinity. Through them He creates, preserves, and destroys the universe."

Another misconception must also be removed. It is not reasonable to think of any cause prior to Prakriti and Purusha, for that only leads to a *regressus in infinitum*. The truth is, that to deny the eternity of the powers of God, called Prakriti and Purusha, is to deny the existence of God; because God without His nature and His independence of nature is nothing. It is distinctly to be stated that God really or interiorly is the Absolute.

20. In the production of cause and effect, the cause is said to be Prakriti:[1] in the production of experiencership of pleasure and pain, Purusha is said to be the cause.[2]

"Cause" may here be interpreted in two ways; either as meaning the five senses, five organs, manas, ahankâra, and buddhi, or as

[1] "Cause is said to be Prakriti;" that is, the initiating cause of all action in the universe. "Is said" refers to Kapila, the divine sage, with whom were born righteousness, knowledge, dispassion, and power. The Blessed Lord says, "Among the perfect I am Kapila" (Chap. X. v. 26.)

[2] "Purusha is said to be the cause." Purusha does not here mean the Supreme Spirit, but the Ego as connected with Kshetra, by the connection called ignorance (avidyâ). He is the cause by reason of this connection.

the seven secondary causes; namely, buddhi, ahankâra, and the five subtle elements. The connotation of "effect" will depend upon that given to "cause." If this term is accepted in the former sense, then "effect" would mean the gross physical frame; in the other case it would include the sixteen non-producing products of root-nature as accepted by Sânkhya philosophers; namely, five senses, five organs, manas, and five gross elements.

These two powers are the cause of the universe; because, without the productive capacity of Prakriti, and the cognizing power of Purusha, the universe cannot exist. But the universe is the connection called ignorance, existing between the objective Prakriti, which contains cause and effect, and the subject Purusha.

The experiencing of pleasure and pain is the perceptible universe, which is only another expression for the bondage of the Ego. According to the Sânkhya philosophers, Prakriti, being unconscious, cannot be the experiencer; but there is no objection to her being the agent, only performing action when cognized by consciousness by relation to her through the mysterious power of ignorance. It is observed that the teats of the cow exude milk when the calf is near; thus by the rational, not spacial, proximity of Purusha, Prakriti works, — in the same way as a blind man makes his way out of a forest even if a cripple mounts upon his back to direct him.

The experiencership of Purusha has been mentioned. To what is it due?

21. Purusha seated[1] in Prakriti[2] experiences the qualities born of Prakriti: the cause of his birth in good and evil wombs is self-identification with qualities.

The acceptance of the experience of pleasure and pain and indifference existing in Prakriti as belonging to the Ego, is the chief cause of birth, disease, and death. The sacred authority declares, "What he desires, that becomes a determination; and what he determines here, that he becomes on passing away."

Two causes of birth are here mentioned, — self-identification with qualities, and Prakriti, in which the Ego is seated. Prakriti is the material cause, and supplies the material for the construction of this

---

[1] "Seated," that is, accepting Prakriti as the Self.
[2] *Prakriti*, in the sense of avidyâ, or the binding and not the liberating aspect of Prakriti as explained by Sânkhya philosophy. (See Sânkhya Kârikâ, Aph. XLIII.) In the latter aspect she is Vidyâ, or spiritual knowledge.

"baseless fabric of a dream." Self-identification with qualities is the instrumental cause in this construction.

The mention of the extremes, good and evil wombs, includes birth as a god, a human being, or an animal. The ego, said to vary in one body from that in another body, is celestial, terrestrial, or bestial, according to the attributes with which it is identified. Stripped of the "muddy vesture of decay," it is none of these, but pure consciousness, which is the spirit of God. Upon the birth of a creature upon the earth, the ego does not start from absolute nothingness, but it was in the purpose and design of God from beginningless past time. The purpose and design of God is Prakriti, which is ceaselessly at work. An ego dwells in Prakriti by undergoing endless incarnations until it knows what Prakriti is; in other words, until it knows the Divine purpose of its existence. When this is realized Nirvâna is attained.

The bondage of the ego is neither essential nor accidental, but false, being due to ignorance or illusion. The ego thus bound is liberated by the realization that in truth it is not subject to such bondage. The thinking principle is the cause of bondage as well as of liberation. When operating in relation to objects it is bondage; when not operating in relation to objects by reason of the perception of their falsehood and the reality of the ego alone, it is liberation.

22. The Purusha in the body is supreme,[1] is upadrashtâ,[2] anumantâ,[3] bhartâ,[4] bhoktâ,[5] Maheçvara,[6] and also called [7] Paramâtmâ.[8]

[1] "Supreme;" that is, superior to Prakriti.

[2] *Upadrashtâ;* that is, the innermost in us, as well as the witnessing spirit; in other words, that which is the centre of all, body, mind, and intelligence, and at the same time is not an object, but is absolute consciousness. The term also implies that the spirit is merely the on-looker, and is not concerned about the body and its acts.

[3] *Anumantâ;* that is, producer of satisfaction in the doer of an act, though not himself concerned in action, still appearing as such; witnessing the work of all, and never forbidding any.

[4] *Bhartâ;* that is, the true consciousness which is reflected as the consciousness in the assemblage of the body and the interior faculties; hence, "the supporter."

[5] *Bhoktâ;* the consciousness which, pervading the buddhi as units of consciousness, appears as conscious beings.

[6] *Maheçvara,* "the great Lord." Consciousness as connected with the whole universe. "This is the Lord of all, the great master of all things, this the ruler of worlds," says the sacred text.

[7] "Called," in the Vedas.

[8] *Paramâtmâ;* the âtmâ, or spirit as the consciousness in the First Cause. The term is explained in Chapter XV. verse 17.

Know that which thou callest "I" and blindly givest attributes to is the Absolute Emperor of the universe, the Creator, Destroyer, and Preserver of all. The being within thee which experiences objects is the personal ruler of the universe; the true Self is the consciousness which manifests this knowledge, and therefore identical in all but name with the consciousness in the First Cause. Existence as man and its good and evil experiences are entirely false. Die to the falsehood and thou shalt live in truth. The realization or true knowledge of this annihilation before God is liberation or eternal life.

23. Whoso thus[1] knoweth Purusha and Prakriti,[2] together with the qualities, he, though engaged[3] in everything, is not born again.

"Again" refers to the time after the dissolution of the present body. What happens to his beginningless past Karma, as well as to that of the present and of the future time in which the existence of the body continues? The sacred authority says, "His Karma is destroyed by realizing Him who is the superior as well as the inferior nature."

Does death of the body then follow the attainment of spiritual knowledge? No; as in that case no spiritual teacher could have existed; and without spiritual teachers the acquirement of knowledge is quite impossible.

What Karma is it, then, that keeps him alive? The Karma that was in operation at the time when knowledge was attained. It is difficult to understand how this residue is left on the consumption of Karma by the fire of knowledge. The explanation is that all acts done by the sage, after his illumination, are not done by him, because he knows himself to be the unknowable consciousness which is identical with the Absolute and Actionless Spirit. Consequently such acts produce no change or effect in him such as could be the seed of future Karma.

[1] "Thus;" that is, directly realizes Purusha, — "I am he."

[2] *Prakriti;* owing to this realization he destroys avidyâ, together with all its modifications, by vidyâ. "As light destroys the mass of darkness, so vidyâ, avidyâ," says the revered commentator. When the darkness is destroyed there remains no further use for the light, and then the ineffable life in God, the true Self, is found.

[3] "Though engaged," etc.; even if he does things that are enjoined or prohibited by scriptural authority.

The stored-up Karma is destroyed because its root, avidyâ, and desire are destroyed by knowledge and dispassion. But the Karma already in operation is not destroyed, because it is not perceived by the sage, as his body is to him like a shadow, or as one of the illusions created by avidyâ and previously considered as himself. He now realizes that his body has nothing to do with him, the Ego, or true Self; but as knowledge is no impediment to the operation of illusion in regard to others, so in the case of the body its acts are perceived by them to continue as begun.

An illustration may be given. A man is surprised in the night by a robber, as he thinks. He shoots at the untimely visitor, and instantly sees, by a flash of lightning, that he had mistaken a friend for a robber. He throws down his weapon, but that does not prevent the shot discharged from wounding the friend.

In the first twelve chapters the conception of the individual spirit and of the universal spirit is purified; in this chapter their identity is declared. "Know Me to be even as the Kshetrajna." The Blessed Lord now proceeds to unfold the various ways of realizing this life-giving truth.

24. By meditation [1] some realize the âtmâ in the heart by the buddhi; [2] others by Sânkhya Yoga, [3] and others again by Karma Yoga. [4]

The condition of the very lowest is next considered.

25. Others, again, not knowing this, [5] worship assiduously, [6] hearing from others, even they go beyond death, [7]

---

[1] "Meditation," which consists in withdrawing all the senses from their objects and merging them in the mind, and then the mind in the individual spirit. This is appropriate for the moderately spiritual, who cannot perceive the truth from its simple declaration, but must quiet all disturbing influences by concentration of mind on the scriptural declarations about Truth which is the real nature of the Spirit.

[2] *Buddhi;* the purified inner faculties.

[3] *Sânkhya Yoga;* realization of the Ego as distinct from the three qualities which constitute avidyâ. There is no reference here to the philosophy of Kapila. This is possible to the most spiritual only.

[4] *Karma Yoga;* the dedication of all action to the Deity. Fit practice for those incapable of the others.

[5] "Not knowing this;" that is, unable to believe in it from personal examination of the Scriptures, they receive it on the authority of others.

[6] "Worship assiduously;" that is, meditate on it constantly.

[7] "Go beyond death;" that is, escape from conditioned life by slow degrees.

making the hearing of the Scriptures[1] their supreme goal.

26. Whenever the least thing, animate or inanimate, is born, know that to be from the union of the Kshetra and the Kshetrajna.

Unions are usually of two kinds: 1. Like the union of the rope to the water-jar round the neck of which it is tied; 2. Like the union of blackness and an object, together forming a black object. The "union" here spoken of is different from these; it consists in the ascription of the properties of one to the other. The Ego is absolutely different from the non-ego, yet a relation between them is perceived. This is due to the ascription of objectivity to the Ego and of consciousness to the object. This false knowledge disappears when it is perceived that consciousness has no relation to objects. The result of this realization is the disappearance of objects; namely, the universality of the universal spirit and the individuality of the individual spirit, and then liberation is accomplished, suffering is extinguished, and the Truth is known. He who once attains this knowledge is deluded no more, whether he lives or dies, and whatever he may do. He is free as the air, bound by no laws of any kind. (Cf. John iii. 8.)

The extinction of false knowledge is further treated of in order to impress us with the fact that this is the supreme consummation of existence.

27. Whoso sees the supreme Lord[2] remaining equal[3] in all creatures, undestroyed in the destruction of them all,[4] sees indeed.

28. Perceiving the Lord as differenceless, existing equally everywhere, he does not destroy the Self by himself, and therefore goes to the supreme end.

---

[1] "Hearing of the Scriptures," etc.; hearing includes all requisites of proper study. This is the chief expedient for the lowest.

[2] "Supreme Lord;" from the standpoint of the consciousness dwelling in "union" with the body.

[3] "Equal;" although the Supreme Spirit is in all creatures, it still has no differences.

[4] "Undestroyed in . . . them all;" destruction includes all the six changes to which every creature is subject. To be destroyed, a creature must have passed through birth, existence after birth, growth, decay, and change of substance.

The Deity is differenceless since he is the one and secondless consciousness; there is nothing either similar to or different from the Deity. It must not be forgotten that in the Deity the idea that " I am and nothing but I am " does not exist. The meaning of the saying that " the Supreme Spirit is one and secondless " is the negation of such an idea, which would imply a searching for something, and then feeling that the impulse to search finds rest without finding anything. This, being a mental process, is to be negatived with regard to the Deity, who is " without life and without mind," according to sacred authority.

The Deity is the plenitude of bliss, is unconditioned consciousness, the absolute perfection, and therefore devoid of all impulse of any kind which, being the invariable sign of want and imperfection, do not belong to the real nature of the Deity.

" Existing equally everywhere " is a paradox ; for " everywhere " implies differentiation, and " equally " is the negation of all differences. All that is, is the Supreme, yet the Deity is nothing but the Deity. There is no simile for the wide expanse of the heavens, nor for the waters of the ocean ; how much less can there be a simile for the unsearchable God, whose image the universe cannot hold, in search of a perfect representation of whom Brahmâ is said to be eternally creating and abandoning creation in despair. Here lies the great difference between Truth and Pantheism. The Pantheist says, " Nothing but God is, and He is the Universe." The true devotee says, " Nothing but God is, and He is not the Universe." The great commentator says, " The Supreme Spirit is different from the universe. Besides that Spirit nothing is ; that which is different from the Spirit is a false seeming, like a mirage of the desert."

" Does not destroy the Self by himself." It is well known that even the most foolish do not consciously injure themselves. The wise man who knows his identity with God does not seek to kill himself by casting out God.

The unwise, who do not know that the Self is identical with God, are guilty of suicide, and must therefore wander in the utter gloom of unrest. The Scripture says, " Sunless are those spheres, wrapped up in blinding gloom, whither repair after death the creatures who are murderers of the Self," meaning in the above sense.

It has been said that "the Lord is equally everywhere." How can this be harmonized with the observable differences in personalities ?

29. Whoso sees every variety of action as performed by Prakriti,[1] and also the Ego[2] as non-actor,[3] he sees indeed.

Not only is the Ego undifferentiated while existing in all things, but also the things themselves are not different from one another, being but various modifications of Prakriti, which is one. To show this it is said: —

30. At the time when he recognizes[4] the distinctions of things as merged in one,[5] and therefore also the manifestations, then he becomes the Supreme Spirit.

How the absoluteness of the Deity remains unaffected, even though manifested in various forms, is next spoken of: —

31. By reason of being causeless,[6] attributeless,[7] this, the Supreme Spirit, is changeless, and though in the body,[8] O Kuntî's son, he neither acts nor is attached.

The Supreme Spirit "neither acts nor is attached" to the result of action or to action itself. If the Supreme Spirit is the Ego and does not act, who is the actor? This question the Blessed Lord

---

[1] *Prakriti*, the illusive power of the Deity, the same that the Sânkhya school calls the "rootless root," the unconscious producer of all that is produced.

[2] "Ego," the Kshetrajna.

[3] "Non-actor," that is, unconditioned.

[4] "Recognizes," that is, following the teaching of the Scriptures and the preceptors, he gradually acquires a vivid realization of the truth underlying those teachings, and feels that the truth he realizes is what they taught him.

[5] "Merged in one." He perceives that all this is the Self; therefore life, mind, expectation, the elements, appearance, and disappearance are in reality but the Spirit. In other words, all that appears to exist is really Self appearing in so many forms through the power of illusion, which is also called the creative energy.

[6] "Being causeless" or beginningless, the Ego which is realized as identical with the Supreme Spirit can have no limbs or parts strung together and harmonized into a whole. That which has no limbs cannot act except when action is its essential characteristic, as in the case of Prakriti. But unlike Prakriti, the Ego is

[7] "Attributeless," while Prakriti is the union of the three qualities. Therefore the action implied in having different qualities does not apply to the Supreme Spirit; and further, the Supreme Spirit cannot have any action through nature, because there is no nature that can be regarded as peculiarly his, as the great nature is but his power. Therefore the Spirit is changeless.

[8] "In the body," that is, perceived through misconception as connected with the body.

answers, "Nature only acts;" nature being the same as avidyâ (Chap. V. v. 14).

The freedom of the Ego from action and attachment is explained by illustrations.

32. As space, though all-pervading, is not attached, by reason of its subtlety, so the âtmâ, though seated in all kinds of bodies, is not attached.

33. As one sun manifests all this world, the Kshetrajna manifests all Kshetras, O son of Bharata.

The illustration of the sun applies to the unity of the Kshetrajna in spite of the variety of Kshetras, and also to its want of attachment to conditions. The sun manifests this world with its mountains and valleys, sea and land; but the sun does not thereby become many, nor is the sun defiled by the impurities it brings to sight.

If we take the sun as the Ego, and consider a number of saucers full of water as human beings, then it will be seen that although there is one sun in reality, yet each saucer seemingly has a sun of its own. While the reflected sun is taken for *the* sun, the motion of the water from the breezes will give a seeming motion to the sun. If the saucer is broken and the water runs out, then a man who has never known the sun except by attributing reality to a reflection, will think the sun is destroyed; but not so the man who recognizes the sun in the saucer as merely the reflection of the blessed sun in the heavens. As a child may imagine the sun to be extinguished when clouds prevent his seeing the sun, so when the knowledge within us is veiled by ignorance we imagine non-identity with the Deity.

The chapter concludes with a summary of its contents.

34. Those who, with wisdom's eye,[1] thus perceive the difference between the Kshetra and the Kshetrajna, and also the extinction of the nature of objects,[2] go into the Supreme.[3]

[1] "Wisdom's eye;" the instruction of Scriptures and preceptors. The Vedas are called the eye of the ancestors, gods and men.

[2] "Nature of objects;" avidyâ, the illusive power which brings into existence objects essentially unreal.

[3] "Go into the Supreme;" escaping from the wheel of migratory existence, attain Nirvâna.

Thus ends chapter the thirteenth, called "RIGHT KNOWLEDGE OF THE DISCRIMINATION BETWEEN KSHETRA AND KSHETRAJNA," in the blessed BHAGAVAD GÎTÂ, the sacred lore, the divine wisdom, the book of divine union, the colloquy between the blessed KRISHNA and ARJUNA, and contained in the Bhîshma Parvan of the blessed MAHÂBHÂRATA, which is a collection of one hundred thousand verses by VYÂSA.

By the realization of objectivity and its distinctness from the Ego, which is in reality pure unconditioned consciousness, not different from the Supreme Spirit, all and every suffering comes to an end, and the crown and consummation of being is reached.

Salutation to Krishna, who is that truth which separates the Kshetra from the Kshetrajna.

CHAPTER XIV.

RIGHT KNOWLEDGE OF THE DIVISION OF THE THREE QUALITIES.

ALL that is produced is due to the union of the objective Prakriti and the subject Purusha (Chap. XIII. v. 26). This chapter is intended to show that this union is dependent upon the will of God, and not — as is held by the Sânkhya philosophers — that in the production of the universe, with all its functions, Prakriti and Purusha are independent.

The cause of birth in good and evil wombs is said to be self-identifying attachment to the qualities. This is rendered clear by amplification; the subject is treated by dividing it into six different topics, namely : —

1. Depending upon the Divine will, the confusion of identity between Prakriti and Purusha, and the attachment of the latter to qualities of Prakriti, is the cause of the universe (vv. 3, 4).
2. The different kinds of attachment according to the difference of the qualities to which the attachment is made (v. 5).
3. The different qualities defined.
4. How the Ego is bound by them (v. 10).
5. How liberation from the qualities is gained (vv. 17-20).
6. What liberation implies (vv. 21-27).

THE BLESSED LORD *spoke:*

1. Again[1] I shall declare the supreme,[2] excellent[3]

---

[1] "Again;" although the purport of what follows is found in what has been said, it is again presented on account of the great difficulty in properly comprehending the truth.

[2] "Supreme;" that is, relating to that which is the supreme end of existence. This epithet refers to the object-matter of knowledge.

[3] "Excellent," that is, yielding the ultimate end of being. This refers to the value of this knowledge to the wise.

knowledge of the wise.[1] Knowing this the sages have attained supreme success from here.[2]

The reason for declaring the value of this knowledge is to increase the hearer's receptivity.

2. Having taken refuge[3] in this knowledge, those who attain to my state[4] are not born at the time of creation, nor are they pained at the season of dissolution.[5]

According to sacred authorities creation is of three kinds: (1) That which is taking place every moment; (2) That which takes place when all the inferior products of Nature are absorbed into the universal mind; (3) That in which the universal egotism (ahankâra) is dissolved into the First Cause. Here the last is referred to.

It may at first appear as if the declaration of a specific result meant that even in Nirvâna there is a sense of separateness; but this is not so. The specific result is here mentioned only to attract the hearer to the right path. By the figure of speech called understatement, the absolute being, or Nirvâna, is intended to affect the hearer for whom the absolute would be a mere word.

3. My great Prakriti is the womb into which I cast the seed; from that, O Bharata's son, is the birth of all creatures.

"Prakriti" is called "great" because it is all-comprehending; and "my" because I (meaning the Supreme) am not dominated

---

[1] "Of the wise;" that is, the knowledge about to be imparted is not one among the class of qualities beginning with want of consciousness of merit, described in the preceding chapter (v. 7 *et seq.*).

[2] "From here," after the dissolution of the body.

[3] "Having taken refuge;" that is, performing all that is needed for the reception of truth; namely, studying revealed philosophy, meditating on it, assimilating it, and then being effaced in the truth thus made manifest.

[4] "My state" does not mean a state similar to mine, because that would be opposed to the identity of the individual and universal spirit which is uniformly taught by the Blessed Lord, "Know me as the Kshetrajna in every Kshetra" (Chap. XIII. v. 2).

[5] "Dissolution," the period of universal dissolution.

by it. Prakriti means matter in every form, and is the assemblage of the three qualities, and by true knowledge is shown to be unrelated to consciousness; consciousness is the spirit of God from the standpoint of one who is aspiring to the knowledge of God. Hence the Deity is not touched by the false knowledge from which the aspirant seeks to escape, and without this false knowledge there is no bondage to Prakriti. Consequently Prakriti depends upon the will of God, by which the power of true knowledge is shaded. It is to be understood that the Prakriti of the Sânkhya philosophers is here spoken of.

The "seed" was for the birth of the creator Brahmâ, and corresponds to the power referred to in Genesis: "the spirit of God moved upon the face of the waters." This seed is false knowledge, desire, and regulation of desire. I, the Deity, the lord of the two powers Kshetra and Kshetrajna, unite the unchanging Kshetrajna to object-producing power consisting of the three qualities.

Prakriti and Purusha are united by a power called false knowledge, and disunited by a power called true knowledge. The series of phenomena, creation, preservation, and destruction, is the relation between knowledge, true and false. Time is the relation between these three great classes into which existence is divided.

Both true and false knowledge exist. That which is now is the false knowledge; true knowledge is its opposite, and disunites Prakriti from Purusha. Consequently true knowledge makes Prakriti disappear, first as containing Purusha and then as separate from Purusha. In other words, through true knowledge Purusha is independent of Prakriti. True knowledge is eternal because unrelated to Time, which touches only the three, which are nature, consciousness conditioned through illusion, and the relation between them, or illusion itself; therefore Purusha is eternally unrelated to Prakriti. In other words, God is, and through mere being is the ruler of Prakriti.

On the other hand, false knowledge is eternal because time is included in it; therefore the universe is eternal, and the bondage of Purusha is eternal in the sense of not ending by mere lapse of time. The whole cannot be changed by the relative change of its parts. But true knowledge is the opposite of false knowledge; therefore they cannot co-exist except by destroying each other, leaving a third thing; namely, the Ego, which is the witness of both. This realization is liberation.

Purusha, or consciousness, neither is nor is not related to Prakriti, which is the co-inherence of the true and false knowledge, of bondage and liberation. Therefore it is justly said, the Ego is never bound or loosened; that is to say, one who is liberated is not conscious of being liberated after bondage or desiring to be liberated, — the Ego is the Ego *per se*.

4. In all wombs, O son of Kuntî, whatever forms are born, of them the great womb is Prakriti, and I am the seed-giving father.[1]

This verse refers to gods, men, and animals. Whatever apparent cause exists there is but one real cause, and that is the union of Purusha and Prakriti. Even the Creator, Brahmâ, is an instrument of the Deity. The whole universe may be considered as the objective form of the Supreme Spirit, who really has no form.

The qualities are now described.

5. O thou of mighty arms, sattva, rajas, and tamas, these Prakriti-born[2] qualities bind[3] to the body the unchanging lord of the body.[4]

6. Among them sattva, illuminative on account of its transparency and restfulness, O sinless one,[5] ties through attachment to happiness and knowledge.

Sattva is transparent in the sense that the all-pervasive consciousness is manifested by it as sunlight is by a transparent medium. Those objects which have the least of this power are considered as unconscious by us. The sattva quality is the most spiritual part of nature. Its manifestations are the higher virtues and spiritual

---

[1] "Seed-giving father;" that is, the fructifying cause.

[2] "Prakriti-born." The perfectly harmonious commingling of the qualities is Prakriti, and as any action takes place, one or other of the three qualities asserts its prominence; in this sense alone are the qualities born of Prakriti.

[3] "Bind;" that is, connect it with the experience of pain and pleasure by reason of the error that the body is the spirit, which it is not.

[4] "Lord of the body;" Kshetrajna, the consciousness as connected with the body.

[5] "O sinless one." Those whose sins have been exhausted through the means prescribed by the Scriptures are alone able fully to comprehend spiritual philosophy.

insight. The universal spirit possesses the acme of this power or quality as one of his powers. He only is good,—all other beings are evil,—and that which is manifested as good in us is really this power of the Deity, the fruits of the Spirit of God (Gal. v. 22 *et seq.*).

Through sattva the Ego appears to be happy and wise. To be happy is an experience; therefore happiness is an object, and consequently its relation to consciousness is not essential, but is produced by false knowledge. Similarly, when wisdom is attributed to the Ego it is through false knowledge. The true Ego is absolute. "I am that I am."

7. Know rajas to be the embodiment of desire, and the producer of thirst and relish; that, O Kuntî's son, ties the ego through attachment to action.[1]

Rajas seems, as it were, to lay the colors on the transparent sattva. "I am happy, I know," is the expression of the pure, calm state of the heart. On this ground, like patches of color, arise such thoughts as, "I want this, I have it, I like it, and want to keep it." Thus it manifests itself in thirst for absent things and relish in possession of them.

8. Know tamas as born of insensibility,[2] the deluder[3] of all embodied creatures, O Bharata's son; it ties through heedlessness,[4] laziness,[5] and sleep.[6]

9. Sattva attaches to happiness, rajas to actions, while tamas, veiling[7] the power of discrimination, attaches to heedlessness.

The mode of operation of the three qualities is next shown.

---

[1] "Attachment to action," both present and future.
[2] "Insensibility," that power in Prakriti which does not reflect consciousness.
[3] "Deluder," the cause of the acceptance of falsehood for truth.
[4] "Heedlessness," the non-performance of what is intended to be done, on account of attachment to some other things.
[5] "Laziness," lack of energy and enthusiasm to complete what is begun.
[6] "Sleep" includes stupor.
[7] "Veiling," etc.; that is, obscuring the clearness of perception due to sattva, causes non-performance of right action. The power to perceive spiritual truths belongs to sattva, but tamas causes their oblivion at time of action.

10. Overcoming rajas and tamas, sattva asserts itself, O Bharata's son; similarly, rajas, sattva and tamas, and tamas, sattva and rajas.

Those who desire the cultivation of sattva must overcome the other two qualities. In order to impress this upon the mind, the mode of the operation of the qualities is given. The effect of one of the three is perceived when the other two are overborne.

11. When at every gate[1] of the body there is the illumination of knowledge, then know that sattva is dominant.

12. Greed,[2] initiation of action,[3] energy in great worldly achievements, unrest, and thirst, these are born on rajas becoming dominant.

13. Non-illumination,[4] non-initiation, heedlessness, and delusion,[5] — these, O son of Kuru, are born on tamas becoming dominant.

The future condition of creatures is due to attachment and desire, and is therefore dependent on the power of the qualities.

14. If the embodied self experience death when sattva is dominant, he obtains the stainless[6] spheres of the knowers of good.[7]

15. Experiencing death when rajas is dominant, he is born in spheres of attachment to action.[8] And so,

---

[1] "At every gate," that is, all the senses and faculties attain the fullest manifestation of power, and thereby remove all sense of effort or inability.

[2] "Greed," desire of that which is possessed by others.

[3] "Initiation of action," striving for objects in general without any special end in view.

[4] "Non-illumination," want of discriminating power, external and internal.

[5] "Delusion," stupidity and gross folly.

[6] "Stainless," free from rajas and tamas.

[7] "Knowers of good," those who know the nature of buddhi, or are worshippers of the cause of the physical universe.

[8] "Spheres of ... action," as a human being.

one dead when tamas is dominant is born in deluded wombs.¹

The varieties of disposition due to the qualities, and the consequences of such dispositions, have been enumerated in the three preceding verses. The influence of the qualities on actions is next declared.

16. They² call the fruit of righteous acts as pure and pertaining to sattva: of rajas the fruit is pain³: and the fruit of tamas is insensibility.⁴

Rom. vi. 23.

17. From sattva arises knowledge,⁵ from rajas greed, from tamas heedlessness and delusion, as also spiritual blindness.

18. Those established in sattva⁶ go upwards;⁷ those belonging to rajas remain in the middle;⁸ and those established in the functions of the lowest quality — those belonging to tamas — go below.⁹

The preceding chapter briefly says (v. 21): "The cause of his birth in good and evil wombs is self-identification with qualities."

The foregoing verses of the present chapter explain the nature of false knowledge and the qualities which cause bondage. Liberation from attachment to the qualities comes from right knowledge, as is shown in the following verses.

---

1 "Deluded wombs," as creatures in whom the power of consciousness is very limited.

2 "They," that is, the wise. One authority says Kapila, the founder of Sânkhya philosophy, and his disciples.

3 "Pain" is the consequence of action in which right is mixed with wrong; pain predominates, while there is still some pleasure.

4 "Insensibility." The consequence of vice is pain varied by insensibility to pain.

5 "Knowledge," right perception by all the senses and faculties.

6 "Established in sattva;" acquiring spiritual knowledge and acting under the influence of sattva.

7 "Go upwards;" are born in celestial spheres.

8 "Middle;" the human sphere.

9 "Go below;" born as irrational beings, or as some say, in hell.

19. While the wise man who does not perceive the actor as different from the qualities,[1] and also perceives what is different[2] from the qualities, attains to my state.[3]

20. The ego in the body transcending these three qualities from which the body is produced, and being liberated from birth, death, decay, and sorrow, attains immortality.

Whenever the three qualities, or Prakriti and Purusha, are discriminately known, liberation is reached.

The question naturally arises as to what characteristics are found in one who has attained such liberation, because characteristics natural to him are to be acquired by the aspirants as means for the accomplishment of the desired end.

Arjuna *said:*

21. By what characteristics does a man become known, O Lord, as having transcended these three qualities? What is such an one's behavior, and how does such an one transcend these three qualities?

The Blessed Lord *spoke:*

22. Illumination, engaging in action, as also delusion, O Pându's son, when in activity he does not hate,[4] nor wish for when ended,[5]

---

[1] "Different from the qualities;" that is, the qualities are being modified into cause and effect, and under their influence it appears as if the ego were the actor.

[2] "What is different;" that is, consciousness, by relation to which through false knowledge the qualities exist at all.

[3] "My state," Nirvâna. Realizes that all this is really the ego.

[4] "He does not hate;" that is, when any one of the three qualities asserts itself he does not wish to check it.

[5] "Wish for when ended;" that is, one established in sattva wishes for the domination by sattva of the other two qualities when they assert themselves. This answers the question as to the characteristics of one who transcends the qualities.

23. Who, remaining as disinterested,[1] is not perturbed by the qualities;[2] "the qualities prevail, overcoming one another;" who, thus fixed, is not moved;

24. Equal towards enjoyment and suffering, seated in Self;[3] equal towards a clod of earth, stone, and gold; equal towards the desirable and the undesirable,[4] wise, equal towards blame and adulation;

25. Equal towards honor and disgrace; equal towards friendly and hostile sides;[5] abandoner[6] of all initiation, is called beyond the qualities.

26. And also Me[7] whoso worships in unwavering union of love,[8] he, completely transcending the qualities, is able to become the Supreme God.[9]

This answers as to how the qualities are transcended. The path of love is mentioned because the condition of sages illuminated by knowledge is comprehended in the two previous answers.

27. Even of the Supreme Ruler, immortal and unmodifying; of the eternal law of righteousness; of the acme of bliss, — I am the support.

---

[1] "As disinterested;" that is, unattached to the qualities and their actions.

[2] "The qualities," etc. In consequence of the realization of the distinctness of the Purusha from the qualities, it is perceived that all that is cause and all that is effect are but the three qualities and their modifications. This answers the question as to behavior.

[3] "Seated in Self;" that is, independent of all objects.

[4] "Desirable and the undesirable," from the point of view of others.

[5] "Equal towards friendly ... sides;" not only disinterested as regards his own apparent interest, but also for that of others; the true object of spiritual interest of the human race is one and the same, — the Deity, who is the true and only Self.

[6] "Abandoner;" engaging in no action not indispensable for the maintenance of the body.

[7] "Me;" the Spirit, which though one yet dwells in every heart.

[8] "Unwavering union of love;" an all-exclusive, changeless love; never thinking of the condition of bondage.

[9] "Able to become ... God;" that is, attains Nirvâna through the grace of God, even before the dissolution of the body. "To become God" in scriptural language means "to be in the form of God."

Here ends chapter the fourteenth, called "RIGHT KNOWLEDGE OF THE DIVISION OF THE THREE QUALITIES," in the blessed BHAGAVAD GÎTÂ, the sacred lore, the divine wisdom, the book of divine union, the colloquy between the blessed KRISHNA and ARJUNA, and contained in the Bhîshma Parvan of the blessed MAHÂBHÂRATA, which is a collection of one hundred thousand verses by VYÂSA.

The Blessed Lord as the Spirit is the spirit of the Supreme Ruler whose nature is immortality and eternity; perfect spiritual illumination reveals the truth that the Spirit of God is the only true Spirit in Being. The "eternal law of righteousness" is the power or ability to attain Nirvâna; the knowledge by which the identity with the Deity is manifested to the devotee is also the Deity; the power and the powerful being the same. In this sense the Blessed Lord is the support of the Supreme God. God is, because the true Ego is the Spirit of God.

In this chapter has been explained how the union between Kshetra and Kshetrajna causes the universe; the extinction of conditioned existence by perfect knowledge is declared. The natural characteristics of one who has transcended the qualities are also explained, for the purpose of indicating the proper means to the aspirant for liberation; and finally, it is said that all-exclusive love of the Deity is the easiest road to salvation.

Salutation to Krishna, whose devotee easily crosses over the ocean of existence produced by attachment to the three qualities.

CHAPTER XV.

RIGHT KNOWLEDGE OF THE SUPREME SPIRIT.

It has been said that by right knowledge the bondage of conditioned existence is cut asunder (Chap. XIV. v. 19). It has also been said that this knowledge can be acquired only through the grace of God, who grants it to the aspirant either through another human form, called his preceptor, or in some inscrutable way (Chap. IV. v. 34). The truth that the fruit of all action and the realization of identity with God in real essence, or as consciousness, are dependent finally upon God's will, and not upon human will, is declared as supreme. In the last verse but one of the foregoing chapter the Blessed Lord says that He grants liberation to His devotee.

As knowledge of God is the only road to salvation, the Blessed Lord proceeds to declare the right knowledge of the Self, by the bestowal of which He rescues His devotee from death. This knowledge which saves is not a mere intellectual form, but real consciousness, — a new life, in fact.

The Blessed Lord *spoke:*

1. Exhaustless they call the Açvattha,[1] with roots above[2] and branches below,[3] the leaves whereof are the Vedas;[4] who knows this knows the Vedas.[5]

---

[1] *Açvattha* — literally, fleeting, evanescent — here means the sacred fig-tree, *Ficus religiosa.* It symbolizes the universe, which is called exhaustless because it is without beginning, and ends only by spiritual knowledge and not in time.

[2] "Roots above;" that is, the Supreme Spirit, through the power called the first cause, is the root of the universe. Above, because the subtlety, permanence, and comprehensiveness of the cause transcends the effect.

[3] "Branches below;" the branches are the product of the first cause, which is Prakriti, under the oversight of the Spirit. These products are buddhi, ahankara, and the five subtle elements.

[4] "The leaves whereof are the Vedas;" because as leaves protect a tree, so the Vedas protect the universe by revealing the law of righteousness.

[5] "Knows the Vedas;" that is, whoever knows the Truth knows the Vedas, as they are but the embodiment of the Truth.

The endless stream of evolution is represented as a tree for the purpose of teaching that without complete purification through dispassion no one can ever know the mystery of God's being. At the same time it is not true that every pure and dispassionate man necessarily attains that knowledge of God which gives salvation. Besides purity of heart it is necessary to have the aspiration to know God; and this aspiration may be called love of God, love of liberation, love of Nirvâna, or love of truth.

This symbolism occurs in the Vedas: "This Açvattha, with roots above and branches below, is eternal." Elsewhere it is said:—

"Prakriti is the root, and supported by it this tree is raised, and buddhi is its trunk, and the crevices in it are the senses and organs; the subtle elements are its branches, and it is leafy with gross objects; good and evil are its flower, and pleasure and pain are its fruit; suited to the life of all creatures is this tree of Brahmă. This is also the abode of Brahmă; perpetually Brahmă dwells here; with the great sword of knowledge piercing and cutting it asunder, and thence obtaining the enjoyment of being the true Self, one does not revolve."

The idea is that nothing exists but God, and His nature has two aspects, as inseparable as sunshine and shadow. The first aspect is all that appears to be, and the other is His own independence of it, — otherwise called bondage and liberation. To realize this opposition of the two aspects of the Divine power — in other words, to see that what appears to be is not — is to know God. That which supports the existence of two mutually destructive things is beyond both and is the real nature of God, — Himself. This is the absolute majesty of God which is untouched by the universe that seems to be its negation, as also by the disclosure of the true character of the universe as seeming. He to whom this truth is as real as the pen is to the writer who holds it in his hand is in Nirvâna; he knows even as he is known.

2. Its branches,[1] having objects of sense for shoots and invigorated by the qualities,[2] spread above and

---

[1] "Branches;" that is, various creatures who are distinguished from one another by the difference of surroundings proceed to regions above or below according to their merits.

[2] "Qualities," meaning the three qualities, — goodness, passion, and ignorance.

below; and the roots,[1] having actions for their consequences in the world of men,[2] also penetrate down below.

3. Its form in this world is not perceived as such;[3] it has not end[4] nor beginning[5] nor middle,[6] — this Açvattha with roots[7] struck deep, having cut asunder with the firm sword of dispassion,[8]

4. Then[9] that seat, from which those who attain it fall back[10] no more, is to be sought by taking refuge in that Primeval Spirit, from whom is the beginningless flow of conditioned existence.

5. Without egotism and indiscrimination, having subdued the fault of attachment,[11] devoted to the thought of the nature of the Spirit,[12] with desires at rest,[13] free from the pairs of opposites called pleasure and pain, the undeluded go to that exhaustless seat

6. That is not manifested by Sun or Moon or Fire, and having gone there they fall not back; that is my Supreme abode.

Rev. xxi. 23; xxii. 5.

[1] "Roots;" that is, secondary causes, such as attachment and hatred, which produce the inexorable chain of causation, which by the will of God governs the experiences of conditioned beings.

[2] "World of men;" because in other worlds creatures are more contented and less changeful than men.

[3] "Is not perceived as such;" because if the true character of worldly existence is once perceived it vanishes like mist before the sun.

[4] "It has not end;" no man knows when it will end, because it can only end by illumination which comes according to no law. (Cf. Matt. xiii. 32.)

[5] "Nor beginning;" no man can say when the universe began.

[6] "Nor middle;" even its present condition cannot be understood.

[7] "Roots" etc., that is, the stream of worldly existence will not end if left to itself.

[8] "Firm sword of dispassion;" that is, with the face resolutely turned towards the Supreme God, perpetually practising dispassion with right discrimination.

[9] "Then;" after renunciation the supreme seat is to be sought.

[10] "Fall back;" that is, into migratory existence.

[11] "Having subdued . . . attachment," that is, being equal to friends and enemies.

[12] "Nature of the Spirit;" the mystery of the connection between the Absolute and the conditioned Self.

[13] "Desires at rest," as in sages who have perfected renunciation.

The sacred text says: "Not there shines the sun, nor moon, nor stars, nor shine these lightnings; where is there this fire? That light reflecting, these all shine; by the light of that all this is manifested."

Every union in nature is followed by disunion. Even then how there is no falling back from that seat is now explained.

7. Even a portion[1] of Me becoming the beginningless apparently conditioned ego in the world of such egos, draws in the six senses (together with the manas), existing in their proper relation of harmony.

The word "portion" might suggest the thought of the division of the Supreme, but in reality this division can appear through delusion alone. The usual illustration is that the light within an earthen pot which is pierced with holes issues from each opening as a distinct line of light; but if the pot is broken, the lines of light are merged in *the* light and do not again appear in those individual lines. For clearness other illustrations are given. By reflection on a number of surfaces the sun appears as many suns, but on the destruction of the reflectors the sun-images are lost in *the* sun forever. When the space occupied by an object merges into infinite space on the destruction of the object, it remains a part of *the* space. Immortality consists in the knowledge that the sun-image and the sun are one. The ego is the same as the Supreme Spirit, but immortality is an object called by some recognition, — of the oneness, of the want of change in the quality of consciousness, despite the infinitude of objects that exist by dependence on it.

The portioning of the Supreme Spirit into personal egos is due to false knowledge or creative power, and these illusive entities circulate in the wheel of evolution by causing a coherence of the various powers of sensation and reflection in a definite way, the whole system of evolution being as real or as imaginary as those egos. The immediate agency which causes this aggregation may be called pre-existing desires; this naturally gives rise to the inquiry as to what gives this power to desires. Philosophers solve this problem in two ways, according to their respective schools.

---

[1] "Even a portion," etc. The truth is that the conditioned ego, which never falls back after attaining the Supreme, is at no time really different from the Supreme.

By some it is called *Svabhavat*, or *natura rerum*, while others call it the will of God. Whichever term is used, the explanation is the same; the mysterious, ultimate cause is beyond comprehension, like the yellowness of gold. Both schools will admit that from our present point of view the Cause is conscious, and both will agree that by spiritual illumination the cause is seen to be separate from consciousness, and therefore non-existent except as the power of consciousness, and therefore *really* identical with it.

8. The Lord,[1] carrying these, proceeds to the body he receives, from the body he leaves, as the wind bears fragrance from the source thereof.

As the subtle perfume of flowers is borne away by the wind, so the conditioned ego carries with it the six powers before mentioned. The metaphor goes further. The ego is really all-pervading, like air; but as currents of wind circulate in reference to objects different from the air, so in reference to the body the ego appears to migrate; and this appearance is due to the operations of the mind and senses.

The individual ego — in other words, the conditioned ego considered at the lowest limit of conditions — is unfettered by human conceptions of time and space; mind and senses are necessary to relate it to these two classes of conditions. The individual and the universal spirit are coeval, the former not knowing the latter. Because, in order that the universal should be known by the individual it is necessary that their identity as *the* Spirit should be manifested, as knowledge is nothing more than the manifestation of the knower's relation to the object known.

The manifestation of this identity is but another way of saying that the co-related attributes of the Spirit which form the individual and universal spirit are rejected from consciousness, and the Absolute is itself. Ignorance of the universal Spirit is the essential condition for the existence of the individual spirit. It may be urged in opposition that the relation between the two is not identity, but some other which would enable the two to exist, and yet the individual know the universal; this is self-contradictory. The idea of individuality does not admit of the existence of things similar to itself. That is not individual which is unrelated to the universal, and it is

---

[1] "The Lord" of this assemblage of body and faculties.

obvious that that which is related to many can have no relation to the universal, which to be must absorb every variety within itself.

All being thus reduced to duality, it is clear that the universal Spirit must know the individual spirit. Otherwise where would the consciousness be to support the latter's existence by knowing it? It cannot know itself as the individual spirit except it also knows the universal Spirit, in relation to whom alone the individual is the individual, as has been said before.

The individual spirit can, therefore, exist only as "I do not know myself;" this is the meaning of individuality. The universal Spirit is "I know myself;" the "myself" in both cases being the same, and identical with the real nature of God.

This "I do not know myself" considered apart from consciousness is the primeval darkness over which the spirit of God or consciousness broods, and contains within itself the whole warp and woof of all that has been, is, or can be. The Son of God or universal Spirit knows this darkness is not I, and in this way is omniscient. Thus divested of self-identity with all objectivity, the self-existent consciousness is perceived not as an object but as the Self; while the individual knows that there is an I which he does not know, and is also contented with the want of knowledge. In other words, the individual believes himself to be an object; the stuff of this false belief about the Ego or Spirit is false knowledge (avidyâ), because the Ego is not an object. This seeming or false knowledge by its own nature counterfeits the I. The knowledge that the Ego is not an object is the only true knowledge of the Ego, which does not require to be known in order to be. Spiritual knowledge is not an intellectual acquirement; it is dispassion, universal love, and the faith that I am pure consciousness and nothing that can be the object of any operation; its consummation is Nirvâna.

9. Dominating ear, eye, skin, tongue, and nose, as well as the manas, he enjoys objects.

"He" is the personal ego, the being who feels in connection with the body that "I am the actor" and "I am the enjoyer." Ahankâra, apparently impregnated by consciousness, or, as it is technically called, receiving on it the reflection of consciousness, is the personal ego.

10. The deluded[1] do not see him, migrating, stationary, or experiencing qualities; but the wisdom-eyed[2] do perceive.

11. Men of tranquil hearts,[3] striving for it,[4] perceive him, seated in the buddhi;[5] but those of impure hearts,[6] and devoid of discrimination,[7] though striving for it, do not perceive him.

12. The splendor in the sun which illuminates the whole world, that which is also in the moon, that also in the fire, — know that splendor as mine.

The various luminous powers are but reflections of the same light, and that light is the Deity. It is to be understood that the Divine influence pervades everything; but all things do not manifest it equally, through the influence of the quality called tamas. This is an enlargement of the idea as to the illusive manifestation of the Deity as conditioned egos.

13. Also entering into the earth,[8] I uphold these creatures by my power,[9] and I nourish all vegetables by becoming Soma,[10] the embodiment of sapor.

Heb. i. 3; Gen. i. 29.

[1] "Deluded," that is, engrossed in material life.
[2] "Wisdom-eyed;" that is, those whose minds have been purified by spiritual knowledge.
[3] "Men of tranquil hearts;" those who are carnally dead, and alive in spirit.
[4] "Striving for it;" that is, through meditation and Scriptural study.
[5] "Seated in the buddhi;" that is, though connected with the body, yet separate from it.
[6] "Impure hearts;" those who have no control over their senses, and cannot concentrate their minds on one thing except for a short time; who have not abandoned evil habits, and whose egotism and vanity are not subjugated.
[7] "Devoid of discrimination;" turbulence of the senses causes defective perception.
[8] "Entering into the earth;" as its soul the divine power makes the earth what it is.
[9] "By my power;" that is, the fitness of the earth to be the dwelling-place of all creatures really comes from the Deity.
[10] *Soma* is the sacred plant said to embody all the sapor of the entire vegetable kingdom. If this sapor (or essence of taste) did not exist, no vegetable would have been eatable, and creatures could not have lived. The fitness of vegetables for food to sustain life is here indicated.

14. I, becoming Vaiçvânara,[1] and entering into the bodies of living creatures, digest the four kinds[2] of food, being joined with the upward and downward life-breaths.

15. I am also seated in the hearts of all;[3] from Me is recollection[4] and knowledge, as well as their removal; by all the Vedas I am to be known,[5] and I am also the author of the Vedânta,[6] as well as the knower of the Vedas.[7]

The remaining verses of this chapter contain an epitome of the whole book.

16. Two spirits[8] are there in the world,—the destructible[9] and the indestructible.[10] The destructible is all creatures, and the kûtastha[11] is called the indestructible.

17. But different is the Supreme Spirit,[12] called the Paramâtmâ,[13] who, the exhaustless God, having entered into the three spheres, supports[14] them.

[1] *Vaiçvânara* is the internal fire or energy which causes digestion in connection with respiration.

[2] "Four kinds;" according as the food is chewed, sucked, lapped, or drunk.

[3] "Seated in the hearts of all;" all creatures, from the ant to the highest god, are conscious because of the same Ego; each taking it as himself, through false knowledge.

[4] "Recollection:" that is, the righteous remember the law under all circumstances, which the unrighteous cannot do.

[5] "By all the Vedas I am to be known." The Lord is no other than the Supreme Spirit revealed by the Vedas.

[6] "The author of the Vedânta;" that is, the Primeval Teacher who was the first expounder of the true meaning of the Vedas.

[7] "The knower of the Vedas;" he who realizes the truth embodied in the Vedas is identical with the Supreme Spirit.

[8] "Two spirits;" the Supreme Spirit is seen through two different veils.

[9] "Destructible;" the material of all things, from the body of the most exalted creature to the fibre of wood. It is called spirit in accordance with popular usage, and for the purpose of indicating the Supreme Spirit by the process of elimination.

[10] "Indestructible;" the power of the Deity which causes the destructible.

[11] *Kûtastha;* the indestructible spirit is thus named because it is unaffected by all differentiation. These two are really the Supreme Spirit manifested to man's conception through two correlated forms.

[12] "Different;" that is, unrelated to the conditions which form the other two.

[13] *Paramâtmâ;* of all things called âtmâ from any point of view, this is the supreme, the innermost reality, the Most High.

[14] "Supports;" that is, without effort, by His mere being. The Absolute does not lose its character in supporting the universe.

18. Because I[1] am beyond the destructible,[2] and superior even to the indestructible;[3] therefore in the Vedas as well as in the world I am called the Supreme Spirit.

19. Thus whoever, undeluded, knows Me as the Supreme Spirit, he, the knower of all, worships Me in all forms.

20. Thus this most secret instruction has been declared by me, O sinless one; knowing this, a man becomes, O Bharata's son, the doer of all that is to be done.

> Thus ends chapter the fifteenth, called the "RIGHT KNOWLEDGE OF THE SUPREME SPIRIT," in the blessed BHAGAVAD GÎTÂ, the sacred lore, the divine wisdom, the book of divine union, the colloquy between the blessed KRISHNA and ARJUNA, and contained in the Bhîshma Parvan of the blessed MAHÂBHÂRATA, which is a collection of one hundred thousand verses by VYÂSA.

Salutation to Krishna, who has revealed the right knowledge of the Supreme Spirit, which is realizable only by cutting down the tree of conditioned existence.

---

[1] "I;" not the human being called by the world Krishna, but the Spirit which he knows to be the true Ego, — the real Himself.

[2] "Destructible;" the perpetually changing universe.

[3] "Indestructible;" the divine omnipotence which is the basis of the universe.

CHAPTER XVI.

RIGHT KNOWLEDGE OF THE DISCRIMINATION BETWEEN GODLIKE AND DEMONIAC ATTRIBUTES.

In Chapter IX, verses 12, 13, it has been said that human nature is divisible into three classes, — godlike, demoniac, and impish. This subject is now further explained, in order to teach that those who aspire for salvation must cultivate the godlike attributes and abandon the others. This chapter is also intended to elucidate the last verse of the preceding chapter by showing how "the knowledge of the being of the Deity" is to be obtained which makes a man the "doer of all that is to be done."

The Blessed Lord *spoke:*

1. Want of fear,[1] sincerity of behavior,[2] assiduity in regard to knowledge[3] and its realization,[4] gifts,[5] external restfulness,[6] sacrifices,[7] study,[8] austerities,[9] rectitude.

---

[1] "Want of fear;" acting fearlessly, without doubt or misgiving, in accordance with scriptural instruction.

[2] "Sincerity of behavior;" not influencing others artfully or by falsehood, sophistry, or by causing perplexity.

[3] "Knowledge;" instruction about the real nature of the ego and non-ego given in the Scriptures and by preceptors.

[4] "Realization;" constant effort to verify these truths by personal experience. These three are the most important of the attributes called godlike. The nature of a man in whom these attributes exist is said to pertain to the quality of sattva.

[5] "Gifts;" sharing one's possessions with others.

[6] "External restfulness;" repose of manner; absence of nervousness.

[7] "Sacrifices;" according to the Scriptural injunctions.

[8] "Study;" that is, of the Scriptures other than those which deal directly with liberation.

[9] "Austerities;" as explained further on.

2. Inoffensiveness, truth, want of anger, renunciation, internal restfulness, not speaking of the faults of others, compassion towards creatures, superiority over temptations,[1] gentleness, shame,[2] freedom from gesticulation.

3. Power,[3] forgiveness,[4] patience, purity, want of desire to cause harm, want of over-esteem of self, are the godlike attributes wherewith a mortal is born,[5] O son of Bharata.

"Purity" means both mental and bodily cleanliness. External impurity can be removed by water and other purifiers. The mind also requires purification whenever anger is felt, or a falsehood is told, or the faults of another needlessly disclosed ; whenever anything is said or done for the purpose of flattery, or any one is deceived by the insincerity of a speech or an act. Habits of internal cleanliness should be cultivated with even greater care than those of outward purity. The agent of internal purification is shame and repentance. Entertaining anger or hatred is more loathsome than falling into a sewer; and self-gratulation and self-praise are as offensive as foul sores.

Godlike attributes are spoken of as "the fruit of the Spirit" by Saint Paul (Gal. v. 22, 23). Against such, as the apostle says, "there is no law," because they lead to liberation, as is expressed here in verse 5.

4. Ostentation religious and worldly, egotism, anger, sarcasm, false knowledge,[6] are, O Prithâ's son, the demoniac attributes wherewith a mortal is born.

5. Godlike attributes are for liberation, and demoniac[7]

---

[1] "Superiority over temptations;" freedom from agitation in the presence of temptation.

[2] "Shame;" all genuine repentance must be preceded by shame.

[3] "Power," to overcome opposition.

[4] "Forgiveness;" absence of anger, even when injured; this distinguishes it from "want of anger."

[5] "Mortal is born;" these attributes are godlike as indicating the future well-being of the soul.

[6] "False knowledge;" perverted ideas of right and wrong, truth and falsehood, spirit and matter.

[7] "Demoniac;" pertaining to the quality of rajas, and here includes impish attributes pertaining to the quality of tamas.

for continued bondage, — this is meant by Me, O Pându's son;[1] grieve not; thou art born with godlike attributes.

6. In this world the creation of creatures is twofold, godlike and demoniac. The godlike has been fully declared; hear from Me, O Prithâ's son, as to the demoniac.

Gal. v. 17.

For facility of detection and avoidance the rest of this chapter describes demoniac attributes in a concrete form.

7. Demoniac creatures do not know what to do and what not to do, neither purity nor right behavior; there is no truth in them.

8. They call the creatures truthless[2] and lawless[3] and Godless,[4] produced by the union of the sexes, having lust only for cause.

Among the various systems of Indian philosophy this view is not unrepresented. Chârvaka, said to be a demon in the form of a Brâhman, is the leader of Indian materialists. The main feature of his doctrine is the rejection of both Scriptures and reasoning by inference, as legitimate organons of right knowledge. His ground for discarding inference is noteworthy as being in anticipation of many modern thinkers. A general proposition is inferred from observed instances; and again instances are employed to prove the validity of the conclusion drawn by inference; hence all universal and general propositions are inadmissible and illegitimate. Such is the reasoning of Chârvaka and his modern successors. It is to be noted, however, that the assertion of the validity of perception by the senses and exclusion of inference and revelation involves the universal proposition — all revelation and inference are inadmissible. The whole fabric of materialist philosophy is thus based upon a contradiction.

---

[1] "O Pându's son;" the Blessed Lord, knowing the thought of Arjuna, now proceeds to remove his anxiety as to his own attributes.

[2] "Truthless;" that is, as they are deceptive, so is the whole race, they think.

[3] "Lawless;" there is neither good nor evil, and all Scriptures are produced by fools and knaves.

[4] "Godless." There is no conscious cause or righteous judge in the universe.

9. Relying upon this view,[1] those of cruel deeds, perverted natures,[2] and of little reason,[3] enemies of the world, are born in order to destroy.

10. Full of ostentation, self-glorification, and pride, fixed firm in insatiable desire, steadfast in false faiths[4] through blindness, and impure of conduct,[5] they prevail on earth.

11. Also holding fast to measureless anxiety terminated only by death, and convinced of this that the enjoyment of objects of desire is the supreme end.[6]

12. Bound by hundreds of bonds of desire, taking supreme resort in lust and anger, and for the enjoyment of objects of desire working unrighteously[7] for many possessions.

13. This has been gained by me to-day, and that desired object I will gain; this treasure is, and that also will become mine.

14. This enemy by me has been slain, others I shall also slay; I am lord, I am enjoyer, I have gained my end, I am powerful, I am happy.

15. I am rich and high-born; who else is there equal to me? I shall perform sacrifices, I shall give alms, I shall rejoice. By such blindness deluded,

16. With hearts confused by many desires and covered by the net of delusions, and engrossed in the enjoyments of objects and lusts, they fall into impure hells.

---

[1] "This view;" that is, the view of Chârvaka.

[2] "Perverted natures," having no means of working for their own well-being hereafter.

[3] "Little reason;" because confined to that which can now be perceived.

[4] "False faiths;" perverted view of the destiny of man; or worship of false gods, as one authority says.

[5] "Impure of conduct;" because their religious rites involve the taking of life, drinking intoxicating drugs and liquors, and other similar impure practices.

[6] "The supreme end;" according to Chârvaka the supreme end of existence is to enjoy all possible pleasures.

[7] "Working unrighteously;" by committing thefts, frauds, etc.

17. Honored in their own eyes, arrogant, full of pride and delusion of riches, they perform sacrifices in name,[1] irregularly,[2] and for the purpose of ostentation,

18. Embracing egotism,[3] tyrannical power, self-conceit,[4] lust and anger, the enemies of the righteous hate Me in their own[5] bodies and in the bodies of others.

19. Them, the haters,[6] cruel and worst among men, I cast endlessly[7] into impure, demoniac wombs, in this sphere of migratory existence.

20. Falling into demoniac wombs, deluded from birth to birth, and not finding Me, O son of Kuntî, thence they go to even worse[8] conditions.

The demoniac attributes are the "lusts of the flesh" against which Saint Paul warns (Gal. v. 19–21): "They which do such things shall not inherit the kingdom of God."

21. Threefold is this the gate of hell, causing perdition of the soul,[9] lust, anger, and also greed; therefore abandon these three.[10]

---

[1] "Sacrifices in name;" this teaches that even Vedic ceremonies are valueless when performed in such a spirit.

[2] "Irregularly;" that is, in violation of established rules.

[3] "Embracing egotism;" ascribing real and imaginary qualities to one's self through false knowledge.

[4] "Self-conceit;" which makes it intolerable for them to be thought of as obeying any authority except their own or set up by themselves.

[5] "In their own," etc.; that is, violate the scriptural commands of the Deity. The Supreme Spirit, as consciousness, witnesses all that a man does.

[6] "Haters" of God and righteous men.

[7] "I cast endlessly," etc.; by reason of their perverted nature they go from bad to worse. God does not treat them thus from a personal feeling of anger, but their evil deeds, violating divine commands given for their welfare, draw them into evil births, in which they work evil and are again born in evil wombs.

[8] "Even worse;" it is not to be imagined that left to themselves they ever turn to God, but eternally go from bad to worse.

[9] "Causing perdition of the soul;" that is, preventing the soul or conscious creature from gaining the supreme end, Nirvâna. It does not mean annihilation.

[10] "These three;" the chief among the demoniac attributes; if these three, the root of all evils, are abandoned, the rest will soon disappear.

22. O Kunti's son, the man secure from these three, the gates of hell, works for his well-being and then proceeds to the supreme goal.[1]

23. Whoso, abandoning scriptural injunctions, remains in self-wilful conduct,[2] attains no heavenly sphere,[3] nor happiness,[4] nor the supreme goal.

24. Therefore, in the decision as to what ought and what ought not to be done, the Scriptures are to be thy authority; thou oughtest to perform action on earth, knowing what is enjoined by the Scriptures.

> Thus ends chapter the sixteenth, called "RIGHT KNOWLEDGE OF THE DISCRIMINATION BETWEEN GODLIKE AND DEMONIAC ATTRIBUTES," in the blessed BHAGAVAD GÎTÂ, the sacred lore, the divine wisdom, the book of divine union, the colloquy between the blessed KRISHNA and ARJUNA, and contained in the Bhíshma Parvan of the blessed MAHÂBHÂRATA, which is a collection of one hundred thousand verses by VYÂSA.

The supreme authority of the Scriptures is emphatically declared by Jesus Christ by fulfilling the Scriptures himself, and also by explicit words, — "The Scriptures cannot be broken" (John x. 35).

In all spiritual difficulties the best course is to follow the Scriptures when there are any express declarations pertaining thereto; if not, the practice and opinion of sincere men of religion is a good precedent; failing even in that, the conscience trained by the study of the Scriptures is a safe guide to follow.

According to the influence of the three qualities, the attributes forming men's characters are divisible into two classes; namely,

---

[1] "Proceeds to the supreme goal;" avoiding the trinity of evils, the man not only attains the supreme goal, or Nirvâna, but also lives a happy, peaceful life on earth.

[2] "Self-wilful conduct;" following the corrupt impulses of carnal nature.

[3] "Heavenly sphere;" that is, imperfect vision of God, in lower celestial spheres.

[4] "Happiness;" that is, on earth.

godlike and demoniac. Those who wish for salvation ought to avoid lust, anger, and greed, — the chief among the demoniac attributes,— and cultivate the godlike attributes of courageous obedience to the Scriptures, study of spiritual philosophy, and perseverance in its practical realization.

Salutation to Krishna, who by describing the godlike and demoniac attributes has shown what is to be followed and what avoided in order that the truth which is liberation may be received.

CHAPTER XVII.

RIGHT KNOWLEDGE OF THE THREEFOLD DIVISION OF FAITH.

IN the preceding chapter the Scriptures are said to be men's eyes in regard to spiritual matters. Those who have no faith in any revealed Scriptures are liable to be the victims of their own fancies; for the natural man receiveth not the things of the Spirit of God (1 Cor. ii. 14).

Yet at the same time it is to be borne in mind that the Scriptures are not the truth, although they point out the path to truth. "The Vedas have for their object only the assemblage of the three qualities; be free from the three qualities, O Arjuna. . . . As much benefit as there is in a limited expanse of water, so much is there in water stretching free on all sides; similarly, as much benefit as there is in all the Vedic rites, so much is there for the truth-realizing Brâhman (Chap. II. vv. 45, 46). When the forest of delusion thy heart shall cross over, then shalt thou attain dispassion both as to what is heard and what is yet to hear" (Chap. II. v. 52). These and many similar passages in the Gîtâ condemn an idolatrous veneration of the letter of the Scriptures. In brief, the Scriptures are invaluable as means for the attainment of truth, but only as the means; if accepted as the end they are not only not good, but evil. The letter killeth.

The faith which manifests itself in the godlike attributes described in the last chapter is the best and highest faith, being faith in the only true God; but it is not easily attainable, and is rarely seen. The Blessed Lord uses this occasion, offered by Arjuna's question, to explain the nature of the inferior faith, which has three forms.

Arjuna *said:*

1. How, O Krishna, is the devotion of those who, leaving scriptural injunction, worship in faith, — is it sattva, rajas, or tamas?

This does not refer to those who, knowing the scriptural injunctions, abandon them in favor of human innovations; such cannot be said to worship in faith. If the God whom they worship is the true God, they can find no knowledge of Him outside the Scriptures; and external worship is not necessary to one who finds God within himself. Consequently, when a man who is acquainted with the Scriptures renounces them and is not yet holy enough to worship God in the form which transcends all Scriptures, namely, "in truth and in spirit," he cannot be said to have faith, and is included in the demoniac class (Chap. XVI. v. 23). The worshippers here spoken of are those who, through incapacity and want of development, rest contented with traditions and the opinions of authority.

The question is answered by showing the nature of this inferior faith, which can belong to any one of the three qualities. Faith in the true God of the Scriptures is of the purest sattva quality.

The Blessed Lord *spoke:*

2. The faith of embodied creatures is born of their innate nature; it is of three kinds, namely, belonging to the qualities of sattva, of rajas, and of tamas; hear about that now.

The "innate nature" here means the tendencies of the beginningless past, not purified by any spiritual influences; it is here used to distinguish it from a nature which has been produced by obedience to the will of God as revealed in the Scriptures.

The only way to change the character of man as produced by past evolution is to study the Scriptures and have faith in them. This study of the Scriptures is a sacred duty, incumbent upon all capable of it, and no study is perfected unless the knowledge acquired from it is conveyed to at least one other person. Those unable to study fulfil their duty completely by simple obedience to the lawful authority.

3. The faith of all, O son of Bharata, proceeds from the quality of sattva; this being[1] is made of faith;[2] whatever is one's faith, the same he is.

True faith comes only from the Scriptures directly, or indirectly through the instructions of holy men.

4. Those of the sattva quality worship gods;[3] those of the quality of rajas worship Yakshas[4] and Rakshas;[5] other men of the quality of tamas worship ghosts[6] and spirits.[7]

From the time that faith germinates the external appearances become of secondary importance, for they are but fading echoes thenceforward. The doctrine of justification by faith as given in Chapter IX. verse 37 is a practical application of this great spiritual truth.

5. Those men who perform terrible austerities unenjoined by scriptural authority, and are full of vanity and egotism,[8] and full of the strength of desire[9] and attachment, —

6. Those deluded creatures, — torture the powers and faculties that inhere in the body, and also Me,[10] presiding over his innermost heart; know them to be possessed of demoniac purpose.

[1] "This being;" the embodied ego, the ordinary creature.

[2] "Made of faith;" a man can have genuine faith in that alone which he *really* is. Faith comes of the quality of sattva and varies according to its power over the other two.

[3] "Gods," that is, the powers of the true God, as manifested in the quality of sattva.

[4] *Yakshas*, spirits who preside over treasures.

[5] *Rakshas*, malignant spirits, enemies of piety.

[6] "Ghosts," disembodied human beings inhabiting the world of shadows.

[7] "Spirits," the powers of the elements.

[8] "Vanity and egotism" are the causes of their being addicted to cruel austerities.

[9] "Desire" refers to absent, and "attachment" to present objects. These characterize the quality of rajas.

[10] "And also Me." The Deity is said to be tortured by the violation of his commands. The "deluded creatures" here described are those overpowered by the quality of tamas.

These two verses treat of those unscriptural worshippers who are demoniac; the other class is left out on account of its infrequency. Those described must be avoided.

7. Food, sacrifices, austerities, gifts attractive to creatures, are also of three kinds; hear of their differences now.

All that are mentioned here are threefold according to their relation to the qualities. Those desirous of spiritual well-being must adopt that which cultivates the quality of sattva and avoid the others.

8. Foods which promote longevity, mental tranquillity, industry, harmony of bodily functions, cheerfulness, and sympathy with those of like temperament, and are succulent, oleaginous, producing permanent benefit to the body, and the composition of which is ascertainable at sight, are attractive to those in whom the quality of sattva is dominant.

9. Foods excessively bitter, sour, salt, hot, pungent, dry, and ardent are attractive to those in whom rajas prevails, and are productive of unpleasantness,[1] suffering,[2] and disease.

10. Foods insufficiently cooked, deprived of savor, offensive in odor, not fresh, and unfit for sacrificial offering,[3] are attractive to those in whom tamas prevails.

11. That sacrificial ceremony belongs to sattva quality which is enjoined by scriptural authority, and performed by men who expect no benefit,[4] and fix the mind in this, that "it is to be done."

12. O best of Bharata's sons, know that sacrifice which

---

[1] "Unpleasantness" while being eaten.

[2] "Suffering," that is, after-effects, such as depression of spirits.

[3] "Unfit for sacrificial offering," that is, food which has been irregularly tasted by any one before it is blessed by sacrifice, which corresponds to the saying of grace among Christians.

[4] "Benefit;" outside of the desire to perform it.

is performed, looking to the result,[1] and also for a purpose of pride,[2] as belonging to the quality of rajas.

13. That sacrifice is said to pertain to tamas which is unfounded on sacred authority, in which food is not given to Brâhmans, nor holy texts recited, concluded without making gifts, and performed without faith.

Sacrifices and offerings, and indeed all kinds of religious works, are good because prescribed by scriptural authority, and not in themselves; consequently no good comes from their performance according to personal pleasure, or without faith in the Scriptures.

Having condemned all violent and unscriptural mortifications, the Blessed Lord declares the nature of proper austerities.

14. Doing reverence to Gods,[3] Brâhmans, superiors,[4] and wise persons, purity and straightness,[5] chastity,[6] and uninjuriousness[7] are called bodily austerities.

15. Words that cause no anxiety, that are truthful, soothing, and beneficial,[8] and also repeated readings of the Scriptures, are called verbal austerities.

16. Transparency of the mind,[9] cheerfulness manifested in the countenance,[10] restraint of speech,[11] self-

[1] "Looking to the result," that is, for the purpose of specific rewards in heaven, or for acquiring reputation for righteousness.
[2] "Purpose of pride," that is, for self-gratulation.
[3] "Gods," that is, the Deity under all names and in all aspects.
[4] "Superiors," that is, parents and others worthy of honor.
[5] "Straightness;" this is a technical term which implies not using the limbs in prohibited acts, and keeping them engaged in the opposite.
[6] "Chastity;" here meant in the absolute sense.
[7] "Uninjuriousness," that is, inflicting personal harm on no one.
[8] "Words that cause ... beneficial." Righteous speech must have all these elements: 1. It shall cause no anxiety; 2. It shall be in harmony with the real experience of the speaker; 3. It shall be soothing or pleasant in relation to apparent objects; 4. Also beneficial in relation to spiritual things. For example, "Be collected, my son; study the Scriptures or perform religious works; that will promote your well-being."
[9] "Transparency of the mind," from absence of anxiety.
[10] "Cheerfulness," etc.; the function of the mind which suppresses all thoughts injurious to others and entertains only such as are for their well-being. This faculty is the source of saintly calmness depicted on the countenance of holy men.
[11] "Restraint of speech;" the determination of the mind which causes it is here meant.

restraint,[1] and sincerity of conduct[2] are called mental austerities.

17. By men not desiring benefit, and tranquil in heart, austerities practised in excellent faith are said to belong to sattva. Thus[3] is austerity of three kinds.

18. Austerities that are practised for obtaining fame, honor, and favor, that are uncertain, transitory,[4] and confined to this world, are said to belong to rajas.

19. Austerities that are practised in consequence of a conviction founded upon folly, for the torturing of one's self, or for the destruction of another, are said to belong to tamas.

20. "Gifts have to be made;" thinking thus, gifts that are made to those who make no return, in proper place[5] and time[6] to a recipient,[7] also otherwise proper, are considered as belonging to sattva.

21. But that gift which is given for the purpose of a return of benefit, or expecting some definite spiritual benefit, or given unwillingly, is considered as belonging to rajas.

22. The gift that is made in improper time and place, and to improper recipients, who are not honored but treated with contempt, is said to belong to tamas.

---

[1] "Self-restraint;" withdrawing the mind from worldly objects. This is meant to include all things which are not specifically mentioned as fit objects for the exercise of self-control.

[2] "Sincerity of conduct;" absence of desire to influence others by any deviation from straightforwardness.

[3] "Thus," as is about to be described.

[4] "Uncertain and transitory;" their effect is entirely confined to this life, even when they do not disappoint the performer.

[5] "Proper place;" according to Brâhmanical custom holy places, such as Benares, are proper places in which to make gifts.

[6] "Time;" by the same authority the last day of the month is a proper time for making gifts.

[7] "Recipient;" a Brâhman versed in the Vedas is the proper recipient of a gift when he makes no return.

It being extremely difficult to preserve perfect purity of gifts and other works, here follow the directions for the removal of unavoidable shortcomings.

23. OM, TAT, SAT, these are considered as the three designations of Brahmă.[1] By these, in the beginning, the Brâhmanas,[2] the Vedas, and sacrifices were sanctified.

24. Therefore, uttering the syllable OM, the Scripture-enjoined acts — pertaining to sacrifice, gift, and austerity — of those who declare the Supreme Spirit[3] become always blameless.

25. By those desirous of salvation, uttering the syllable TAT, are performed various acts of sacrifice and austerity as well as acts of giving alms.

26. On birth of sons, on adopting righteousness of conduct, the syllable SAT is to be employed, and also on occasion of marriage, O son of Prithâ, the word SAT is suitable.

27. In sacrifice, austerity, and almsgiving, the permanent good result is called SAT, and also works for the sake of the Deity are called SAT.

The repetition of these syllables, or any of them, has the efficacy of purifying works from rajas and tamas qualities.

28. Whatever offering is made into the fire, whatever is given, whatever austerity is practised, and whatever is done, without faith, O son of Prithâ, that is called Asat,[4] and that is not for well-being here or hereafter.

---

[1] *Brahmă* is the Supreme Spirit.
[2] "Brâhmanas," that is, knowers of Brahmă. No special reference to caste is here meant.
[3] "Declare the Supreme Spirit," that is, those who, having attained identity of nature with the Deity, afterwards lead others to that goal according to the instructions contained in the Vedas.
[4] *Asat*, that is, unrighteous, and not bringing the actor to God; the opposite of SAT, which literally signifies Truth or Beingness.

Thus ends chapter the seventeenth, called "RIGHT KNOWLEDGE OF THE THREEFOLD DIVISION OF FAITH," in the blessed BHAGAVAD GÎTÂ, the sacred lore, the divine wisdom, the book of divine union, the colloquy between the blessed KRISHNA and ARJUNA, and contained in the Bhîshma Parvan of the blessed MAHÂBHÂRATA, which is a collection of one hundred thousand verses by VYÂSA.

Abandoning rajas and tamas, the sattva quality is always to be aspired for in austerities, sacrifices, and almsgiving. Faith being present, all imperfections in such works are removed by pronouncing the name of the Deity.

Salutation to Krishna, who has shown the path to knowledge by purification of heart through the cultivation of faith pertaining to the pure sattva quality.

CHAPTER XVIII.

RIGHT KNOWLEDGE OF LIBERATION.

In this final chapter is given the summary of the other seventeen, and all that is to be found in the Vedas is also to be found here in a concise form. The immediate occasion for the discourse of the Blessed Lord is the uncertainty of Arjuna as to the distinction between the renunciation of all works and giving up the expectation of personal benefit in the fruit of works by dedicating them to the Deity, since it is said that the same result, liberation, comes from both these courses.

ARJUNA *said:*

1. I wish to know, O Thou of mighty arms, the essential truth as to renunciation and as to the giving up of results; and also their difference, O Slayer of Keçi.

THE BLESSED LORD *spoke:*

2. The renunciation of all works for specific purposes is known by the wise as renunciation; the sages call the abandonment of the fruit of all actions the giving up of results.

"Works" here means the sacrificial and other ceremonies as prescribed by the Vedas. Renunciation consists in not performing all works, to which the Scriptures attach some specific gain. Renunciation, then, is the performance of the prescribed every-day duties, and such as are enjoined for special occasions; as, for example, on the birth of a son. Some among the wise also consider the giving up of this class of duties as renunciation.

The "giving up of results" is not expecting any personal benefit from the performance of such every-day and special duties. Although the sacred authority promises no specific reward for the performance of such duties, yet in a general manner they are said to "lead to the sphere of the righteous," and to "diminish sinfulness."

If all desire for benefit from action is to be given up, what reason can there be for acting at all?

First of all it should be impressed upon the mind that no man can be saved by acts, because salvation is not an act, but a new life or consciousness. Suppose a prince to be stolen at birth and brought up among swineherds, with no knowledge whatever of his royal descent. Can he by any act change his consciousness of being a swineherd's son? It can only be changed when the statement of some other person as to that fact proves to be true.

In a similar manner no conditioned creature can cease to be conditioned by any act. It can only be changed by a new consciousness arising from a source different from the conditions which seem to limit the ego. It is also true that this new consciousness cannot be given unless its recipient has faith in the source from whence it comes. From the moment that this is realized, it will be clearly seen that there is but one thing to be done, and that is to acquire this faith. Every one knows that what is unfamiliar is not believed; no great confidence is felt in a stranger, however friendly his professions may be. Suppose it to be shown that if the stranger can be trusted great good will come to those who believe in him, which cannot come in any other way. It would be reasonable then to give a trial to the stranger's words, and to feel confidence in him after a time if nothing occurs to disprove his veracity.

Works are nothing more nor less than this trial. "Faith without works is dead." In other words, works are of value only as accessories, faith being the principal. Therefore, in order to attain supreme faith which is not merely the assent of the intellect,— the approbation of the stranger which influences one to test him,— but a new consciousness or life, works also are needed. At the same time, if the works are done with some other purpose than to prove the stranger's veracity, no good comes from them; the real end for which works are prescribed is defeated. The true purpose of religion is not to direct and facilitate the self-improvement of the faithful, but to lead them to the life hidden in God, ethical improvement being one of the preliminary requisites. For this cause let him, who aspires for salvation, do whatever he has to do with the sole object of gaining God by faith; and when perfect faith comes, action will cease because its purpose is fulfilled.

Therefore it is said that "actions or works purifying the heart turn it towards the Spirit, and then, their purpose being consummated, they disappear like clouds at the end of the rainy season;" "the Yogi does not leave action, but action leaves him;" and many other texts to the same effect. The liberty of the Spirit is the consummation of spiritual culture. Therefore the right course for those who aspire to salvation is to perform their duties in life, as well as such good works as their conditions permit, believing them to be commands of God, and desiring only to strengthen the faith which by grace will save them.

The distinction between renunciation and the giving up of results is here made for a definite reason; otherwise the two might be included in the resignation of the personal will. Absolute resignation characterizes the state of those who have reached the supreme condition of spirituality described in the concluding verses of the second chapter, and in the fifth verse of the twelfth chapter. But here the Blessed Lord is not speaking of those; He speaks of such as are devoid of wisdom and in bondage to action, but are desirous of escaping from bondage by realizing identity with the Deity in the manner described in Chapter XIII.

It is necessary for these seekers for spiritual life to know that after a time the road is divided into two paths. It is absolutely necessary to give up all special works, such as would secure a livelihood, longevity, and other kinds of worldly prosperity. Let no one who desires salvation strive for these things himself, or by deputy, or advise any one to do so. Other works are not to be necessarily given up, but the expectation of personal advantage therefrom must be resigned, absolutely and forever.

3. Some sages say that all works should be given up as impure; while others say that sacrifices, gifts, and austerities must not be given up.

Those who renounce all works are the followers of Kapila, the founder of the Sânkhya system of philosophy; the others are the orthodox Brâhmanical ritualists, who form the Mimânsaka school.

The "works" especially referred to here are the Vedic ceremonials; and the chief objection against them, made by Kapila and afterwards by Buddha, is that they involve the taking of life. Attachment and aversion are also to be given up as impurities.

It is clear from the nature of the objection against works that it does not contemplate the illuminated sage. For to him nothing is impure, since he knows that all objects are included in the Kshetra, from which the Kshetrajna or Ego is distinct. Further reasons in support of this view will be stated presently.

4. It being so,[1] hear my words, which leave no uncertainty, O best of Bharata's sons, in regard to giving up;[2] giving up is perfectly declared to be of three kinds.

5. Sacrifices, gifts, austerities, are works that must not be given up; they must indeed be performed. Sacrifices, gifts, and austerities are purifying for the wise.

This teaches that for those who renounce the thought of personal benefit these works are purifying, and should not be given up. Here also we perceive that the spiritually illuminated are not spoken of, for they can need no purification. "There is nothing more sanctifying than knowledge" (Chap. IV. v. 38).

6. Even these works are to be done renouncing all personal interest in them or in their fruit; this is, O son of Prithâ, my indubitable and supreme declaration.

Whenever any act leaves in the mind any feeling other than that the command of God has been fulfilled, that feeling is produced by egotism.

7. The abandonment of obligatory works is not proper; the abandonment thereof through delusion is the result of the quality of tamas.

These works are not obligatory on those who seek for liberation, according to the doctrine of the Sânkhya philosophers. Upon

---

[1] "It being so;" there being this difference of opinion.
[2] "Giving up" does not include the supreme resignation of the spiritually illuminated, but as practised by those not illuminated is here "perfectly declared."

all men under it the Brâhmanical law imposes certain duties without reference to any such special occasions as the birth of a son, etc.

8. Whoso gives up these works through fear of bodily trouble, thinking they are painful, the giver-up, impelled by the quality of rajas, does not gain the fruit of renunciation.[1]

No man does right who gives up the unmistakable duties of life, resting on divine command, excepting when, through realization of identity with the Deity, these duties naturally become impossible of fulfilment.

9. O Arjuna, when obligatory works are performed with the thought "They ought to be done," and abandoning attachment and result,— that giving up is considered to be of the quality of sattva.

He who performs duties thinking that if they are not performed some evil will come to him, or that their performance will remove difficulties from his path, works for result. Duties should simply be done because commanded by God, who may at any moment command their abandonment.

10. The true giver-up, full of sattva quality,[2] spiritually wise,[3] and with doubts cut asunder,[4] hates not unfavorable works,[5] nor is attached to favorable works.[6]

11. It is not possible for an embodied creature completely to abandon action. He who gives up the fruit of action is called a giver-up.[7]

[1] "Fruit of renunciation," which is salvation. On the contrary, this kind of giving up brings on suffering, owing to domination by passions.

[2] "Sattva quality" fits one for spiritual illumination.

[3] "Spiritually wise;" and therefore at rest in the realization of identity with the Deity.

[4] "Doubts cut asunder;" that is, false knowledge extinguished by true knowledge.

[5] "Unfavorable works;" that is, unfavorable to the attainment of liberation, such as forbidden works, or those which only lead to personal benefit.

[6] "Nor is . . . works;" that is, has no special pleasure in them; performs them involuntarily, without thought, in the same way as he breathes.

[7] "A giver-up;" that is, in a secondary manner; so far as a man in that condition can be.

He who, by leading the life of works, renouncing egotism and expectation of personal benefit, becomes sufficiently pure to abolish from his mind every impulse towards activity through the realization of the absolute independence of the Ego, rests in the "city of nine gates, neither working nor causing work to be done" (Chap. V. v. 22). But to an "embodied creature," in whom the false idea that the body is the ego is still entertained, this is not possible. He is therefore commanded to perform his scriptural duties, moral and religious, as an "unprofitable servant," in order to attain the salvation described in Chapter V. v. 22.

The connection of the illuminated sage with the body which is called his is of no personal use to him. It is entirely for the good of the world.

12. The three kinds of result of action,[1] desirable, undesirable and mixed, come after death to those who do not practise renunciation; but never to those who practise supreme renunciation.[2]

In the next five verses the reasons are given which makes complete renunciation possible for the illuminated only. The sage has realized that the Ego never acts, and knows that all acts are done by the five agents now to be enumerated, which are brought into existence by the illusive identification of the Ego with objects. Those who accept these agents as the Ego are naturally unable to free the mind from all impulse to action.

13. Learn from me, O thou of mighty arms, these five, the agents for the performance of all actions and declared in the Vedânta,[3] which extinguishes all action.[4]

[1] "Action;" mental, verbal, and bodily.
[2] "Supreme renunciation;" as described in Chapter V. verse 22. He who simply renounces fruit of action gradually attains this condition.
[3] *Vedânta;* some take this to mean Sânkhya philosophical treatises. The Vedânta consists of the Upanishads, the Bhagavad Gîtâ, and the Brahmâ Sûtras. No teaching, not founded on these, can be authoritative for the followers of this school.
[4] "Extinguishes all action;" because spiritual knowledge comprehends all action (Chap. IV. v. 33).

14. The body,[1] the actor,[2] the different instruments,[3] the various and separate efforts,[4] and fifth, the supporting divinities.[5]

15. Whatever act a man performs with the body, speech, or mind,[6] whether lawful or the opposite,[7] these five are the causes thereof.

16. This being so, whoso perceives the Self, which is unique, as the agent, he, of perverted heart,[8] does not perceive by reason of unpurified understanding.[9]

17. He, in whom there is no consciousness of egotism,[10] and in whom buddhi does not adhere[11] to anything, — he, even though slaying all these worlds, does not slay, nor is bound.

The Blessed Lord in the beginning says, " This neither slays nor is slain " (Chap. II. v. 19), for the reason that " it never is

---

[1] " The body " is the location of desire, liking, and aversion.
[2] " The actor ; " egotism, or the ahankâra.
[3] " The different instruments," twelve in number; namely, five powers of sensation, five of action, and the powers of reflection and determination.
[4] " Various and separate efforts ; " which are the vital powers, usually called life-breaths. They are divided into five, according to the difference of their functions, — digesting, circulating vitality through the body, inspiring and expiring, and causing upward currents to the head.
[5] " Supporting divinities ; " that is, the internal and external instruments considered as conscious beings.
[6] " Body, speech or mind ; " the classification here refers to the different ways in which the results of action are experienced, and does not contradict the above enumeration of the five agents.
[7] " Lawful or the opposite ; " these include the functions of the body because good or bad health is caused by prior deeds, good or bad.
[8] " Perverted heart ; " that is, a nature which binds one to the wheel of repeated births and deaths.
[9] " Unpurified understanding ; " not refined by the instructions of the Scriptures, religious teachers, and philosophers. Those who believe in doctrines that imply the actorship of the true Ego are included in this class, because such doctrines are not meant for those of purified understanding.
[10] " Consciousness of egotism ; " that is, realizes that essentially the Ego is independent of the powers of action, will, and cognition.
[11] " In whom buddhi does not adhere ; " realizing the true character of the Ego, does not feel " I have done this, and in consequence will have to go to hell or suffer in some other way." Those who have realized identity with the Deity in the sense in which it is understood in the Vedânta, namely, identity of will and design with God, in consequence of participation in Divine nature, are beyond all rules, and the responsibility of their acts belongs to the Deity, who is absolute.

born," etc. (Chap. II. v. 20). Therefore how can he "kill or cause to be killed"?

This has been repeated again and again, and is here finally summed up. Every one is liable to be visited by the three classes of the results of action, except the man of true renunciation, from whom all actions have fallen off. This, the revered commentator says, is also the truth taught in all the Vedas.

18. Knowledge,[1] the object known, and the knower[2] are the three varieties of causes exciting action;[3] the actor, the object, and the instrument are the threefold basis of action.[4]

19. From differences in respect to the qualities,[5] knowledge, action, and also actor are said to be of three kinds in the philosophy of Kapila;[6] listen to them, properly[7] expounded.

The three kinds of knowledge are next declared.

20. Know that knowledge[8] as belonging to sattva, by which is perceived the one exhaustless essence, undistributed,[9] though in distributed bodies.

[1] "Knowledge" is that by which an act of cognition takes place; the broadest instrument of cognition.

[2] "The knower;" that is, the Ego appearing as such by the mysterious power of false knowledge.

[3] "Causes exciting action;" that is, a cognition of loss or gain is followed by the operation of the five causes and not of the Ego (Chap. V. v. 14). Then the acts produced are of three kinds, according to whether they inhere in the body, speech, or mind.

[4] "Basis of action;" that is, that which contains an action. For instance, no action can exist except as a certain relation between the actor and the object and the instrument used by the actor. In grammar, the basis of action is formed by the nominative, accusative, and instrumental cases; the other cases are not directly related to the action.

[5] "Qualities," the three qualities.

[6] *Kapila*, the author of the Sânkhya philosophy.

[7] "Properly," that is, in accord with reason and authority. Although the Sânkhya philosophy is not to be followed in regard to the being of God, it is authoritative in regard to the present subject.

[8] "That knowledge" whereby the identity between the Ego and the Deity is attained.

[9] "Undistributed;" that is, though bodies are different, there is but one Ego reflected in them all.

21. Know that knowledge to belong to rajas whereby different egos of different descriptions are perceived in all the various creatures.

22. But that worthless knowledge which, unreasonably, without spiritual insight, perceives[1] the totality as attached to some one form, is of tamas.

The three kinds of action are next defined.

23. That action is said to belong to sattva which is obligatory,[2] not done with attachment[3] or from liking or aversion, by one who desires not its fruit.

24. That action is said to be of rajas which is done by one desiring its fruit, or again, in pride, and which involves great trouble in its performance.

25. Without regard to consequences, loss, injury, and one's own capacity, whatever action is begun in delusion is of tamas.

The three kinds of agents are next described.

26. An agent who is devoid of personal interest, not self-assertive,[4] possessed of zeal and perseverance, undisturbed by success or failure, is said to be of sattva.

27. The agent who is attached, desirous of fruit of action, covetous, harmful to others, unclean, full of rejoicing and grieving, is declared to be of rajas.

28. The agent who is heedless, dull, unbending, deceptive, preventing others from gaining a livelihood,

---

[1] "Perceives," etc.; that is, vainly imagines God to dwell in any one form, in the way He dwells in the whole universe. This is the view of all idolaters who select some special object as God. Such beliefs are wanting alike in reason and spiritual insight.

[2] "Obligatory;" that is, such actions as are not prescribed for any special purpose, — gifts, penance, and sacrifice (v. 3).

[3] "Attachment," that is, self-identification with it through the feeling of being the actor; the power to do it is really of God, who can remove it whenever He chooses.

[4] "Self-assertive;" that is, does not speak about his own share in the work. Charity "seeketh not her own."

lazy, desponding, and procrastinating, is said to be of tamas.

> The three kinds of agent include the three kinds of knower; action includes what is to be known, and buddhi similarly includes the instruments.

29. Listen to the differences of buddhi, as well as of the recuperative powers,[1] which are of three kinds by reason of the qualities, and which are being exhaustively and discriminatively declared, O Dhananjaya.

30. The buddhi,[2] that knows initiation and renunciation, also what ought and what ought not to be done, and what is to be feared and what not, also bondage and liberation, is of sattva.

31. That buddhi, O son of Prithâ, is of rajas, whereby are imperfectly known what is righteous and what unrighteous, and also what is to be done and what not to be done.

32. That buddhi which, wrapped up in gloom, makes unrighteousness appear as righteous, and all things the opposite of what they are, is of tamas, O son of Prithâ.

33. That recuperative power which through fixity of mind becomes unwavering, and by which the action of the mind, vital powers, and senses are kept in control, is, O son of Prithâ, of sattva.

34. That recuperative power whereby moral excellence, enjoyment, and desires are upheld[3] in a man desiring fruit of action, is of rajas, O son of Prithâ.

35. That recuperative power by reason of which a man of impure understanding does not give up drowsi-

---

[1] "Recuperative powers" includes perseverance, patience, and endurance.

[2] *Buddhi.* The functions of this faculty are to give knowledge and recuperative power.

[3] "Upheld;" by being always perceived as desirable.

ness, fear, grief, internal and external lassitude, and vanity, is determined to be of tamas.

The agent and instrument have been described; the result is now declared.

36. Now hear from me, O best of Bharata's sons, the three kinds of happiness, in which enjoyment comes through repetition and in which pain comes to an end.

37. That happiness which is like poison in the beginning, and in the end is like nectar, and is produced by the transparency of the understanding[1] directed towards the Spirit, is said to be of sattva.

38. The happiness that is consequent upon the contact of sense with objects, is in the beginning like nectar and in the end is like poison,[2] and is known as of rajas.

39. That happiness which in the beginning and end is delusive to the embodied ego, arising from sleep, indolence, and heedlessness, is said to be of tamas.

40. No such creature[3] is there on earth, or among the gods in heaven, who is free from these three nature-born qualities.

By the descriptions of the agent, action, and instrument, and the results gained, as influenced by the three qualities, it has been shown that the real enemy is the illusive power embodying the three qualities. Since this power is the stuff of which the entire universe is the varied manifestation, nothing in the universe — agent, action, instrument, or result — can destroy it, any more than fire can extinguish fire.

Therefore it is said that salvation is not obtained by much learning nor many acts, but by a new consciousness unlimited by the

---

[1] "Transparency of the understanding;" that is, the purified understanding, or heart, becomes transparent to the light of the Spirit.

[2] "Is like poison;" by causing loss of strength, reputation, health and vigor, discernment, memory, and energy. Sensuous pleasures are undesirable for this reason.

[3] "Creature" includes plants, and is, in fact, equivalent to "object."

power of illusion, and showing illusion to be illusion. This is the destruction of illusion; for to show an error to be an error is to destroy it. Everything in the universe is error, and knowledge is that which reveals the true nature of the universe to be a gigantic error. No one attains eternal life except through this knowledge, faith, or new consciousness, and this knowledge never dawns until the tree of false knowledge, described in the opening of Chapter XV., is cut down by the firm sword of dispassion. This, says the revered commentator, is the teaching of all the Vedas and other Scriptures, and, it may be added, of all religions.

Dispassion is extremely difficult of attainment. It does not consist in simply suppressing the outward activity of the body, but in complete unconsciousness of any impulse of the mind or body colored by the feeling that these impulses are from within, or that they should or should not be suppressed. It is foolishness for a man to imagine that by a particular course of action he can be freed from personality. Such a thought is the most powerful manure for a luxuriant growth of the upas-tree. A personal man can only become impersonal through what is very rightly called a supernatural means, or an act of grace generating a faith in that which is absolute and beyond the reach of mind and sense.

To escape from personality, and consequently from suffering, a man must look for an expedient which is beyond experience. In fact, he must accept a mystery. So long as this faith is wanting there is no hope for salvation. But when this faith is obtained, one of two equally good results will follow; either a complete abandonment of the world, or else remaining in it and working as an unprofitable servant carrying out the commands of a master whose will is not subject to question or full comprehension.

Let no one think under these circumstances to enlarge one's duties and responsibilities in life by one's own initiation, but simply to keep the divine commandments; not even attempting to do something not commanded, thinking that it would be acceptable to the Master. For nothing is acceptable to Him but perfect resignation to His will, under the conviction that he is the Master, even of those who do not consciously submit to His will.

This resignation cannot be an act which brings about a new relation between the Master and His servant, but is the recognition of a fact which always exists. With this in view the divine commandments to the Brâhmanical people are next declared. The duties pertaining to their system of castes are divine commands; in other words, a declaration of the latent possibilities of the soul which could not have been otherwise discovered. These commands must be obeyed without questioning, always recognizing the fact that the power for performing these duties does not belong to the performer who gains no special merit, because they are intended for his own spiritual well-being and for no other purpose.

41. The duties of Brâhmanas, Kshatriyas, Vaisyas, and also[1] of Çûdras are divided into classes by the qualities arising from nature.[2]

42. Internal and external self-control, purity, forgiveness, rectitude, learning, spiritual perception, and faith are the nature-born duties of Brâhmans.

43. Heroism, vigor, patient endurance, presence of mind, not turning back in battle, liberality, lordliness, are the nature-born duties of Kshatriyas.

44. Agriculture, breeding of cattle, and commerce are the nature-born duties of Vaisyas; and of Çûdras the nature-born duty is that of which the essence is to serve.

Men are said to be the body of the Creator, and the various castes are His different limbs. As each member of the body has its peculiar function, so are there appropriate duties for each of the four castes. The conception of the caste system in the Theocratic Brâhmanical Law is paralleled by the Christian idea that the Church is the Body of Christ. It would be very instructive to compare the *dicta* of the Sacred Law of the Brâhmans on caste with the parable of the vine, and with the utterances of Saint Paul in Romans xii. 4–6, and I Cor. xii.

---

[1] " And also " is intended to show that only the first three castes are entitled to study the Vedas.
[2] " Qualities arising from nature ; " " nature " is the power of the Deity consisting of the three qualities ; otherwise it may be taken to mean the tendencies resulting in birth in the different castes. The scriptural commands relating to the different castes are founded upon the difference of inherent tendencies or qualities.

45. Men devoted to their own proper duties attain full perfection. Listen how they attain perfection by devotion to their own duties.

The usual teaching is that those who perform their caste duties properly obtain celestial enjoyment after death and are then born in a country inhabited by religious men, in a worthy caste and family, full of intelligence, knowledge, wealth, etc. But here it is said that by the right performance of caste duties men attain perfection. Not only Brâhmans, but all others, when purified by the right performance of their duties, are fitted for the reception of spiritual knowledge, which is salvation.

46. Worshipping by the performance of one's duties Him[1] from whom is the endeavor of men,[2] by whom all this is pervaded, a man attains perfection.[3]

47. Better are one's own proper duties, though devoid of merit, than the duties of another,[4] even though well performed. Performing acts in obedience to nature, a man does not incur sin.[5]

48. Nature-born duties,[6] even though stained with faults, must not be abandoned.[7] All acts are wrapped up in faults as fire is by smoke.

[1] "Worshipping," etc.; that is, the interior spirit of devotion and self-surrender to God makes the performance of the ordinary duties of life acts of worship.

[2] "From whom is the endeavor of men;" that is, He who, dwelling in each human heart, engages it in action and regulates its course.

[3] "Perfection" does not here mean liberation, but the fitness to become a man of true renunciation and devoted to the acquirement of spiritual knowledge which brings liberation.

[4] "Duties of another;" because a thing is right in the abstract it does not become right for every one to do it.

[5] "A man does not incur sin;" as an insect born in a mass of poison does not die from that poison, so a man who does his duty does not incur sin, even if those duties involve acts which are hateful to others.

[6] "Nature-born duties," are the duties to which a man is born in consequence of pre-existing tendencies.

[7] "Must not be abandoned;" it is possible for those, who have realized the Ego, and know that it is immortal and therefore unaffected by time, to be actionless. But those whose impulse to action has not been removed by spiritual knowledge should perform their natural duties; otherwise they infuse new vitality into their tendencies and thus frustrate the desired end; namely, the realization of the true Ego, which is actionless.

49. He whose buddhi is everywhere unattached, who is victorious over his heart and devoid of desire, obtains through renunciation the perfection which is actionlessness.

The greatest result which can come from action is independence of action.

50. Hear from me, in brief, the way in which the Supreme Spirit is attained after obtaining freedom from all action. This is the ultimate end of the application to the pursuit of knowledge.

The path to the supreme goal is now described.

51. Possessed of pure[1] buddhi, controlling the self[2] with patience,[3] abandoning all objects, beginning with sound,[4] and also giving up attachment and aversion,

52. Dwelling in secluded spots, eating little,[5] regulated in speech, body, and mind, engaged in concentrated contemplation,[6] and joined to unwavering detachment from all objects.[7]

53. He who, abandoning egotism, strength, vanity,[8] desire, anger, acceptance,[9] is in peace and devoid of the

[1] "Pure;" that is, free from the idea of within and without; Buddhi as influenced by the quality of sattva (v. 30).

[2] "The self" means the body, senses, and mental faculties.

[3] "Patience," as influenced by the quality of sattva (v. 33).

[4] "Beginning with sound;" that is, the objects of the senses. Such a disciple abandons everything not absolutely necessary for the support of the body, and even for that has neither attachment nor aversion.

[5] "Light in food;" and therefore free from drowsiness, heedlessness, and idleness, as well as healthful in body, mind, and speech.

[6] "Concentrated contemplation;" that is, the thinking principle at rest after being turned towards the Spirit.

[7] "Detachment from all objects;" including divine worship through body, mind, or speech, which interfere with unbroken contemplation.

[8] "Vanity;" the emotion which succeeds the feeling of satisfaction with anything, and leads to the violation of the law of righteousness. "From being pleased a man becomes satisfied, and satisfaction leads to the violation of the righteous law governing him," says a sacred authority.

[9] "Desire, anger, acceptance;" through perfect purity of nature the sage does not feel that he accepts anything, even that which is necessary to maintain life; but he does not resist the natural workings of the body.

feeling of possession,[1] is worthy to be the Supreme Spirit.[2]

54. Attaining the Supreme Spirit, he, having his nature perfectly purified, neither grieves nor desires, but equal towards all creatures[3] attains supreme devotion[4] to Me.

55. By devotion he knows Me, how[5] and what I am in reality;[6] then,[7] having known me in truth, after that he enters into Me.

56. He who is always the performer, even of all actions, depending upon Me,[8] attains through my favor[9] the eternal, exhaustless seat.

57. Having placed all action in Me, through power of discrimination, and regarding Me as the supreme goal, and also taking resort in firm faith, be always with heart fixed in Me.[10]

58. Having thy heart fixed in me, thou shalt cross over all troubles by my favor; but again, if from pride thou listenest not to Me, thou shalt perish.

---

[1] "Devoid of the feeling of possession;" even in regard to life and person.

[2] "Is worthy to be the Supreme Spirit;" meaning that the realization of identity with the Supreme Spirit takes place at this stage.

[3] "Equal towards all creatures;" that is, perceives the grief and joy of all creatures by comparison with his own.

[4] "Supreme devotion;" that is, true knowledge of the Deity. (See Chap. VII. v. 17.)

[5] "How;" that is, appearing as varied by being reflected in different objective bases.

[6] "What I am in reality;" attributeless consciousness.

[7] "Then." This does not show that after the Supreme Spirit is known the final consummation comes; for the knowledge of the Supreme Spirit is Nirvâna. Each one knows the Supreme Spirit as himself; so, although the Supreme Spirit is one, and Nirvâna also one, yet, as each one who attains Nirvâna realizes the Supreme Spirit as himself, each one is absolute.

[8] "Depending upon Me;" that is, fully convinced that God is the Ego in him, and therefore not wishing for reward.

[9] "Through my favor;" the knowledge that sets man free is not attained by any acts; it is a gift of divine grace. Salvation, or Nirvâna, cannot be gained through action.

[10] "Heart fixed in Me;" do not turn to any other source for help. Put your trust in Him even though He should slay.

59. If resting on egotism thou thinkest "I shall not fight," vain indeed is thy determination; thy nature shall engage thee in it.

All men are under the domination of God; some know this,— others do not.

60. Tied to thy natural tendencies [1] by what has gone before,[2] thou shalt, powerless to resist, do that which thou, through delusion, wishest not to do.

61. The Lord, O white-souled one, seated in the heart of all creatures, by His illusive power revolves all creatures, who are as though mounted on a machine.

62. Take sanctuary with Him, O Bharata's son, with all thy soul;[3] by His favor thou shalt find supreme peace,[4] as well as the eternal abode.

This verse is intended to deny fatalism. Although God is the performer of all action, yet each man feels that he has a free will; and unless the free will is freely resigned to the will of God, the ceaseless assertion of it will continue. Consequently, no peace can come to such a man. All that is necessary for salvation is spoken in the one word "obey."

63. This knowledge,[5] the most mysterious of mysteries, has by Me been thus declared unto thee; considering this in its entirety, act according to thy will.[6]

For the benefit of those not able carefully to consider the profound doctrines set forth in the Bhagavad Gîtâ, the Blessed Lord Himself sums up its teaching.

---

[1] "Thy natural tendencies;" this refers to the warlike character of Arjuna.
[2] "Gone before;" that is, all past Karma,—all causes of every kind leading to the present situation.
[3] "With all thy soul;" in mind, body, and speech.
[4] "Find supreme peace;" this favor lasts until divine knowledge arises.
[5] "This knowledge" is the Bhagavad Gîtâ.
[6] "According to thy will;" that is, adopt the path of knowledge, or that of action, as seems right in thy sight.

64. Listen again to my supreme words which are the most mysterious of all; thou art ever beloved of Me, therefore I am declaring what is thy welfare.[1]

65. Be with thy mind fixed in Me, be my devotee, be my worshipper, bow down to Me,[2] and thou shalt come even to Me; this I verily swear unto thee; thou art beloved of Me.

66. Abandoning all acts, take sanctuary with Me alone. I shall liberate thee[3] from all sins; do thou not grieve.

When the heart has been purified by following the precepts in verse 65, then abandon all acts, knowing that there is none else but God. This is the teaching of all Scriptures. So long as the restlessness of our nature is not reduced to tranquillity we must work, consecrating to the Deity all the fruit of our action, and attribute to Him the power to perform works rightly. This is not, however, an injunction, but a restriction.

The true life of man is rest in identity with the Supreme Spirit. This life is not brought into existence by any act of ours; it is a reality, the truth, and is altogether independent of us. The realization of the non-existence of all that seems to be opposed to this truth is a new consciousness, and not an act. Man's liberation is in no way related to his acts. In so far as acts promote the realization of our utter inability to emancipate ourselves from conditioned existence, they are of use; after this is realized acts become obstacles rather than helps. Those who work in obedience to Divine commands, knowing that the power thus to work is a gift of God, and no part of man's self-conscious nature, attain to freedom from the need for action. Then the pure heart is filled by the truth, and identity with the Deity is perceived.

"Knowing Him alone one goes beyond death; there is no other path for going," says the sacred text. Another text completes this declaration: "When men shall fold up space as though it were a piece of skin, then only will suffering end without knowing the

---

[1] "Thy welfare;" that is, the attainment of supreme truth.

[2] "Bow down to Me;" that is, surrender to Me thy goal and the means thou employest for its attainment.

[3] "I shall liberate thee" by the resplendent lamp of wisdom (Chap. X. vv. 2–5).

Deity." This knowledge is the only immortality; works and action of themselves can in no sense liberate man from his present bondage.

Then follow the rules that must be observed in the study of the Truth declared by the Blessed Lord.

67. This must never be declared by thee to one who does not practise mortifications, has no devotion, and is unwilling to serve the spiritual instructor; and also, not unto one who reviles Me.[1]

68. Whoever shall expound this supreme mystery[2] to those who have love for Me,[3] shall without doubt come to Me, having obtained supreme love for Me.[4]

69. Than he, there is among men no better performer of what is dear unto Me, nor shall there ever be on earth any one more beloved of Me.

70. Also, whoso will study this colloquy between us two, which makes for righteousness, by him I shall be worshipped by the sacrifice of knowledge; this is my mind.

71. The man who shall listen to it in faith, and without cavilling, even he, freed from sins, shall obtain the blessed abodes of those who work righteousness.

72. Has this been heard by thee, O Prithâ's son, with thy heart one-pointed? Has thy confusion arising from ignorance been destroyed, O Dhananjaya?

This verse shows the duty of the righteous teacher. If one method fails in its effect on the pupil, some other must be adopted.

---

[1] "Reviles Me;" thinks Me a vainglorious man who has pretended to be one with God.

[2] "This supreme mystery;" the dialogue between Krishna and Arjuna.

[3] "Those who have love for Me;" this shows that the purity of devotion to Krishna, even in the absence of other qualifications, renders the devotee fit to receive these doctrines.

[4] "Having obtained supreme love for Me;" whoever expounds these doctrines as an act of service to the Primeval Teacher, Vâsudeva, will attain liberation through His favor.

An obedient pupil must never be given up simply on account of his dulness. The question is asked here in such a manner as not to discourage the pupil.

Arjuna *said:*

73. My delusion is ended, and by me has been attained right recollection[1] through thy favor, O Achyuta;[2] I am firm,[3] free from doubts,[4] and will perform thy bidding.

Sanjaya *said:*

74. Thus I have heard this dialogue between Vâsudeva and Prithâ's son, of great soul; unheard ever before, and making the hair stand on end.[5]

75. Through the favor of Vyâsa,[6] this supreme mystery[7] of yoga[8] has been heard by me; from the lord of yoga,[9] Krishna himself speaking.

76. O King, again and again remembering this wonderful and sanctifying colloquy between Krishna and Arjuna, I am again and again rejoicing.

77. And also again and again remembering that wonderful form of the Lord, my wonder is great, O King, and I again and again rejoice.

---

[1] "Right recollection," or the faith that the Ego is truly independent of material conditions.

[2] *Achyuta* is Krishna, "he who never falls"—the eternal Lord, the Primeval Teacher.

[3] "I am firm" in my obedience to thee.

[4] "Free from doubts" as to what is right; there is nothing right that is not done in obedience to Divine command.

[5] "Hair stand on end," through spiritual joy.

[6] "Favor of Vyâsa." In the Mahâbhârata it is said that the sage Vyâsa bestowed spiritual perception on Sanjaya, by which he heard this dialogue.

[7] "Supreme mystery;" because relating to the supreme consummation of existence.

[8] *Yoga;* the liberation of the Ego from all conditions with which it is connected through the power of false knowledge.

[9] "Lord of yoga." He by whose favor those striving for isolation of the Ego become successful.

78. Wherever is Krishna, the lord of yoga, wherever is Prithâ's archer-son, there unwavering are Fortune, Victory, Increase, and Wisdom of action; this is my mind.

> Thus ends chapter the eighteenth, called the "RIGHT KNOWLEDGE OF LIBERATION," in the blessed BHAGAVAD GÎTÂ, the sacred lore, the divine wisdom, the book of divine union, the colloquy between the blessed KRISHNA and ARJUNA, and contained in the Bhîshma Parvan of the blessed MAHÂBHÂRATA, which is a collection of one hundred thousand verses by VYÂSA.

In reverence and devotion to the teachers of old, and the Primeval Teacher of all, this Scripture is ended.

SYNOPSIS.

By the affliction of sorrow which overcomes Arjuna in the beginning of the Lord's Lay it is shown that the root of all evil is the false self that hides the real spirit within man and asserts itself in the vain conceit of its own sufficiency and the lust of possession. The spirit of falsehood which says "*I* have done this; these are mine" is the enemy to be overcome to attain the eternal life which is the heritage of all human beings. This is made clear in the second chapter by exposing the deceitfulness of this false self and despoiling it of the pretence of being the real Self, which is immortal and perfectly pure. It is also declared there that to realize the true nature of the Self is the attainment of salvation. But for all but a very few this realization is not at once possible because of the impurities of human nature that tie them to the exterior life of action. Although the highest perfection is only gradually attainable by a life of action, yet the forcible repression of tendencies to action is reprehensible. A life of right action is the means of purifying the heart for the reception of true spiritual consciousness by which the life of darkness and evil, our common human nature, is ended. The third chapter teaches this, and points out that the performance of right action consists in the fulfilment of duties to God and man, accepting duties as the commands given by God for the well-being of man and doing them for the love of God alone, and not for the purpose of any personal gain. The peculiar efficacy of the religious works resting upon scriptural authority is also declared.

The fourth chapter discloses the source of the teacher's authority. He interiorly is the Logos who, for the salvation of mankind, from time to time reveals to the world through human forms selected for the purpose the path of truth and righteousness. It then goes on to teach that when the man of pure heart has seen

God he becomes invested with that liberty of spirit which makes it optional for him to engage in action or abstain from it. As all personal desire becomes extinguished by the sight of God, all the subsequent acts of such an one are really performed by the Divine power for the benefit of the world. The relation of morality to the spiritual life is expounded. The laws of morality are instituted for the purpose of giving man the right appreciation of life by the comprehension of inaction and forbidden and enjoined acts. When in this manner the true nature of the restless human spirit is understood, all obstacles are removed from the attainment of spiritual consciousness by which God is known. This knowledge of God is to be sought after by reverent obedience to those who possess it, and by cultivation of faith in their words and in the words of the Scriptures. The relative position in spiritual culture of right performance of action in the world and adoption of a life of seclusion away from the world is elucidated in the fifth chapter. Without renunciation of personal desire no one can perform action rightly, and without right performance of action no one can attain to thorough detachment from the world. Thus they form together one harmonious whole. It is true that between complete detachment and the rise of spiritual illumination in the heart nothing intervenes; yet it is better not to wrench one's self away from the life of action, but wait patiently for its dropping off in right time. The sixth chapter sets the limit to the life of action by the birth within the devotee of that purity and dispassion which serve as a barrier which the world cannot pass. At this stage the devotee becomes fit for self-effacing contemplation of the Divine Spirit. Contemplation is attainable through dispassion and long-continued loving annihilation of self before God, accepting him as the only Self that is real. The task of reaching this state is beset with great difficulties, but they can be conquered by perseverance and faith. If the final consummation of contemplation, namely, the vision of God, is not attained even at the close of life, the devotee may rest in the confidence that he never shall come to an evil end, but that through perseverance success will be finally his.

With the first six chapters concludes the first topic of the Lord's Lay; namely, the real nature of the individual spirit, — what man really is. The immortal spirit in the breast of man is the witness of all that he does and all that he is, and yet the man cannot know it because he is always going outwards and not inwards. The spirit is the innermost of all that under any conditions he calls himself. It is his very ownness.

Having thus declared the real nature of the spirit within man to be pure consciousness, incorruptible, attributeless, and perfect, the Blessed Lord begins the declaration of the real nature of the spirit outside of man. What the devotee really is has been shown; the next topic is, Who is the object of devotion? With the seventh chapter begins the revelation of the mystery of the being of God. As there is nothing higher than this in the whole universe, all devotees cannot possibly receive it in the same way, in consequence of the difference in their spiritual states. The seventh chapter declares the mystery so as to enable the most pure and spiritual devotees to feel after God and recognize Him as identical with the true Self within them. The spirit of God is absolute consciousness; this is the Supreme Deity as He is in Himself. By His mysterious will He unites consciousness, without causing any alteration in its nature, with the objective which is His power and no substance in itself. Whoever knows that the Spirit of God as present in the ant is the same as in the highest celestial being and also in Himself, is liberated. The eighth chapter declares Him as the object for the contemplation of those who through impurity of nature are not able to find Him without loving, all-excluding contemplation. He who with all his heart and all his soul and all his mind seeks through contemplation to find God, who, though attributeless, is the Spirit present in the devotee's own heart, in the sun, in the cause, in the effect, and in the mutual relation of cause and effect, and is the superintendent of his acts, attains to Him by progress through various celestial states. The ninth chapter declares the mystery of the Divine Being for the benefit of those who are unable to approach Him in either of the before-mentioned ways. The tenth chapter continues the declaration begun in the ninth of the omnipotence of the Deity as manifested in nature, human and super-human. This is intended for the contemplation of devotees of immature spirituality. Those who in faith and perseverance contemplate the wonderful evidences of Divine Almightiness given by nature, and in a pre-eminent degree by godlike beings, may hope by the grace of God to know Him as the Soul of which the universe is considered to be the body. In the eleventh chapter Arjuna is favored with the vision of the Deity in that aspect. The twelfth chapter declares the relative position of the different classes of the devotees. Those who realize that the Deity is in the veriest reality the true Ego are His very Self. Among the rest, those who lose themselves in Him through the power of all-absorbing love are the best devoted. The chapter closes with commandments to those whose spirituality is lower than what has been described; by keeping these they can by degrees attain to perfect devotion and find God.

The second third of the Lord's Lay terminates the declaration of the mystery of God's being. In His real nature God is absolutely unknowable, and nothing more can be said about it than that it is the purest BEINGNESS, the mysterious essence of Being, the Consciousness. Yet God is not entirely incomprehensible when diligently sought after through His works. The whole universe is but a manifestation of His imperial will and can be destroyed by the same will. All laws are really not laws, but the modes in which the imperial will chooses to work. That which is called cause can produce effect because God wills it so, and not through any inherent power of its own. God is not limited by any ethical laws, it is His eternal lordly pleasure to reward virtue and punish sin. He forgives the sins of those who seek after Him, love Him, and work for Him alone. He searches our hearts by dwelling in us, and is our Father, Mother, and Friend.

The last six chapters of the Lord's Lay deal with the relation between man and God, by the realization of which immortality is attained, and man becomes a "partaker of divine nature" (2 Pet. i. 4). The thirteenth chapter declares that the supremely real nature of man is the Spirit of God and nothing else. The consciousness in man when disconnected with everything else is the same as the consciousness which is the Deity; there is not the least difference in that. The reason why man can be saved is because he is always immortal. But the identity of the real nature of man with the Spirit of God is of no practical use to him unless he knows it; and this knowledge he can never attain except by the grace of God. There is but one Self in the universe, and that is God. The one Self dwells in all creatures, not by a change of nature but merely by His will so to dwell; the true Self is God, and in supreme reality unknowable and attributeless; and the Self as perceived is nothing but the image of that Divine Self which as itself can never be perceived. In an impure heart the image of God is dark and distorted, but in a heart that is pure the image is perfect. The perception through which God is known in the way explained, and immortality is attained, can never exist in a being devoid of the virtues described in this chapter and called knowledge. The same note is heard in the Lord's Lay as in a Western Scripture, — "Behold, the fear of the Lord, that *is* wisdom; and to depart from evil *is* understanding" (Job xxviii. 28). The identity with God, which is the highest spiritual hope contained in the Vedas for the Brâhmans, is nothing more or less than a participation in the real nature of God and identity with Him in will and design. The fourteenth chapter further elucidates the nature of this identity. The power of God works in three characters usually called qualities of nature, named sattva, rajas, and tamas, — purity, passion, and darkness. He who attains to identity with God does nothing of himself, but through the Divine power. He is in the perfect form of God. The three qualities of nature and their operations are described in the fourteenth chapter. The state of the devotee who is identical with the Deity is described in the succeeding chapter. He sees all the operations of the Divine power in its fulness; the universe constitutes the apparent bondage of the spirit, and its liberation is achieved by perceiving the Spirit of God which pervades and supports all things. He sees how the Spirit of God enters into us as our spirit and carries on the work of birth, life, and death. In brief, the whole purpose and design of God is manifest unto the glorified spirit. Knowing the Supreme Spirit as above and beyond all things, he makes the most perfect adoration; and all labor and work for him is ended for ever and ever! The Blessed Lord then proceeds to illuminate the path of salvation. There are two paths in the world eternally established by the inscrutable will of God, — the path of salvation and the path of damnation. Those who are on the former road possess godlike attributes, the fruits of the Spirit; and those upon the latter are possessed by demoniac attributes, the fruits of the flesh. Knowing this, the devotee must seek after the first and kill out the latter, which leads to ceaseless mutations in evil and suffering. The Lord casts them into demoniac wombs and they never come to Him. The aspirant for God must implicitly follow the authority of the Scriptures. This is the highest and purest form of faith. Those not following the authority of the Scriptures, the seventeenth chapter goes on to say, can have an inferior kind of faith according to the tendencies of their natures; but that faith cannot bring them to the only true God. According to the predominance of one of the three qualities in man, faith, austerities, sacrifices are of three kinds. But all things done in faith in the Supreme God can be only of one kind, namely, pure. Faith sanctifies all things. In the final chapter the Blessed Lord gives a summary of His teachings, and firmly establishes the truth that the eternal life is not the outcome of man's acts, but the gift of Himself made by the Father of All when the heart is purified by right performance of duties to God and man, in obedience to the Scriptures and the spiritual experience of those who have followed them and attained to perfection.

Human nature is one, God is but one, and the path of salvation, though many in appearance, is really but one.

INDEX.

INDEX.

ABSOLUTENESS of the Deity, 80, 84, 162, 196, 197, 212.
Achyuta, 268.
Action, bondage of, 47, 94.
    freedom from, 65, 263, 266.
    man of, 144.
    philosophy of, 46, 47, 50, 64, 70, 256.
    right performance of, 104.
Action-born, 89.
Açvattha, 225, 226.
Adhibhûta, 136, 137.
Adhidaivata, 136.
Adhiyajna, 136.
Adhyâtma, 136, 137.
Ahankâra, 76, 125, 230.
Âkâsa, 111, 124.
Anger, results of, 58, 73.
Anumantâ, 207.
Arjuna, 23, 24, 25.
    despondency of, 32.
    his duty to fight, 44.
Asat, 247.
Âtmâ, or true Ego, 39, 40, 41, 42, 207, 232.
Attachment, abandoning, 51, 55.
    and repulsion, 59.
Attributeless, worship of, 182.
Attributes, demoniac, 238.
Aught, 35.
Austerities, sacrificial, 88, 89, 245, 246.
Avidyâ, 206, 208, 209, 213, 230.

BATTLE, resolve fixed on, 45.
Bhagavad Gîtâ, 3, 14, 179, 265.
Bharata, son of, 132.
Bhartâ, "the supporter," 207.
Bhîshma, 22.

Bhoktâ, 207.
Birth, causes of, 206, 221.
Births, many, 130.
Blind, spiritually, 51.
Bliss, absolute, the attainment of, 155.
Body, conquered, 96.
    the Lord of, 74.
Bondage of the Ego, 207.
Brahmâ, 141, 217.
Brahmă, the supreme, 7, 136, 137, 247.
Brahmachâri, 108, 140.
Brâhman, 50.
    caste, 83, 98.
Brâhmanas, 247.
Brâhmanical ritualists, 251.
Brâhmans, theocratic law of, 27, 66.
Buddha, 9.
Buddhi, 76, 111, 124, 258.

CASTE system, 261.
Castes, described, 83, 261.
    results to, from confusion of, 28.
Cause, First, 203, 205, 208.
Chakravartin, 17.
Character defined, 71.
Chârvaka, the Indian materialist, 236, 237.
Christs of God, 78.
City of nine gates, 97.
Cognitive power, 59.
Conscious existence, 164.
Consciousness, facts of, 35, 123, 137.
    pure, unconditioned, 214.
    the Supreme Spirit, 30, 71, 79, 100, 126, 199.
Content, the meaning of, 54.
Cow, rajas, 98.
Creation, 149, 216.

Creator, Brahmâ, 218.
Creatures, origin of, unperceived, 42.
Çudra caste, 83.
Culture, spiritual, 121, 242.

DAY of Brahmâ, 141.
Deadly sin, belief in plurality of gods, 79.
Death, meditation at time of, 138.
    spiritual, 74.
Declare the Supreme Spirit, 247.
Deity, absolute, 80, 84, 162, 196, 197, 198, 205, 212.
    attributeless, 133, 198, 212.
    knowledge of, 199, 211.
    the form of, 169, 171.
    the true Self, 80, 112.
    unchangeable, 69, 79.
    unsearchable, 150.
    with attributes, 172.
Delhi, 17.
Delusion, results of, 58, 128.
    the forest of, 52.
Demoniac dispositions, 128.
Dependence on God, 123, 133.
Desire, absence of, 114, 263.
Desires, broods of, 48.
<u>Devotee, how emancipated, 96.</u>
Dhananjaya, 24, 51.
Dhristadyumna, 24.
Dhritarâshtra, 17, 18.
Dispassion, 52, 260.
Divine incarnation, mystery of, 78.
    power, 148, 158, 160.
Divinity, not proved externally, 55.
Domination of God, 265.
Doubt, dangerous, 91.
Duryodhana, 17, 21.
Duties, unmistakable, 253.
Duty, the law concerning, 73, 262.

EARTH, defined, 124.
Earthen pot illustration, 35.
Easy path, 181.
Ego, 32, 33, 36, 37, 41, 56, 57, 58, 218, 229, 254, 256.
    bondage of, 207.
    identical with God, 58, 61, 74, 75, 190, 218, 228.

Ego, immortal or real, 36, 37, 38, 40, 202.
Egos, plurality of, 33.
Egotism, 96, 111.
Elephant, tamas, 98.
Emperor, Absolute, 208.
Equal-sighted, 98.
Essence of Bhagavad Gîtâ, 179.
Eternal, 39.
    life, 9, 34, 82.
Ethical codes, 44.
Ethics, highest benefit of, 84.
Everlasting life, 102.
Evil-doer, 90.
External objects, how removed, 101.

FAITH, certainty-souled, 47, 48.
    described, 71, 130, 151, 242.
    how obtained, 243.
    persevering in, 133.
Fatalism denied, 265.
Father, the, 126, 136, 204.
Fire of knowledge, 91.
First Cause, 203, 205.
Food, the effect of, 109, 263.

GÂNDÎVA, 25.
God, absolute, 31, 80.
    attributeless, 678.
    Christs of, 78.
    grace of, 223.
    is consciousness, 75.
    life in, the true Self, 208.
    personal, 30.
    the love of, 155, 156.
    the will of, 229.
God's mercy, 11.
    nature, 80, 226.
Gods, belief in a plurality of, a deadly sin, 79.
    concourse of, 173.
    false, 131.
Govinda, 26, 32.
Grace, Divine, 78, 126, 183.

HEARING Scriptures, 210.
Heedlessness, 219.
Holy Ghost, 98.
Hrishîkeça, 24, 32.

IÇVARA, the Son, 204.
Identity, 113, 123, 189.
    with Supreme Spirit, 266.
Idolatry condemned, 83.
Ignorance destroyed by fire of knowledge, 91.
Ikshvâku, 77.
Illumination, inner, conditions for, 56, 129.
    spiritual, 51, 68, 102.
Illusion, 50, 72, 129.
Illusive power, 128.
Immortality, 141.
Incarnation, mystery of divine, 78, 81, 131.
Incarnations, purpose of, 81, 207.
Indwelling spirit, 43.
Infinity, 56.

JANÂRDANA, 26.
Jehovah the Creator, 203.
Jesus Christ on the supreme authority of the Scriptures, 239.

KAPILA, 251.
Karma, 105, 136, 137, 208.
Keçava (rays of omniscience), 53.
Knowledge, how gained, 91.
    lamp of, 161.
    sacrifice through, 90.
    union with, 51.
Krishna, 25, 79, 113.
    slayer of foes, 31.
Kshatriya, military caste, 43, 44.
Kshetra and Kshetrajna, knowledge of, 189, 210, 217, 252.
Kshetrajna, consciousness, 199.
Kuntî, son of, 31.
Kuru, 17, 21.
Kurukshetra, 17, 18.
Kûtastha, the indestructible spirit, 232.

LAMP, 110.
Laziness, 219.
Liberation attained, 144, 155, 202, 221, 222, 262, 266.
Life-breaths, 88.
Life everlasting, 102.

Logos, the, 124, 125, 132.
Lord of all worlds, 102.
    of the body, 74.
Love of God, 156.

MÂDHAVA, 23, 117.
Madhu, 136.
    slayer of, 26.
Maheçvara, the Lord of all, 207.
Manas, 76, 111, 124, 138.
Man, the Temple of God, 4.
Man's duty, 44.
Manu, 77, 160.
Master, the, 260.
    of great car, 21.
Materialists, Indian, 236, 237.
Meditation, mounting to, 104.
    the man of, 116.
    to sit for, 107, 108.
Me, how attained, 141, 153, 154, 155, 156, 264.
    how tortured, 243.
Mental states, three, 108.
Milch-cow of desire, 66.
Mimânsaka school, 251.
Modes of worship, 152.
Moods, 128.
My-ness, 32.
Myself, 129.
Mystery, supreme, 268.

NATURE, godlike, 151.
    inferior and superior, 125.
    of God, 80, 97.
    of objects, 213.
    the totality of qualities, 65, 71.
Naught, things that are caused, 35.
Nirvâna, 4, 8, 33, 34, 47, 66, 82, 112, 130, 230.
    attained, 47, 77, 87, 97, 99, 100, 102, 105, 109, 123, 133, 181, 193, 223, 239, 264.

OBEDIENCE to divine commands, 73, 242.
Objects, nature of, 213.
Offerings, the doctrine of, 245.
Om, 127, 135, 140, 152.

Omission, results from sins of, 45.
One-ness, spiritual, 113.
Opposites, pairs of, 34, 86, 132.

PAIN-WOMBED, 99.
Pairs of opposites, 34, 86, 132.
Pându, 17, 18, 21.
    son of, 23.
Paramâtmâ, 207, 232.
Path of ancestors, 144.
    of gods, 144.
Peace, 156, 184.
Perfection, 262.
Persevering in faith, 133.
Personal God, 30.
Philosophy, purely spiritual, 46.
    the Sânkhya system, 251.
Pleasure and pain, 206.
    craving in, 55.
Pot of earth, 35.
Power, divine, 160.
Powers, vital, 140.
Praise, lovers of, 48.
Prakriti, 111, 192, 193, 200, 201, 202, 203, 215, 216, 217.
Prakriti-born, 218.
Pranava, 127, 140.
Prostration, 90.
Purity, 235.
Purusha, 111, 137, 200, 202, 215, 217.

QUALITIES, 200, 223.
    arising from nature, 261.
Question, 90.

RAJAS, 65, 73, 128, 219.
Rakshas, 243.
Reality, 50, 110, 125.
Realization of the spirit, 53, 199.
    right knowledge of, 123.
Religion and Scriptures, 139.
Religious duties, 67.
Renunciation, 66, 94, 95, 100, 102, 103, 249.
Resolve fixed on battle, 45.
Rest in Supreme Spirit, 53, 97.
Restraint, 88.

Results, giving up of, 250.
Righteousness, 73, 81.
Rites, Vedic, 152.

SACRIFICE, 66, 67, 87, 244, 245.
Sage, the illuminated, 39, 40, 54, 61, 68, 100, 164.
Sages, the seven, 160.
Salvation, life in the Deity, 100.
    not of works, 63, 123, 245, 259.
    through love of God, 156.
Samâdhi, 56.
Sankarâchârya, 3.
Sanjaya, 18, 21.
Sânkhya system of philosophy, 251.
Sapor, essence of taste, 231.
Sattva (goodness), 49, 65, 83, 98, 128, 218, 242, 244, 247.
Scriptures, the, 138, 139, 242.
    the supreme authority of, 239, 242.
Self, 105, 106, 122.
    (and not self), 36, 38, 53, 54, 80, 105.
    the supreme, 105, 110.
Self-restraint, 246.
Senses, 88, 200.
    the control of, 60.
Sensuous pleasures, 259.
Service, 90.
Shadows of speech, 49.
Sincerity of conduct, 246.
Slayer, the, 38, 45.
Sleep, the effect of, 109.
Smell, sacred, 127.
Soma, the sacred plant, 231.
Son of God, 30, 126, 136.
Speech, shadows of, 49.
Spirit, exhaustless, 142, 143.
    right knowledge of, 68, 165, 225.
    the indwelling, 43.
Spiritual death, 74.
    philosophy, 47.
Spiritually blind, 51.
Studies, necessary, 44.
Supporter, 32.
Supreme Spirit, 32, 53, 61, 68, 84, 87, 95, 97, 98, 135, 177, 183, 186, 196, 198, 229, 264.
    actionless, 84, 85.
    declare the, 247.

INDEX.

TAINTS, 98.
Tamas, 65, 128.
Teachers, spiritual, 191.
Tendencies, how removed, 105, 116.
That, 135.
Time, its meaning, 53, 143.
Tortoise, limbs of, 56.
Troubleless seat, 52.
Truth held back, 129.
    its essence, 62.
    righteous, 147.

UNIVERSE, the false nature of the Ego, 194.
Unknowableness, 80.
Unmanifested, 142.
Upadrashtâ, innermost spirit, 207.
Upanishad, 2.

VAÇISHTHA, 201.
Vaiçvânara, cause of digestion, 232.
Vanity, 263.

Vâsudeva, 130.
Vedânta, 254, 255.
Vedic rites, 152.
    texts, 38, 83, 95, 139, 226.
Veiling, 219.
Vital powers, 140.
Vivasvat, 77.
Vyâsa, 18, 268.

WISDOM'S eye, 213.
Word, the, 126, 204.
    made flesh, 80.
Works, 249, 250, 251, 252.
Worship, modes of, 152.
    of true God, 130, 242, 262.

YAKSHAS, 243.
Yoga, Karma, 209.
    Sânkhya, 209.
    what it is, 51, 52, 110, 112, 114, 268.
Yoke of God, 155.
Yuga, 141.

University Press: John Wilson & Son, Cambridge.

www.ingramcontent.com/pod-product-compliance
Lightning Source LLC
Chambersburg PA
CBHW032052230426
43672CB00009B/1564